BEST OF BRITISH BIKES

Patrick Stephens Limited, part of Thorsons, a division of the Collins Publishing Group, has published authoritative, quality books for enthusiasts for more than twenty years. During that time the company has established a reputation as one of the world's leading publishers of books on aviation, maritime, military, model-making, motor cycling, motoring, motor racing, railway and railway modelling subjects. Readers or authors with suggestions for books they would like to see published are invited to write to: The Editorial Director, Patrick Stephens Limited, Thorsons Publishing Group, Wellingborough, Northants, NN8 2RQ.

BEST OF BRITISH BIKES

JIM REYNOLDS

PATRICK STEPHENS LIMITED

First published in 1990

British Library Cataloguing in Publication Data

Reynolds, Jim, *1938-*
  Best of British bikes.
  1. British motorcycles, history
  I. Title
  629.22750941

  ISBN 1-85260-033-0

For Valerie
Always my inspiration

Patrick Stephens Limited is part of the Thorsons Publishing Group, Wellingborough, Northamptonshire NN8 2RQ, England

Printed in Great Britain by The Bath Press, Bath, Avon

10 9 8 7 6 5 4 3 2 1

CONTENTS

ACKNOWLEDGEMENTS

This book would not have been possible without the help of the people whose machines are shown in it. My thanks to them all.

Thanks also to those who helped with the valued photographs: Keith Simmonds, Brian Holder, Malcolm Carling, Island Photographic, *Motor Cycle News* Archives, EMAP Classic Archives, Bob Culver, Martin Barnwell, Peter Wileman, Peter Howdle, Ron Langston, Titch Allen, Eric Houseley, David Tye, Bob Collier, Deryk Wylde, Don McKeand, Mike Griffiths, Barrie Scully, Patrick Gosling, John Davies and the ever-helpful Jim Davies.

INTRODUCTION

In the early 1970s, it would have been tempting to write the obituary of the British motorcycle industry. Almost every great name had gone or was only a shadow of its former self. Yet today the names live on, powered by the enthusiasm that bonds motorcyclists together, and the old wheels keep turning, even if spare parts have to be specially made or adapted from another vehicle to replace those worn out by long years of use. A long involvement with the old-bike scene leaves me in no doubt that they will continue to flourish.

It has been my privilege to meet British bike riders from ex-World Champions to everyday ride-to-work riders, occasionally to ride their precious machines, but always to share an enthusiasm. I hope this book will convey some of that love of quality, toleration of faults and simple enjoyment of what was once the industry that led the world. Owning a British motorcycle is the entry into a very exclusive club, and I am proud to be a member.

Jim Reynolds
Cleobury Mortimer
South Shropshire

In 1948 the famous Brands Hatch circuit was a grass track, an unlikely place for a major factory to show its new road race model in action for the first time. But that was where the AJS 7R first barked down its huge megaphone exhaust, ridden by Jock West in a demonstration of what the factory in Plumstead, London, was offering the racer with ambition.

The engine was a clear descendent of the 1930s type used by aces like Bob Foster and George Rowley in the TT and at European events. But even in those days the racer had only survived because Rowley had found an old model and entered it at Brooklands, despite the factory's clear instructions that his racing days had finished when the old AJS factory in Wolverhampton had been taken over by London-based Matchless. George rode like a hero on a little 350 in bigger company, and the publicity changed minds in the boardroom; when the Second World War was over, AJS were quick to get racing plans into action, and the 7R was the first bike they offered to the public.

The factory team rode the 7R, but in the 1948 TT – a major showplace for sporting British factories – it was a private owner who really shone. The factory riders on their 'Porcupine' twins dropped out of the Senior TT, leaving Ulsterman Artie Bell to bring his factory Norton to first place, but in fourth place was Geoff Murdoch, a name that had not even appeared on a TT leaderboard until this race. And here he was, bringing the new over-the-counter 7R to the best 350 place in a 500cc TT since Howard Davies won on a 350 AJS way back in 1921.

The 300lb 7R went on to become standard wear for fast private owners who wanted something more modern than Norton's plunger-sprung 380 lb Manx and the graceful KTT Velocette with its old-fashioned girder forks. But the Ajay in its two-valve form as offered for sale never won a TT race, even though Bill Doran came within half a lap of winning the 1949 race; it was the very special three-valve version that finally gave AJS TT victory with New Zealander Rod Coleman at the helm in the 1954 race. In

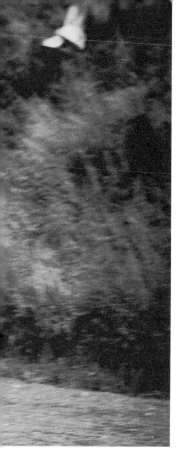

AJS 7R AND MATCHLESS G50

Boy's racer

Left *The 7R gave many rising starts a chance to show off their talents, like Ned Minihan here on his way round Kates Cottage to 13th place in the 1958 350 Manx Grand Prix.*

Below *No AJS 7R or Matchless G50 in classic racing is better-looking than the bikes ridden by Malcolm Clark of Betchworth, Surrey. Here the self-employed builder proves that the two models are closely related, with the tank from his G50 fitted to his 7R after the latter's tank was damaged in transit to a race meeting.*

1952, the great Bob McIntyre won the 350 Manx Grand Prix on a 7R and then rode the same bike to second place in the 500 race, to confirm that the 7R was the best bike for a private owner's hard-earned cash.

The factory changed its racing policy for the 1955 season, dropping the costly three-valve 7R3 and the 500cc 'Porcupine' and campaigning developments of catalogue racing models instead. Jack Williams took over the job of squeezing more horsepower out of the two-valve 7R, and succeeded in raising the output from 37 bhp at 7,500 rpm in 1954 to 41.5 bhp at 7,500 rpm in 1960 by patient honing of the basic design.

So popular was the 350 that pressure for a 500cc version persuaded the factory to introduce a big brother version for the 1959 season, the Matchless G50. Londoner Peter Ferbrache was loaned a 7R and a G50 by the factory and gave the G50 its first International victory in Finland in 1958. For 1959 Northerner Alan Shepherd, whose victory in the 1958 350 Manx Grand Prix on a 7R had pleased the gaffers at Plumstead, was

AJS 7R AND MATCHLESS G50

Engine: Air-cooled vertical single cylinder, with chain-driven single overhead camshaft opening two valves via rockers incorporating roller cam followers. Major castings in magnesium from 1948 until 1961, when aluminium alloy was adopted. 1948 – 7R engine, 74mm bore x 81mm stroke, developing about 33 bhp at 6,800 rpm; from 1956 – 75.5mm × 78mm; final 1962 version – about 42 bhp at 7,800 rpm. Matchless G50 introduced in 1959, 90mm bore × 78m, giving about 45 bhp at 7,200 rpm.

Transmission (all models): Four-speed gearbox with integral footchange, box not in unit with engine. Primary and secondary transmission by chain. Multiplate exposed clutch.

Cycle parts: Welded full cradle type, with telescopic front forks and swinging arm rear suspension. Seven-inch twin-leading-shoe brakes front and rear from 1948 to 1953, then single-leading-shoe rear drum adopted.

Dimensions: Wheelbase – 1948 7R, 56 in; 1960 7R and G50, 55 in. Dry weight – 1948 7R, 298 lbs; 1960 7R and G50, about 285 lbs.

Owners' Club: AJS and Matchless OC and the Classic Racing Motorcycle Club both cater, the latter being very active in promoting racing. OC Secretary – Mrs L. Reeday, 13 Thurlmere Road, Barrow-on-Soar, Loughborough, Leics. CRMC – Mrs A. Murden, Fenn Farm, St Mary's Hoo, near Rochester, Kent.

Sources of help: Spares – Mick Taberer, 325 Coventry Road, Hinckley, Leics; George Beale Motorcycles, Whiteheather, Peggs Green, Coleorton, Leics; R. Lewis Engineering, 321 Crystal Palace Road, East Dulwich, London SE22 9JL; Rutter Developments, 31 Paddock Way, Chedburgh, Bury St Edmunds, Suffolk IP29 4UY. Restoration: George Beale and R. Lewis (as above).

handed the 'development' models, to be entered by selected dealers as private runners. Alan worked with development engineer Jack Williams, 'a top line engineer who wasn't really given a chance,' he remembers. 'They were always short of money and Jack performed miracles on a shoestring budget.' And when Alan asked Williams' advice about an approach from the East German MZ factory, the honest reply was: 'If I was you, I'd get down to the airport, catch a plane to Berlin and sign the contract. The way things are going here, we'll have no bikes for you soon.' Aware of the parent Associated Motor Cycles group's troubles, Williams knew time was running out for the low-cost develop-

ment programme, but it didn't stop him or his chosen rider trying hard to the last. Alan was second in the 500cc World Championship in 1962 and '63, beating the late John Hartle on a Gilera-4 by just one point in the latter instance, while the G50 won a Grand Prix in Finland in 1962 with his calculating skill beating the field.

Alan Shepherd did final preparation at the circuits himself, since the deal with the factory did not include luxuries like a mechanic to help out. He realized the need for ultimate gearing for best performance and engine reliability: 'The 7R used to break at 7,800 rpm, so I normally revved it to about 7,200. The G50 revved to 6,800 rpm.' With only four speeds in the gearbox, the right choice of ratios was essential, and Alan confirmed his skill in this and every other aspect of racing when he took his 500 to the first single-cylinder 100 mph standing start of the TT course in 1962. That achievement was not matched until Dave Pither did it during his winning ride in the 1987 500cc Classic Manx Grand Prix – on a G50-engined Seeley!

After the AMC decision to drop the 7R and G50 in 1962, the supply of bikes and parts continued with the Seeley versions. Sidecar racer Colin, who had campaigned an immaculate G50-powered outfit, bought the manufacturing rights for the engines and produced his own frames. This supply of parts helped keep the G50 engine competitive in International racing when there was no alternative available, and Aussie Jack Findlay rode one to second place in the 1968 500cc World Championship.

The G50 Matchless and its Seeley successor are firm favourites in classic racing today, and demand for them is so high that specialists like George Beale of Leicestershire are planning to make batches of complete, new G50s. Small numbers of a complex engineering structure like a motorcycle mean hand building and consequent high prices, but the 7R and G50 are so much in demand that in 1988 George already had a waiting list, before the first bike had been built! There are few bikes that can give an ambitious racer a realistic chance of success in a competitive field and still not lose value as newer models make their technology outdated. If the 7R and its G50 bigger brother are being priced out of the reach of many competitors today, it is because the craftsmen in the AMC factory and Jack Williams' patient development made them so good in the first place.

1960 Ulster Grand Prix

The AJS 7R was the ideal tool for a serious racer who hadn't reached the heights of a factory ride on something foreign and much faster. At £422.19p in 1960, it was simple enough for the capable amateur to keep in tune, and reliable enough to finish in the money. What it was not expected to do was get in front of the four-cylinder MV-Agustas that dominated Grand Prix racing in the 350 class from 1958 until 1962.

Alan Shepherd thought otherwise at the 1960 Ulster Grand Prix, after a close look at the practice form of John Surtees on the MV that everyone expected to win. 'John came past me just before Deer's Leap,' he remembers. 'He landed badly and got in a wobble, so he slowed down and I went into the next bend with him. I found I could stay with him through the tricky bits because my 7R cornered so much better than his bike, and I tailed him for some miles until I lost the tow from his slipstream.

'Then I did a bit of Bob McIntyre-style thinking, and realized that if I could gear the bike up and get a "tow", I could stay with him on the fast parts of the course. I only had the sprockets I'd known would be needed for the 7R and the G50, so I put the G50 gearing on.

'I knew I had to get a good start to stay with John, and as soon as the engined fired I was slipping the clutch like mad because of the high first gear. He came past me, but at the hairpin he nearly caught me out because he was on the brakes so early – the MV was heavier than in practice because it had a full fuel tank. I got my front wheel between his rear tyre and the exhaust and nearly dropped it, but I caught him up through the bends and managed to stay with him.

'I got past John at the Quarry Bends on the second lap, and with the better handling of the AJS I could stay ahead round the hairpin and through the bends to the finishing line. It made quite a cheer when I came by ahead at the end of that lap,' is Shepherd's modest description of his heroic effort. 'The 7R was much easier to ride on the twists and turns on a road circuit,' he says with authority, 'as I was to find later when I rode the MV. It was like riding a young horse against a spirited stallion.'

A broken timing chain brought Alan's ride to an end at half distance, and Surtees went on to win at 93.39 mph. But the new 350 lap record was given to the AJS rider at 95.42 mph, and the mighty MV-Agusta responded to that news with an official protest that the 7R was using an oversize engine! The protest made almost as much news as Alan's ride, especially when the engine was measured and found legal, just like the bikes lesser men rode.

Geared high and going for a Grand Prix win, Alan Shepherd keeps his AJS 7R ahead of John Surtees and the screaming MV-Agusta Four. The easier handling and road holding helped Shepherd stay with the World Champion until a broken timing chain ended his heroic ride.

AJS TWINS

Three bearings for the Clubman

Right *This 1956 picture of a 600cc Model 30 being assembled shows the Plumstead production methods, with each bike built on a trolley that was pushed along from one stage to the next.*

Below *Frank and Lyn Westworth's 1953 Model 20 was their honeymoon transport in 1980, when the comfort of the AJS dualseat and Jampot rear suspension convinced them that this was a bike they would never sell.*

AJS was the more glamorous of the two famous makes produced in Associated Motorcycles' factory in Plumstead, south-east London. Its Matchless brother was the old-established name that grew up in that neighbourhood, but AJS had been a famous racing name through the years and the factory's racing team used that title. Their 500cc class contender was the E90 twin, nicknamed the 'Porcupine' because of the spiky finning of early model cylinder heads, and even though the engine had to be modified to conform with a ban on super-charging in international racing, it proved fast enough to carry Les Graham to the first ever 500cc World Championship in 1949.

The AJS roadster twin shared everything but its name with the Matchless version, the Ajay Model 20 being known as the 'Springtwin'. The company was happy to have racing development associated with its road machines, and one feature on the Plumstead twins in the technical press told its readers that 'the spring frame is entirely the result of racing tests'. Owners who decided to take their Ajay twins racing didn't entirely agree, like Londoner Mike Apted, who got to know the factory personnel well enough to have special cams in his weekend racer. 'It went well enough, but the handling was like a little puppy dog – it was always wagging its tail,' he laughs at the memory.

A more direct association with the road models was the entry of twins in the International Six Days Trial, with the factory's top off-road men riding in this major shop window of machine reliability. Hugh Viney, maestro of one-day trials on an Ajay single, rode a 500cc twin in the ISDT as one of Britain's Trophy team and won Gold Medals in 1951, '52 and '53. The ISDT

bikes were built in the Plumstead Competition Shop, with cycle parts adapted for rapid roadside repairs if necessary: wheel spindles had built-in tommy bars, an air bottle would reflate the tyres if a puncture had to be mended, an eight-day clock and the speedometer were mounted in rubber for protection from vibration and specially-made Siamese pipes left the transmission side accessible for quick attention. The engines were carefully built, with ports gas-flowed to provide a little extra urge, but, with questionable petrol supplies in some foreign countries, they were not tuned for power. Allen-head bolts on the rocker boxes had hexagon heads welded on to make them more accessible and reduce the number of spanners carried. Very few of this special breed are known to survive today, but Patrick Horton of the AJS and Matchless OC has a 1955 example and knows of a 1954 version in Australia.

The AJS twin was developed to 600cc (72mm bore × 72.8mm stroke) and 650cc (72 × 78.3) in the 1950s, but there were alternative sizes tried for other markets. In 1954 and '55, the USA importer, Cooper Bros of Los Angeles, had all its twins built to 'B' specification, with the bore enlarged to 69mm from the standard 66 and the capacity raised to 550cc as a result. Power went up too, from a claimed 29 bhp to 32 at 6,800 rpm. The arrival of the 600cc Model 21 ended that unusual development.

Below *40,000 miles on the clock, the engine never apart and still giving faithful service. Frank and Lyn Westworth's 1966 Model 31 AJS reflects the mixture of components used for the AMC ranges when times were difficult, with Norton forks and wheels.*

1960 Thruxton 500-mile race

The Thruxton 500-mile race for production machines was the premier race of its type in the 1950s and '60s, with every major manufacturer keen to see his model win. When a BMW won the race in 1959 it was a shock to the British establishment, but in 1960 patriots had their revenge.

Sporting dealers Monty and Ward decided that the 650cc AJS 31CSR 'Sports-twin' would be competitive with the best from BSA, Norton, Triumph and Royal Enfield, and Geoff Monty asked the factory to supply him with two of the new models for the event. 'They were not works bikes,' he recalls. 'All they did was build the bikes in the factory for us – I sold them after the race. 'It was a perfectly straight-forward deal. We entered two bikes, one for Ron Langston and Don Chapman and the other for Alan Shepherd and Michael O'Rourke.'

In the race, Bob McIntyre on the 700cc Royal Enfield took an early lead with a pace round the 2.28 mile circuit that no one could match. But in an attempt to make up time lost while the exhaust system was wired up, Bob and his Constellation parted company at Club Corner and were out of the race. The Langston-Chapman AJS took over the lead and circulated steadily with three 650 Triumphs in vain pursuit.

Langston, the Gloucestershire farmer who excelled at road racing, trials and scrambles,

didn't like endurance racing, even though his road racing debut had been in the Thruxton event on a Velocette. 'It was not an event I enjoyed,' he says. 'I thought it was a bit boring, really. You only stopped for fuel and to change the rider, and just had to go as fast as you could without busting the bike.'

The Shepherd/O'Rourke bike went out with a broken crankshaft, but the Langston/Chapman duo kept their pace without wearing the bike out, observing the 7,000 rpm limit and coming in for regular stops, when one of the riders would fill the fuel tank while Geoff Monty checked the bike over with his experienced racer/tuner's eye.

'I did the last stint of riding,' says Ron Langston, 'and the clutch was slipping like mad, so we had to ease it along very carefully. But the old girl made it to the flag all right before anyone could catch us.'

In fact, the AJS was three laps ahead of the second-placed Triumph and had beaten the 1959 race record by 1.6 mph. The master of understatement, Ron Langston remembers the winning bike to this day: 'A nice bike, really. It went very well and the handling was OK – certainly better than a Triumph.'

Gloucestershire farmer Ron Langston on his way to victory in the Thruxton 500 Miles race on the AJS he shared with Don Chapman. Despite a slipping clutch in the closing stages of the race, the unfancied Ajay set a new record.

The factory was also looking at the need for a small-capacity twin with low compression ratio to suit the African and other third-world markets. Special small pistons were cast and 500cc barrels were linered to produce a 400cc unit, but demand for the bigger versions left no time to develop the idea fully. Two of these very rare engines, survivors of a batch of about 25, are still known to exist on a Pacific island, where some 15 bikes were sent using alloy frames built as an experiment to save weight on the trials models.

The strength of AJS's export sales can be judged by other discoveries in unlikely places. Like new parts stocked in a shop in Bangkok and a 1956 500cc twin found in Malaya and brought back to its homeland for restoration. The Owner's Club boasts four sections active in Australia!

The early versions of the Model 30 (600cc) developed a reputation for breaking crankshafts, but a swap to nodular iron as the material cured that and today any knowledgeable buyer asks if a twin has a 'noddy crank'. The 500cc versions proved to be long-lived bikes with lively performance up to 85 mph, provided they were maintained properly and had their oil changed at regular intervals.

Frank Westworth, editor of the AJS and Matchless Owners' Club's excellent *Jampot* magazine, has lived with AJS twins happily since 1979. He bought his 1953 Model with 20,000 miles recorded on the speedometer, and another 20,000 miles and all-year-round use has required the paintwork to be refurbished twice. But the Argenized rear dampers (a silver stove enamel finish applied when chrome plating supplies were very short) still have the factory finish.

'Cruising two-up at 50 to 60 mph, it gives about 60 miles to every gallon of two-star,' says Frank. 'It's a lovely, docile bike to ride, with excellent handling and awful brakes by today's standards. But if you ask me what problems I've had with it, there's not much of a list – a stud pulled out of the dynamo. That's it, the lot, full stop!'

Sharing space with the Model 20 is one of the last of the AJS Model 31 650s, built after

AJS TWINS

Engine: Air-cooled, four-stroke parallel twin, with separate barrels on AMC engines and two pushrod-operated valves per cylinder. Model 20, 500cc (66mm bore × 72.8mm stroke); Model 30, 600cc (72 × 72.8); Model 31, 650cc (72 × 78.3); Model 33, 750cc (77 × 78.3), made for USA market. Also 20B, 550cc (69 × 72.8) made for USA in 1954 and '55.
Transmission: Four-speed gearbox, early models with Burman, from 1956 with AMC-Norton box. Primary and secondary drive by chain. Multi-plate clutch in oil.
Cycle parts: All models with swinging-arm frame and telescopic forks. Seven-inch drum brakes front and rear until 1964, when Norton 8-inch front brake used.
Dimensions: Wheelbase – Model 20, 55$\frac{1}{4}$ in; Model 33, 55.4 in. Dry weight – Model 20, 394 lbs; Model 33, 400 lbs.
Owner's Club: Very active, 25 UK sections and 4 in Australia. Membership Secretary – Brian Osley, 'Red Roses', Mathern, Chepstow, Gwent NP6 6JD.
Sources of help: Spares – Hamrax Motors, 328 Ladbroke Grove, North Kensington, London W10; Andrew Engineering (Leigh) Ltd, Mather House, Mather Lane, Leigh, Lancs WN7 2PW; Russell Motors, 125-127 Falcon Road, Battersea, London SW11 2PE; AJS and Matchless Owners' Club own scheme. Paint to factory colours – Owners' Club. Restoration – Ernie Merryweather, 14 Rectory Close, Stanwick, near Wellingborough, Northants NN9 6QR.

Associated Motor Cycles had closed the Norton factory in Birmingham, moved production down to Plumstead, and combined parts from the two factories' ranges. So the 1964 Model 31 has Norton Roadholder front forks and wheels, with AJS's own frame. 'The suspension is very hard, typically Norton,' is Frank's opinion. 'The bike has very positive steering, excellent brakes and an immensely reliable engine – I bought it with 17,000 miles on the clock, it's now done 40,000 and the top's never been off.

'I've checked the Owners' Club records, and although the factory made about the same number of AJS and Matchless twins, there are twice as many Matchlesses registered today than AJSs. I think it's because the AJS was so much better, so people used them and wore them out, while Matchless owners just didn't use them, so more of them survived!'

Frank also has a 1968 Matchless G15, a Norton 745cc Commando engine in an AMC competition frame with Norton forks and wheels: 'Very hairy, brutal performance in a straight line, brakes inadequate.'

'All AJS owners know that Matchless twins are rubbish and AJS twins are perfect.'

AMC SINGLES

Plumstead's old faithful

Right *'The Maestro' was the nickname given to Hugh Viney, three times winner of the Scottish Six Days and a man with several International Six Days Trial gold medals to his name. Here Hugh steers his 350 AJS to a Special First Class award in the 1952 Scottish.*

Below *Stan Meir's 1955 350 uses the 'Jampot' rear suspension unit that was a feature of Plumstead-built bikes in the '50s.*

When the British motorcycle industry swung production back to civilian models after the Second World War, Associated Motorcycles had a clear lead over its rivals in the fashion stakes. Its G3L Matchless 350 had been the only British military model fitted with telescopic forms during the war and had built a good reputation for an easy ride across country compared with the old girder forks favoured by rival factories. AMC copied the idea from the German BMW, after a careful look at any patents that covered the design to ensure that they would not be faced with a court case. Not that they were happy when other British makers produced their own versions of the new front suspension, and when Triumph announced that tele forks would be fitted to its bikes, AMC took the front cover advert of *Motor Cycling* to tell the public: 'All that glitters is not gold'.

AMC's factory in Plumstead, south-east London, produced Matchless models from its first day, and AJS models after that company was acquired in the early 1930s. The principle of 'badge engineering' was soon applied, and the only way of telling an AJS 350 or 500 single from its Matchless equivalent, apart from the tank badge, was the AJS tradition of mounting the magneto in front of the cylinder, while Matchless models wore it behind! That didn't stop riders remaining faithful to their own choice, certain that whichever make they favoured was superior.

Both AJS and Matchless singles came in 350 and 500cc form, simple pushrod singles offering 16 and 23 bhp respectively, and were renowned for durability. The Plumstead finish was acknowledged as one of the very best, with cycle parts treated with the factory's own 'Bonderizing' before having three coats of stove enamel applied. The

early rigid-framed Matchless G3L and G80 and AJS 16M and 18 soon became available with swinging-arm rear suspension, a simple 'S' suffix indicating the luxury of a spring frame, and they remained firm favourites with lovers of traditional singles for many years.

The rugged engines were a natural choice for trials and scrambles, with competition giants like Hugh Viney and Gordon Jackson winning National trials and Geoff Ward, Dave Curtis and Vic Eastwood carrying the AJS and Matchless names in scrambles. Hugh Viney became a legend when he won five Scottish Six Days trials, being at the same time AMC's competition manager in the off-road sphere and spotting young talent like Geoff Duke and Mick Andrews in their formative years.

How well AMC singles last is illustrated by owners like Gerry Holdstock, who bought his 1952 Matchless trials model when it was a year old and is still using it in competition today. And road models last well, too, as Andy Lawrence proved when he decided to spend a winter holiday visiting a fellow member of the British Motorcycle Riders Club of Oxford. His friend was on a Voluntary Services Overseas scheme in Sierra Leone, but that didn't stop Andy preparing his 1956 350cc AJS for the trip and heading for the African continent. A special rear pannier frame carried two five-gallon tanks, one for petrol and the other for water on the journey across the Sahara Desert. In a journey of 6,000 miles, the

Below *John Boyes is proud that the paintwork on his 1962 Model 16S is the factory's own, still good enough to make the bike an eye-catcher.*

Below right *Big bikes required big men to ride them across country at speed. Geoff Ward was a long-term star of the Plumstead factory's works team.*

faithful AJS boiled its battery and needed clutch plates replacing after a day fighting through deep sand, the work being done in the dying hours of a sandstorm. After leaving England in the autumn of 1984, Andy and riding companion Barry Jones on a BSA B40 ate a Christmas dinner of guinea fowl and yam before riding into Sierra Leone early in 1985, the AJS still game and breathing through an aircleaner made from an old lunch box and sundry other bits and pieces. Along the way the two Englishmen had helped many riders of more sophisticated machines who had been unable to cope with roadside repairs that required more tools than the simple spanners needed for the British models.

John Boyes, a Worcestershire mental hospital nurse, doesn't cover long distances like Andy Lawrence, but still regards his 1962 AJS Model 16 as a 350 single to keep. With experience of such famous British names as Ariel, Norton and Velocette behind him, John says: 'I buy and sell a bit, like most old bike enthusiasts, but this is a bike to keep.'

John bought his Ajay from an owner who had covered less than 1,000 miles in three years, but it was in a well-preserved original trim, with none of the stainless steel parts that restorers often use to replace worn factory-fitted originals. Paintwork is the factory's own original excellent stoved finish, and with 40,000 miles on the odometer the bike shows how standard Plumstead metal was built to last – even if the dignified black tank with gold lining and transfer had given way to a chrome-plated cast badge that was no favourite with traditionalists.

This Model 16 has the duplex cradle frame introduced in 1960 and the full-width hubs that contain conventional-size brake drums. At the rear, Girling dampers had replaced the traditional 'Jampot' units of AMC's own manufacture, giving a comfortable ride for two-up weekend journeys to club rallies and relaxed visits to country spots. 'Its comfortable cruising speed with the two of us is about 45 to 50 mph,' reports John. 'The brakes have been criticized over the years, but I find them quite adequate for the sort of speeds I do today.

'The carburettor leaks, but the bike has done about 40,000 miles and things do wear out eventually; it just tends to run-on a little when I shut the throttle. The best news is that I get comprehensive insurance for £45 a year if I don't cover more than 3,000 miles.'

To prove how reliable the Model 16 is, even when left standing between outings as John completes another busy shift at the hospital where he works, he wheeled it out of the shed and started it first kick. 'These bikes are so dependable if you get a good one,' he smiled. 'The chap I bought mine from had a Matchless 650 G12 as well. He didn't want to sell that, but I'm working on him.'

The Owners' Club co-operates with specialist parts makers so that rare parts are only produced by one source, and this means that AMC single owners have a very comprehensive back-up for parts from Club or approved dealers. These simple London-made touring singles are among the most highly prized touring classics today.

AMC SINGLES

Engine: Air-cooled, four-stroke single, with two pushrod-operated valves. Early version had iron cylinder barrel and head; alloy head after 1951. Until 1962 – Matchless G3 and AJS 16, 63mm bore × 93mm stroke, 347cc; from 1962 – 72mm × 85.5mm short stroke. Until 1964 – Matchless G80 and AJS 18, 82.5mm x 93mm, 500cc; from 1964 – 85mm × 85.5mm short stroke.

Transmission (all models): Four-speed gearbox with integral footchange. Primary and secondary drive by chain. Multi-plate clutch.

Cycle parts: Rigid rear frame with AMC 'Teledraulic' telescopic front forks, until optional swinging-arm spring frame introduced in 1951; rigid frame dropped at end of 1955. Five-inch drum brakes until 1948, when 7-inch front and rear introduced; full-width hubs introduced in 1954 model year, beginning late 1953.

Dimensions: Wheelbase – 54 in rigid frame (53 in for trials version), 55¹/₂ in spring frame. Dry weight (1952 range) – rigid 350/500, 344/353 lbs; spring frame 350/500, 382/392 lbs.

Owners' Club: Very active, 25 UK sections and 4 Australian sections. Membership Secretary – Brian Osley, 'Red Roses', Mathern, Chepstow, Gwent NP6 6JD.

Sources of help: Spares – Hamrax Motors, 328 Ladbroke Grove, North Kensington, London W10; Andrew Engineering (Leigh) Ltd, Mather House, Mather Lane, Leigh, Lancs WN7 2PW; Russell Motors, 125-127 Falcon Road, Battersea, London SW11 2PE; AJS and Matchless Owners' Club own scheme. Paint to factory colours – Owners' Club. Restoration – Ken de Groome, The Bungalow, Fen Road, Newton, Wisbech, Cambs PE13 5HX (engines only).

1961 Scottish Six Days Trial

Gordon Jackson joined the AJS trials team for the 1952 season, after proving his ability with a 500cc Matchless in 1951 and catching the astute eye of trials team manager Hugh Viney. On the 350cc version of the AJS trials model, Gordon soon proved to be one of the greatest British riders in the feet-up game.

In 1952 he won the 350 class in five of the 12 trade-supported National trials and gave BSA's great star Billy Nicholson a hard fight for the ACU Trials Drivers Star. With 30 events counting towards the final tally, the ACU Star was a season-long test of riding skill, and after 20 results had been counted newcomer Jackson was well ahead of established star 'Billy Nick'. Then Nicholson made a great effort and drew level, the final decision depending on the last event, the Hoad Trophies trial. Jackson needed to win with Nicholson down the field if he was to take the Star, but the wily old BSA campaigner won the trial, beating Jackson by 1.6 seconds on the special test, and took home the title for the second year. 'The 1952 discovery' said *Motor Cycling* magazine of the youthful Kent farmer in second place.

In a career full of successes, Gordon Jackson's victory in the 1961 Scottish Six Days trial was the highlight which set a record that is still unequalled. In six days of battling with the cream of the trials crop, Gordon lost just one mark, for a single cautionary 'dab' throughout the event.

Mounted on 187 BLF, a very special version of the 16CS trials model prepared in the Competition Department by Wally Wyatt, Jackson was on the very top of his form, riding a bike that suited his delicate throttle control that could find grip where others struggled to simply walk. When he had a single touch at the ground on Grey Mare's Ridge on the second day of the trial, nobody realized the significance of what they had witnessed. 'There were seven riders clean up that section,' recalls veteran trials reporter Peter Howdle, covering the event for *Motor Cycle News*. 'It was just an odd dab that nobody thought anything of. It was almost unnecessary, Gordon was so much in control. It was only later in the week that we began to think what he could have done and completed the whole six days clean.'

Howdle himself made reporting history with his picture of Gordon at that historic moment, easing the Ajay over the rock step that kept him from what no man has done, complete the six days of competition in the Scottish Highlands without penalty. But his achievement of 1961 has never been equalled, and probably never will be.

Just one dab! Gordon Jackson's solitary lost mark in the 1961 Scottish Six Days trial was conceded when he eased his works AJS around this obstinate rock on Grey Mare's Ridge.

ARIEL ARROW AND LEADER

Revolution from Selly Oak

Right *The legendary Sammy Miller experimented with the Arrow, including a medal-winning outing in the Welsh Two Days trial.*

Below *The Arrow roadster came after the revolutionary enclosed Leader touring model and was later uprated as the sporting Golden Arrow. In its final form it was produced as a 200cc model, to give learners a better insurance rate.*

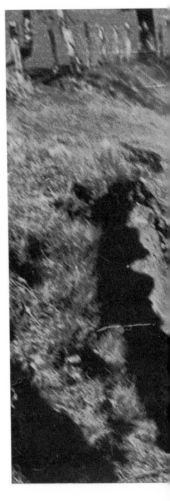

The Ariel factory's first attempt at making a two-stroke was revealed in 1958, and the old-established company's offering was a true revolution. From the fertile brain of designer Val Page, it used a pressed steel monocoque as a backbone, with the 250cc twin and four-speed gearbox unit slung underneath. Pressed steel panelling enclosed the works, with generous legshields to keep the British weather at bay, and a windscreen that shaped around the handlebars kept the rider's fingers out of the draught.

The pressed steel structure of the front forks incorporated trailing link suspension with a conventional damper unit hidden in the fork leg on either side. Rear springing was conventional swinging-arm, but the rear chain came with enclosure. What looked like the fuel tank was actually a glovebox with a lockable lid, and the fuel was really in a tank within the shell of the main frame, less likely to spill in the event of an accident.

The list of extras was extraordinary, from cosmetic touches like a rear bumper and whitewall tyres to the more practical matching panniers with shaped liners that doubled as soft luggage, an inspection light that could also be used as an ignition timing light – and even flashing indicators. Never mind that the Vincent Owners' Club magazine unkindly suggested that the eight-day clock was there to time the Leader over the standing quarter-mile, because the modest performance from the 16 bhp twin didn't stop it selling, giving the lie to the old suggestion that motorcyclists were too

conservative to spend their money on revolutionary models. Production of the four-stroke range was dropped and Selly Oak concentrated on two-strokes with the basic Arrow joining the line and first leaving the factory in December 1959. The Leader had been voted 'Machine of the Year' in the *Motor Cycle News* readers' poll in 1959, and in 1960 the Arrow won the same coveted title.

Sammy Miller took a modified Arrow, with a 20-inch front wheel and a trials rear tyre to tackle the climb to the summit of Ben Nevis. March snows on Britain's highest mountain defeated him at 3,650 feet, but the lowered gearing and siamesed exhaust system helped the Arrow make an impressive attempt. At around the same time, stories

were circulating about an Arrow being modified by Herman Meier for June's TT Races, but that is another story . . .

The Golden Arrow version was announced for 1961, the first models leaving the works in January. Its 27mm Amal carburettor (the Leader and standard Arrow used a 22mm size) combined with a 10 to 1 compression ratio to produce a healthy 20 bhp at 6,500 rpm and a top speed near 80 mph. Finished in white and gold, with whitewall tyres to add a dash of flash, it was an eyecatching bike for covering the miles on country roads where its precise handling was seen to its best advantage. A rather slow gear change and the same six-inch drum brakes that gave Leader riders occasional heart flutter were less impressive, but the little twin's sporting

1960 250cc Lightweight TT

When the Swinging 'Sixties first began to stir into motion, racing men who wanted a British power unit for the 250 class had very little. The obvious choice was the robust little Ariel engine, and even if the parent BSA company would not support racing officilly, there was scope for the right man to convert a tourer into a competitive racer. One man who recognized the potential early on was Herman Meier, a German living in England since 1949 and with a family background of two-stroke tuning.

In February 1960, *The Motor Cycle* told of Meier's work, with a twin-carburettor engine planned for Michael O'Rourke to ride in the 250cc Lightweight TT. Vic Willoughby later tried the bike and reported revs up to 7,200 and power from around the 5,000 rpm mark, thanks to the two Amal 28mm GP carburettors and Meier's own expansion chamber exhausts. By the time the bike was taken to the Isle of Man, top revs were 8,500 rpm, the weight of the standard-framed bike was down to about 200 lbs and the top speed was over 110 mph. Suspension and brakes were basically standard, but subject to Meier's precise preparation.

1960 was a season when the MV-Agusta and Honda teams clashed head-on, and few people gave the little British roadster much of a chance. The race was over five laps of the 37¾-mile Mountain circuit, where the climb towards the top of Snaefell would tax the Ariel, which had only a four-speed gearbox for O'Rourke to play footsie with. But Mike was a racer with a background of getting bikes from scruffy grasstrackers to shining new road race models to the finishing line somewhat near the front of the field, and he proceeded to ride the modest little Arrow to its limit.

Gary Hocking took first place on his works MV-Agusta, with team-mate Carlo Ubbiali second, followed by Provini's Morini and three of the four-cylinder Hondas that were to dominate the 250 class in years ahead. But in seventh place, just off the leaderboard and climaxing a storming ride with a final lap at over 85 mph, came Michael O'Rourke and the little Ariel. It was easily recognized as a close relation of the roadster, which did the model's reputation a great deal of good, and it won the hearts of spectators who could see it as a bike within their own grasp. And O'Rourke's average speed in the race of 80.2 mph was the best ever recorded by a British 250 in the TT. When the engine was stripped for official measuring after the race, it was all in perfect condition – and it had beaten one of the works MVs!

With a best lap at 85 mph on an Ariel clearly based on the Arrow roadster, Michael O'Rourke was the hero of the 1960 250cc Lightweight TT. Finishing seventh, he was beaten only by factory-entered racers from Italy and Japan.

reputation was helped by sprinter George Brown using his own version of the Arrow to break National 250cc records at up to 126 mph.

The Leader proved to be a practical bike for long-distance touring, when 'Flash' Rogers followed the competitors in the 1962 Monte Carlo Rally, starting in Paris and completing 2,312 miles before arriving in Monaco to average 35 mph on the standard tourer. And to show that the model was still capable of long trouble-free miles, Brian Lowe took his across Canada and back through America in 1976, covering 13,400 miles with only a speedometer cable and one set of contact breaker points replaced. Bought for £5 with its gearbox seized and weeds growing out of the panniers, Brian's Leader was rebuilt with a 12-volt electrical system for £75 and covered 30,000 miles before he took it to America tied down on the deck of a Russian freighter. Across the Mojave Desert or climbing 10,000 feet to Cedar City, the Leader took it all in its stride and averaged 63 miles to the gallon!

Driving instructor John Ashcroft doesn't cover high mileage on his beautifully restored 1960 Leader, but prefers to collect awards for this living example of Ariel history that is fitted with every extra the factory listed. Bought as a reminder of the bike that took John through his own driving test many years ago, it was rebuilt after two years of searching for the correct bits in places as far apart as the Shetland Islands and the National Motor Museum's autojumble in Hampshire. A stem-to-stern rebuild included a look inside the engine, where 19,000 miles had left everything in good working order, and a repaint in the popular red and white colour option using Volkswagen Senegal Red and Ford Old English White.

Finished early in 1980, the Leader was ridden to North Wales for the Llanfair Show and came back with its first award tucked in one of the panniers. A week later, John was riding to a local dealer who had helped with parts in the rebuild when a car turned right in front of him and hit the bike. The legshield protected John's right leg, but in the fall he

---

ARIEL ARROW AND LEADER

Engine: Air-cooled, two-stroke parallel twin, with piston ports. Cast iron cylinder barrel, alloy heads. 54mm bore × 54mm stroke, 247cc. Compression ratio 8.3 to 1 (Sports Arrow, 10 to 1); claimed output 16 bhp at 6,200 rpm (Sports Arrow, 20 bhp at 6,500 rpm).

Transmission (all models): Four-speed gearbox in unit with engine, integral footchange. Primary and secondary transmission by chain. Multi-plate clutch in oil.

Cycle parts: Welded pressed steel monocoque backbone, containing fuel tank and glovebox. Front forks of welded structure, with hydraulically damped trailing link; swinging-arm rear suspension. Six-inch single-leading-shoe drum brakes front and rear.

Dimensions: Wheelbase – 51 in; Dry weight – Leader, 360 lbs; Golden Arrow, 300 lbs.

Owners' Club: Very active; 17 UK branches. Secretary – Mike Taylour, Harrow House, Woolscott, Rugby, Warks CV23 8DB.

Sources of help: Spares – Draganfly Motorcycles, Old Town Maltings, Broad Street, Bungay, Suffolk NR35 1EE; Owners' Club own Spares Scheme. Information – Owners' Club specialists.

---

broke his left in four places and he was confined to a wheelchair for months. Not that it stopped him setting about the wreck in his garage, determined to keep his promise to enter the Leader in the very first Belle Vue Classic Bike Show. The job was done in time, and John left the bike for a friend to take to the Show as he and his family took a holiday to forget the pain and worry of recent months. When they came back, he couldn't resist the temptation to look in the garage and make sure the twice rebuilt Leader was safely home. There stood the Leader and the trophy for Best Bike in the Show. Against the glamorous thoroughbreds and select competition models that had drawn thousands of people to Belle Vue, John Ashcroft's Leader had topped the lot!

But this outstanding restoration is not simply a static showpiece, for John uses it in all weathers for leisure riding. Cruising at 50 to 60 mph gives him 80 miles to every gallon and he can't resist the occasional temptation to take it up to a legal 70 mph. 'You don't thrash this sort of bike,' he explains, 'Not with so much work put into it. But it makes me smile when people see it parked and think it's a brand new Japanese model. They can't believe it's an old British bike.'

ARIEL SINGLES

A Red Hunter for all sports

Below *Brian Jones' 1954 NH 350 has won many awards for the quality of the rebuild by its owner. In 1954 the swinging-arm rear suspension was introduced, but the wheels still used the traditional half-width brake drums. The seat-cover in a light shade of beige was an eye-catching feature of the Ariel at that time.*

Ariel built a world-wide reputation for its sturdy singles over many years. One of the oldest companies in the British industry, it started in business in 1902 as Components Ltd and graduated to a bustling factory that dispatched machines from its Selly Oak, Birmingham, factory to every continent. In the 1930s it coined the name 'Red Hunter' for its overhead-valve singles, a name which was used right through until the singles faded from the scene.

1940s models came with a rigid rear end, telescopic front forks and mudguards with deep valances to keep road dirt off both bike and rider. When a sprung rear end was available as an option, the 1950 price was an extra £19.05; quite a lot when the NH350 cost £154.95! In 1954 came the swinging-

arm frame that brought Ariel's comfort in line with others. Through all these years, the distinctive Ariel livery of black cycle parts and deep red on oil and petrol tanks survived styling changes. Enamelling was done in what used to be the Bournbrook Cinema, opposite the main factory in Dawlish Road. It was looked after by the Hook family, father and two sons, with the gout-ridden dad very short-tempered in the mornings until he could get his feet into a hot mustard bath and issue the day's orders in comfort!

Arthur Crook managed operations in the frame shop, where trained craftsmen used the old-established method of brazing and pinning tubes into malleable iron lugs. Their work was checked by Arthur, whose office contained shelves of strong pickles, beer and

Left *The HS 500 scrambler was a natural choice for sidecar men, such as the Rose brothers, on their way to second place in the 1959 Hants Grand National. They were beaten by Frank and Kay Wilkins – on another Ariel.*

Above *Jim Fletcher bought his hard-working VH 500 for just £35 in 1966 and still uses it for commuting to work. 'The secret is to keep the oil clean and keep an eye on the pump,' he says. 'I always have a quick look to see that the oil's pumping around before I start a journey.'*

Above right *The NH 350 engine of the mid-'50s still used an iron cylinder head; in 1955 came an alloy head and a cylinder barrel with the pushrod tunnel cast in.*

snuff. He sat on a stool outside his office and tapped every frame joint with a hammer, in the way that wheel-tappers used to check railway wheels. If Arthur hit the wrong note with his hammer on any joint, the frame went back for remedial work. Today such methods sound archaic, but Ariel built its name for reliable quality with the aid of such knowledge acquired over years of experience.

The 'Red Hunter' singles were the cream of Ariel's sporting crop, and every engine was run for two hours on a bench in the Engine Test shop before being checked for power output on the dynamometer. In 1950 Ariel claimed 19.4 bhp for its NH 350 and 24.6 for the VH 500, more than any other British push-rod single except Vincent's 'Comet'.

Yet the Ariel engine was simple, as a light-hearted competition in the Engine Test shop showed, when fitters raced to assemble the WNG 350 engine of Second World War service that was the basis of the later 350s. Chris Finnelly was the man in charge of the Engine Test shop and showed his mettle by building a complete engine, including fitting the valve seats and assembling the big-end bearing, in just $1^1/2$ hours. Not that the shop had any luxuries – if the weather was warm and fresh air was needed, a panel of the corrugated iron roof was taken out; if it rained, the panel went back in.

Even the delivery man who took new Ariels to dealers made his mark as one of the trade's characters. Terry Mason would pull up outside the showroom with a lorryload of

ARIEL SINGLES

Engine: Air-cooled four-stroke single, with two pushrod-operated valves per cylinder. Early version had iron barrel and head, later with alloy cylinder head. NH 350 – 72mm bore × 85mm stroke, claimed 19.4 bhp. VH 500 – 81.8mm × 95mm, claimed 24.6 bhp. Competition version VCH – 26.0 bhp. HS 500 scrambler – 34 bhp.

Transmission (all models): Four-speed Burman gearbox with integral footchange. Primary and secondary drive by chain. Multi-plate clutch in oil.

Cycle parts: Rigid frame and telescopic forks in 1948, with optional Anstey-link rear suspension until swinging-arm rear end introduced with 1954 range. Seven-inch single-leading-shoe drum brakes front and rear; full-width hubs from 1955.

Dimensions: Wheelbase – 56 in rigid and swinging-arm frames (trials models 52 in): Dry weight – NH 350 rigid, 348 lbs; sprung frame, 365 lbs (500, 375 lbs; claimed, both versions).

Owners' Club: Very active; 18 branches, 7 overseas branches. Secretary – Mike Taylour, Harrow House, Woolscott, Rugby, Warks CV23 8DB.

Sources of help: Spares – Draganfly Motorcycles, The Old Town Maltings, Broad Street, Bungay, Suffolk NR35 1EE; A. Gagg & Sons, 106 Alfreton Road, Nottingham NG7 3NS; Owners' Club own Spares Scheme – rare parts made in batches.

Ariels, and have anxious customers fretting while he rode their new stock down the unloading plank with the works wrappings still firmly in place!

Big singles were the natural choice for top trials men in the '50s, and Ariel's VCH 500cc competition model was popular with solo and sidecar men alike, as was the HT5 introduced for the 1954 season, in rigid frame form only. West Country man Bob Ray won National trials for the factory on a solo, while the sidecar crew of Frank and Kay Wilkins set the standard on three wheels, winning the ACU Trials Drivers Star in 1952 and '53. By the late 1950s the Ariel trials team included the greatest of them all, Sammy Miller, who teamed with Gordon Blakeway and Ron Langston on solos, with Frank Wilkins still the sidecar man to beat. In 1962 Ron Langston made history when he won the sidecar class of the Cotswold Cups Trial; he had won the solo cup in 1956, and thus became the first man ever to win both solo and sidecar awards in the Cotswolds.

Sammy Miller went on to dominate sporting trials on his own Ariel, the legendary GOV 132. Even when the company dropped the four-stroke range to concentrate on the

revolutionary Leader and Arrow two-stroke twins, he kept on winning on his 'obsolete' 500. And when the Selly Oak works was closed in 1962 and production moved to the BSA factory at Small Heath, Sammy kept on with his four-stroke 500 despite BSA's suggestion that he ought to be swapping to the 250 C15T on which its team was mounted to support the road bike sales.

Ariel stunned four-stroke fanatics when it announced in 1959 that it was going to concentrate on the two-stroke Arrow and Leader models, and all four-stroke production would cease. It was the end of a memorable era, as some of the landmarks in motorcycling's history were killed off.

The single still gives good service, as Jim Fletcher confirms. A customer service manager who uses his 1955 VH 500 and other bikes to commute into Birmingham, he bought the Ariel in 1966. 'It had 11,000 miles on the clock and was in incredible condition. Cost me all of £35!' he grins. Jim and his VH have covered testing National and Dragon Rallies together with little or no problems, but when he was on his way to a job interview at the BSA factory in 1969, the Ariel showed its disapproval and ran its big-end bearing. A side-valve VB engine was fitted temporarily, but its lack of power didn't please, and the bike was passed on to his younger brother as a rebuild project. Back together with the right engine, it carried the younger Fletcher to university and served its new master until it came back to Jim again in 1976. 'And just about everything that could move was absolutely shot,' he recalls.

'But getting spares is quite easy, even today, if you're in the Owners' Club. I got a complete bottom end for £8 at a Club autojumble, and when the original tank leaked I fitted a 1956 one that I picked up for five bob (25p)!

'I still use the bike quite a lot, because it's economical even though the original Amal Monobloc is totally worn and it's got no tickover at all. But it still does 60 to 65 to the gallon if I cruise at about 60 mph. I've actually got a new carburettor, and I suppose I'll fit it some day.'

1962 Scott one-day trial

Of all the one-day trials in the British calendar, the Scott is recognized as the toughest. Originally intended as a proving event for Scott machines, it combines long miles over the Yorkshire moors, with the fastest man setting the standard time, and tough observed sections, along the rocky and watery way. Sammy Miller won the event seven times.

In Sammy's career of over 1,000 wins, he has no hesitation in naming the 1962 Scott his greatest victory. 'No doubt about it, that was the one. It was one of those days when everything went well, man and horse had no problems. I suppose we all have exceptional days, and that was mine.'

The trial was run in mist after a week of rain that left every section tougher than usual. Sammy's strongest opposition amongst the 185 starters came from BSA C15T-mounted Jeff Smith and Arthur Lampkin, both men with top line scramble experience, reflected in Jeff Smith setting standard time. Miller on the big Ariel 500 did not have such a light mount to manoeuvre over the bleak moors, but so finely honed was GOV 132 that it needed very little special preparation for the trial. 'Slightly heavier damping in the front forks and the tyres a little harder to prevent any nipping of the tubes over the rocks,' Sammy recalls. 'About six pounds pressure in the front tyre and four in the rear. Only a pound or so up on the normal pressures. I knew I had to get it right, because Arthur was a Yorkshireman and Jeff was from the north, so I wouldn't get the benefit of any doubt.'

Sammy got it right enough to finish only 7 minutes slower than Jeff, to lose 7 marks on time. But Jeff lost 65 marks on observation, and Arthur Lampkin's total was 3 marks lost on time and 76 dropped for footing or stopping over the moors he knew so well. Miller on the big Ariel conceded just 18 marks on observation, giving him a total of 25, a huge margin of 40 marks less than runner-up Jeff Smith. It was a dynamic demonstration of the world's greatest trials rider at the top of his form, on a machine the BSA group had decided was obsolete.

A measure of the conditions in that 1962 Scott was that there were only 40 finishers of the 185 who started, and the only other 500 to finish was Peter Gaunt's Ariel, winning the 500cc class with a total of 164 marks lost. In Miller's glittering career, which included eleven British trials championships (five on his Ariel), that demanding day on the moors is Sammy's choice of his greatest ride ever. The Ariel may have been obsolete in some ways, but when combined with Miller's preparation and skill it made a formidable combination.

In 1958, a young Sammy Miller (right) was still learning how to get the best from his Ariel. Seen here with fellow Ulsterman Benny Crawford, Sammy went on to make GOV 132 the most famous Ariel in the world.

Ariel's first vertical twin was the 500cc KH, designed by the much respected Val Page, and announced in September 1948. Its iron cylinder head and barrel were unremarkable, like the sweet spread of power that its single carburetted 6.8 to 1 compression engine gave; it was just another established company joining the fashion started by Turner's Triumph Speed Twin. Ironically, Page had designed a 650cc parallel twin for the Triumph factory in the 1930s that was not a success.

Sturdy and sweet described the KH. Sturdy because Ariels always were, with a faithful public who bought with confidence in their quality of build and a liking for the standard red tank topping off the sober black enamel of the cycle parts. Sweet because the 63mm x 80mm engine would pull easily from low revs, to an honest 80 mph maximum. Never the top seller, it was given a little more glamour with the all-alloy-motored KHA for 1953, which cost £12.78 more than the £222.33 asked for the iron KH, but when the 1957 list was issued the KHA had gone – which makes it quite a collector's item today! Pushing the alloy twin aside was a 1954 addition, the 650cc 'Huntmaster', with a thinly disguised BSA A10 engine in Ariel running gear.

The Huntmaster was a late move into the over-500cc market, which was surprising as BSA had owned Ariel since 1944 and was enjoying very good business with the solid A10 'Golden Flash'. Maybe the independent satellite at Selly Oak didn't want to do what

ARIEL TWINS

Quality with modesty

Left *Ariel's parallel twin line began with the Val Page-designed 500cc KG, noted for its sweet flexible engine. Colin Aspley's award-winning 1955 example wears period Rodark panniers which complemented the rear mudguard's contour.*

Below *Roly Elliott's 1958 Huntsmaster is a second-time-around love, rebuilt from a wreck with 72,000 miles of accumulated neglect. Cycle parts have been hand painted and the maroon tanks and mudguards sprayed in Austin Rover paint that is a near match to the original colour.*

its masters at Small Heath thought was good for it – they were both in Birmingham, but worlds apart in outlook. Many of the old timers at Ariel never accepted being taken over by 'The Beesa'.

But the market wanted bigger twins, and a slightly uprated BSA gave Ariel its answer. With 40 bhp at 6,200 rpm it was as powerful as the mighty Square Four and offered a top speed in the nineties. *Motor Cycling* said it was 'a mount typical of the modern trend' and when it was given full-width alloy hubs and an optional rear chain enclosure in 1955, *The Motor Cycle* found it '. . . an unusually tractable model' and said that '. . . the smoothness of the transmission permitted optimum use to be made of low-speed punch without harshness.'

The ability to pull strongly from low revs made the Huntmaster a popular choice for hauling a sidecar, and members of the Ariel Owners' Club still use the model regularly with a third wheel. Aeronautical engineer Geoff Thomasson is Technical Adviser to the Club, and his 1956 example with a sidecar hauls a trailer with the Club's own 1911 Ariel veteran aboard with no problems. Fuel consumption for the heavily laden bike driven at speeds of up to 70 mph works out at about 45 miles to the gallon, and Geoff is an admirer of the solid pulling power: 'Bob Brassington, who was our Club chairman, calls it The Gruntmaster for the way it produces its power so low down the rev scale.' Geoff's own bike had about 100,000 miles when he bought it, most clocked up in

1954 round-Britain ride

'Titch' Allen chose Ariel's newly launched 650cc Huntmaster Twin for his epic ride around the British coast in 1954, covering 3,589 miles in 10 days to beat the 12 days of Hugh Gibson for the same route in 1924. With a prototype Nicholson saloon sidecar to protect ACU observer John McNulty, and Feridax screen, legshields and panniers on test as well, the outfit headed north from Liverpool in the first week of May.

The Meteorological Office had advised May as the best time for kind weather in Scotland, but by the time the twin droned into Fort William it was snowing! The northern half of the trip was wet most of the way, which made tough roads even worse. 'It may seem easy to people who live in the south and see the coast road as a highway,' recalls Titch. 'But in northern Scotland it was just loose gravel in parts. In others it crossed bogs where it was laid on brushwood, and you could feel it bounce with the passage of a vehicle.'

A rest day at Holbeach in Lincolnshire – the ACU did not approve of such attempts including a Sunday! – gave a chance to service the bike and swap a rear tyre worn out in 1,700 miles. Hard driving was loosening spokes in the sidecar and rear wheels and in Weymouth, Dorset, one broke and jammed in the drum of the sidecar brake. 'It's not easy taking the stub axle out at the side of the road with stones,' the driver remembers. Not far along the route, ex-Ariel trials teamster Bob Ray had a shop, and there the wheels were rebuilt.

'On the last day, coming up the Welsh coast, the sidecar damper unit broke. The wheel jammed under the mudguard and we ended up in the ditch. It could have been the end, but after nine days you would have picked the outfit up and carried it to the finish,' Titch says. 'McNulty helped me get the bike back on the road, then I walked to a farm and borrowed a saw. I cut a piece of fence post to length and tied it in place of the strut with fencing wire. We finally got into Liverpool within 20 minutes of our schedule.'

The proving run was still not ended. The Huntmaster was driven back to Birmingham to be dismantled for engine inspection; the timing side main bearing was replaced. 'A bit of swarf had got into the bearing and turned the metal out,' Titch says. 'But the rest of the engine was beautiful.'

To prove there was plenty of steam in the engine, the sidecar was removed and the bike taken to Silverstone circuit with solo gearing fitted. There it covered 500 miles in 500 minutes, with a team of riders thrashing the fully kitted tourer hard. But it was a near thing – as final rider Howard German did an extra lap for luck the rear chain broke!

The heavily laden Huntmaster tackles another hill on its way around the coast of Britain. ACU observer John McNulty rode in the sidecar, but his 15 stones could not get the fuel consumption below 48 mpg for ten days of hard driving.

the hands of Owners' Club members. Geoff has rebuilt the twin, but found the sturdy Burman gearbox needed no work at all, which offsets road-test criticisms of a slow change. 'Inside the casings it's an A10 BSA, so spares are no real problem,' confirms Thomasson. 'The little-end bushes rattle loose if you don't watch 'em and I've known some wear in 10,000 miles. I turn my own up in phosphor bronze and make sure they're a good fit.

'You have to watch the timing side main bearing, which is a plain bush. And the splines on the drive side of the crankshaft can wear rapidly if you don't watch them – that's a matter of proper maintenance. The nut on the end of the crank should be tight, with washers to space it out right; if you get a gap because you put the split pin in the castellated nut it can chatter and you get trouble.'

Geoff's son has the 500cc KH twin in captivity, with 25,000 miles in both solo and sidecar form. Dad clearly prefers the smaller engine: 'Sweet as a nut. A lovely, lovely bike.'

High mileages on the long-legged Ariel twin come as a matter of course to Dick Henry, who bought his 650 Huntmaster in 1960 with 5,000 miles on the clock and has added an extra 218,000 since then! 'It's only let me down once on the road,' he boasts. 'A shaft in the gearbox bust in Holland when we were on the way to an Elephant Rally in Germany. But a dealer in Amsterdam had some second-hand bits, so my mate rode in and got them, and we mended it and carried on!

'Most of the miles I've done were with a sidecar on, and it'll go up to 70 and more with a chair. Solo it will cruise in the eighties, and in more normal riding it will do 60 to 65 to the gallon. It used to be my only transport, and I changed the oil every 1,500 miles as the handbook said, but oils have improved and most of us change every 2 to 3,000 miles now; the crankshaft has had one regrind. It did 20 winters without a break for me. It's a good workhorse.'

Roly Elliott went back to the Huntmaster with happy memories of one he owned when

ARIEL TWINS

Engine: Air-cooled, four-stroke parallel twin, with two pushrod-operated valves per cylinder. Iron cylinder head and barrels, except all-alloy KHA. 500cc KH – 63mm bore × 80mm stroke, claimed 26 bhp. 650cc Huntmaster – 70mm × 84mm, claimed 40 bhp.
Transmission: (all models) Four-speed Burman gearbox, with integral footchange. Primary and secondary transmission by chain. Multi-plate clutch in oil.
Cycle parts: All models with telescopic forks, early 500cc version with rigid or Anstey-link rear plunger springing. Swinging-arm rear suspension from 1954. Seven-inch single-leading-shoe brakes front and rear.
Dimensions: Wheelbase – 56 in. Dry weight – 500, 384 lbs; 650, 410 lbs.
Owners' Club: Very active; 18 UK branches, 7 overseas. Secretary – Mike Taylour, Harrow House, Woolscott, Rugby, Warks CV23 8BD.
Sources of help: Spares – Draganfly Motorcycles, The Old Town Maltings, Broad Street, Bungay, Suffolk NR35 1EE; A. Gagg & Sons, 106 Alfreton Road, Nottingham NG7 3NS; Owners' Club own Spares Scheme – rare parts made in batches.

serving his apprenticeship as an RAF engineer. 'I ran it for a year and there were just no troubles. A magic bike.' Buying another to help recapture those days, he learned a lot about what can be worn out and bodged to disguise the result of 72,000 miles. 'There are so many little points that you can miss, like the rear sprocket held on with car wheel studs instead of the correct ones. It took me two hours to get them out.'

Bought as a non-runner, Roly's 650 revealed a host of niggling faults as the RAF Chief Technician stripped it for a complete rebuild and paint. An engine and gearbox rebuilt without gaskets had no chance of being oiltight, and badly worn springs in the advance and retard mechanism left the ignition stuck on full advance, while a bad pattern seat didn't line up with the proper mounting points, and stripped threads left no firm mountings for the oil and petrol tanks.

'I reckon I've put about 150 hours into sorting out the cycle parts,' says Elliott. 'Most of the parts have come from Draganfly, who specialize in Ariels, and the engine spares are easy BSA stuff. The paint was mostly done by hand, using pot scourers to scrub the frame before I painted it, but the tanks were sprayed. To buy one of these, you should research the model and take someone along who knows them well. It's worth it – a good one will go on for ever and a day.'

ARIEL SQUARE FOUR

10-100 mph in top gear

Four-cylinder roadsters are not a creation of modern times – Ariel had one in its range from 1931 until 1958, with production only interrupted by the 1939-45 war. Originally designed by Edward Turner as a 500, the 'Squariel' grew up to be a full 1000cc model that was flexible enough to offer a top gear range from 10 to 100 mph in its later years.

The engine featured two contra-rotating crankshafts, joined in the later versions by straight-cut gears on the drive side of the shafts. The noise from the two coupling gears in their alloy primary transmission case became a characteristic feature of the bike, while the single carburettor feeding four pots through tortuous inlet tracts cast into the head meant that it was never a top-end revver, with peak power coming at 5,800 rpm in the later versions. Just why 1000cc cylinders could not match 650cc twins for power output was explained by Val Page, Ariel's great designer who refined the design and tried to find more power. Of the 4G Mark One with alloy cylinder head, he told Ariel Club historian Jim Lee: 'Actually, the alloy that the heads were made of was very poor quality, that was the real trouble. There was nothing much wrong with the design, and if you got the material right the job was quite satisfactory. We had got hold of the wrong alloy for the head, there was no question about that.' Beefing up the cylinder head studs helped with that problem without the factory having to foot a big bill, but the development of the

Four into a really powerful engine was prevented by basic design.

Near the end of the model's life, experiments were being made to release the four-cylinder power. 'It had some inherent faults,' said Page, 'one of which was the flexible camshaft and the other was the crankshafts; that was the cause of all the vibration we got. But the cranks ran so close together that we could not increase the diameter of the pins by an eighth of an inch.

'We made some tests that were really rather interesting on the deflection of the crankshafts. We hadn't any elaborate tackle to do it, so we put in some adjustable screws with a lead point, two or three around the flywheels. Then we adjusted them so they just cleared the flywheels around the diameter, and ran the engine. The points got knocked right off, and I think we found about fifteen thousands of an inch deflection on the crankshaft.'

Page progressed the Square Four from its cast iron cylinder head and barrel form of 1946 to an all-alloy motor in the 1949 Mark One form, then on to the 1953 Mark Two, with its distinctive style of two exhaust pipes each side of the cylinder block siamesing into one pipe and silencer. And Selly Oak's range topper was part of a flirtation with a different front fork for the summer of 1953. The factory was set to offer the Earles-designed swinging-fork front end as an option on all its models, the Square Four in

ARIEL SQUARE FOUR

Engine: Air-cooled, four-stroke square four cylinders, with two pushrod-operated valves per cylinder. 65mm bore × 75mm stroke on all 1000 cc engines. 1945 – 4G, iron cylinder head and barrels, claimed output 36 bhp at 5,800 rpm; 1949 – Mk 1, alloy head and barrels, claimed output 34.5 bhp at 5,400 rpm; 1952 – Mk II, alloy head and barrel, claimed output 40 bhp at 5,600 rpm.

Transmission (all models): Burman four-speed gearbox with integral footchange. Twin crankshafts linked by straight-cut gears, primary and second transmissions by chain. Multi-plate clutch in oil.

Cycle parts (all models): Rear sprung frame by plunger-style Anstey-link, telescopic front forks (1953 Earles forks not put into production), rigid rear frame optional for sidecar use. Seven-inch diameter single-leading-shoe drum brakes front and rear, with fulcrum adjustment of front brake from 1946 on.

Dimensions: Wheelbase – 56 in (54$^{1}/_{2}$ with optional rigid frame). Dry weight – 1946, 420 lbs; 1949, 412 lbs; 1952-56, 425 lbs; 1958, 435 lbs.

Owners' Club: Very active; 17 UK branches. Secretary – Mike Taylour, Harrow House, Woolscott, Rugby, Warks CV23 8BD.

Sources of help: Spares – Draganfly Motorcycles, Old Town Maltings, Broad Street, Bungay, Suffolk NR35 1EE; Owners' Club own Spares Scheme. Information – Owners' Club specialists.

that form to be known as the Mark Three Royal Hunter. But the death of the very popular Les Graham on an Earles-forked MV in that year's Senior TT brought a public reaction against the alternative to telescopic forks, and the idea was quietly dropped. The Square Four carried on with its lugged frame with telescopic forks and Anstey-link rear suspension until its death was announced in 1958, and the swinging-arm framed model that was under consideration never went into production. Britain's long-running four disappeared; ten years later, Honda started a world-dominating theme with its own four-cylinder model, and in another ten years Britain's Barry Sheene conquered all to win the 500cc World Championship on a Suzuki with its four cylinders in square formation!

A long-term Square Four user is schoolteacher John Bradshaw, who gave up his position as chairman of the Ariel Owners' Club to Lester Grant, another 'Squariel' rider. John Bradshaw's Square Four is a blend of different years that began as a possible spare engine for the later model he was using in the 1970s. 'I was running a Mark Two and using it to get to school in Rubery, near Birmingham,' John recalls. 'One of the lads in my class asked me if I wanted a spare engine for my bike and I finally went along to see it to keep him quiet. I had to peer through this hedge and there was a Square Four engine in a shed! I ended up buying it from the old chap for a fiver, and built the bike around it.

'The engine is a 1946 4G, one of the last of the all-iron units with alloy exhaust manifolds, fitted into a 1953 frame. The tank is 1953 too, with an instrument panel of the 1930s style. I was on the way to a Dragon Rally in Wales, stopped to nip behind a wall because of the force of nature, and found I was almost standing on this rusted Ariel tank! I felt it was almost destiny, so I had the panel fitted in this tank.

'The front forks are a pair that Ken Sprayson made in 1954. I found a pair of the Earles forks like the factory were planning to fit in 1953, and was showing them to Ken. He said I should have a special set of forks for a bike that's one-off like mine and loaned me these forks. I gave the Earles forks to Ralph Hawkins in the Club to fit to his 1953 "Squariel", because that is the sort of bike they would have been on.'

With some 40,000 miles covered during the 11 years he has owned the bike, John is impressed that it still has the original cylinder bores, pistons and camshaft, but early days showed the design's weak spot. 'Soon after I got it, Number Three rod ran the big-end,' he remembers. 'That's the one that goes first – it's furthest from the oil pump. The crankshaft oilways were as usual blocked with sediment and we had to drill them out.

'I paid £45 in 1976 to have the white metal big-ends renewed and they lasted just 700 miles! So my father and I bored the conrods out on his lathe and fitted shell bearings; people said it couldn't be done, but I haven't touched it since. I've done away with the silly little filter Ariel fitted and use a Norton Commando cartridge-type now – everyone who does some miles on a "Square" does that.

'It appeals because it's so smooth. We've done a lot of miles together and it's a lump of metal that I know well. No sentiment, just a nice bike.'

The Healey Four

The Square Four was dropped by Ariel at the end of 1958, but the bike was brought back to life in the 1970s by Tim and George Healey when they offered something really different as a luxury tourer – the Healey Four.

The brothers had been supplying spares and rebuilding Square Fours in their home workshop on Rock Hill, in the Worcestershire town of Bromsgrove, where complete bikes had to be lowered to the road by hoist because the narrow stairway was too steep! They also built and raced a supercharged 'Squariel' in sprints, which taught them a lot about getting the hidden horsepower out of the gentle engine, with a best output of 95 bhp at 4,000 rpm on the testbed – more than double the factory's claimed 42 bhp at 5,800 rpm!

The Healey Four began with a scrap Egli spine frame from importer Roger Slater, which had the engine mounts cut off for racing layout experiments. The combination worked well and attracted a lot of attention at the 1971 London Show; soon the Healey 1000/4 was in production at Bartleet Road in Redditch, not far from the old Royal Enfield factory. The Healeys employed a secretary to take the 'phone calls and look after administration, while Paul Mayhew was trained as a fitter to build the machines with Tim and George. It was a truly shoestring outfit with little capital and no spare staff – when Tim was knocked off his Healey by a car, sustaining concussion and a broken ankle, he worked at the bench from his wheelchair.

Using the Healeys' own version of the Egli spine frame, with Ceriani forks and a huge Grimeca four-leading-shoe front brake, the 1000/4 handled and stopped like a top line sportster. But the engine's flexibility was hardly compromised in its development to give 50 bhp at 6,000 rpm, giving a range from 10 to 110 mph, and with a claimed weight of 355 lbs it was no heavier than the contemporary Honda 250! And a modified camshaft lifted the speed of the prototype to a best of 126 mph with the standard cylinder head and SU carburettor. 'At the end of development we were getting a consistent 126 mph,' claims Tim Healey. 'But the crankshafts were going. If we'd made the cranks we could have overcome that.'

Despite the promise the bike offered, backing was not forthcoming in a world where old-established names like BSA were struggling. Tim Healey went his own way, George struggled on but eventually the factory closed, with 28 bikes and conversion kits made. The attempt to revive a classic design had died, but the ironic twist to the tale of the ill-fated Healey is that it is now even more sought after than the Ariel Square Four!

Tim Healey on the prototype Healey Four takes in another lap of the TT course as he puts in the miles to prove how well Healey development work had been done. The bike covered over 40,000 miles with no attention beyond servicing, with power boosted to 50 bhp.

BIRMINGHAM SCOTTS

The tradition continued

Below *Ken Thirtle's 1946 model still lives in Yorkshire, where it was born, an award-winning example of the way in which the Shipley factory built the post-war models.*

Alfred Angas Scott, a dyer's technician from Bradford, was an original thinker. When the motorcycle industry was in its real infancy, mounting engines on strengthened bicycle frames in positions as diverse as above the front wheel and behind the rear wheel (and most points between), Scott was noting the mistakes of others and laying his own plans.

Most manufacturers were buying engines from abroad, particularly from France, and accepted the limitations of single-cylinder four-stroke units that vibrated and wore their exposed valve gear very rapidly. Scott approached the problem from a new angle and in 1902 he built a water-cooled parallel twin two-stroke in his own workshop. The engine was tested initially on Scott's boat and in his bicycle, but six years later the first complete Scott motorcycle appeared in public and won the Bradford MCC's 1908 hill-

climb. With its engine mounted low to give great stability and an all-chain drive that was not affected by rain, the new Scott set new standards.

By 1911 the design was developed enough for the company's Secretary Frank Philipp to make fastest lap in the Isle of Man Senior TT. And Frank Applebee and Clarry Wood won the 1912 and 1913 Senior TTs respectively, to confirm the ability of the Scott to cope with fast road work. Not content with that, the company ran a trial across the Yorkshire moors in 1914, for its own machines. A strict limit was imposed on gearing, to prevent freak machines being used. Of the 14 starters, nine survived a long day, finding their way across the unforgiving countryside that still beats many riders and bikes in today's Scott Trial, even if most of the moderns would be regarded by Alfred

Above *The purists might not care for modernizing work on Bob Stephens' spotless 'Flying Squirrel', but it makes the bike nicer to ride. 'I don't really push it hard,' he admits. 'She's an old girl now!'*

Left *The gaffer himself. Matt Holder on the 350 racer seems pleased with the team's handiwork.*

Angas Scott as complete freaks.

Scott's thorough approach to proving his machines won him respect, but the company went through varying fortunes. By the 1940s, with the Second World War over, they were still making motorcycles in the old Shipley, Yorkshire, factory, but water-cooled two-stroke twins were out of fashion and sales were slow. In 1951 the company was not listed in *Motor Cycling*'s Year Book, but for 1952 they were shown as trading again, but this time from St Mary's Row in Birmingham. The Birmingham Scott had arrived.

The new owner was Matt Holder, boss of Aerco Jig and Tools, a trained silversmith with a love of Scotts and a streak of independence that casual enquirers found off-putting; Matt sold Scotts to those who knew and revered the marque. His early offerings were simply Shipley-made parts assembled in Birmingham, including the three-speed gearbox and rigid frame that were a long way short of what the opposition had in their specification sheets. But Matt's habit of storing spares, whilst it might turn any newly qualified cost accountant grey, has left a legacy for the Scott enthusiast of the present day. When Matt's son David moved the company and its stock into the old Triumph Number Two factory at Meriden, he found a treasure trove of original parts, including Miller headlight units and Burgess silencers – the sort of parts restorers search the land for and seldom find.

The Birmingham Scott was updated in 1956, with a swinging-arm rear suspension and full-width alloy hubs, but the 596cc water-cooled engine showed its vintage origins with an external Pilgrim oil pump. In

Scott in the '60s – the Bulmer workshop

The Scott's racing history includes more than their successes of early years. In the 1960s, a talented three-man team developed the Birmingham factory's air-cooled 350cc twin to race-winning form. Brian Woolley's two-stroke expertise developed the power, Brian Bulmer's fabricating skills built the bike around the power unit, and newcomer Barrie Scully rode the bike well enough to set a new 350 class record for Barbon hill climb on the bike's 1965 début. That record stood for 11 years!

Bulmer and Scully built the bike in Bulmer Senior's home workshop.'When we were bending tubes, Brian did the heating and I did the pulling,' Barrie remembers. 'It took us about fifteen minutes to do one bend that way, but it made a really good job. Brian's great with a welding torch, and he made all the frame and tanks for the bike.

'I remember we took it to Cadwell Park for a meeting on the Woodlands circuit,' says Barrie. 'I set a new class lap record then. But the problem with the bike was that it used to get tired after two laps or so. We did get it more reliable, but then it was a bit slower.'

Fast enough to impress at a *Motor Cycling* test, with a top speed of 115.4 mph against Paddy Driver's 7R AJS, which managed only 112.5. And fast enough to be in the top ten in the Ulster Grand Prix until a split expansion chamber slowed it. 'I can remember closing on Rod Gould on an Aermacchi at a Cadwell meeting, and wondering how I was going to get past him,' says Scully. 'In fact, I could have gone past him with the speed we had, but I burnt a piston so it didn't matter.

'Occasionally the bike would handle beautifully on a short circuit, but on a long one it could be a bit exciting; it really lacked development in the handling. It had tremendous potential, but Scotts at Birmingham could only go so far – they had a business to run, after all.'

The team also developed a water-cooled 500cc version that was built in unit with the five-speed Albion transmission, using gear primary drive. On the dynamometer at the Bulmer workshop in Yorkshire – where better to have a Scott racing team? – it showed promise with 48 bhp at the rear wheel. After a week of work on settings, the power was up to 52 bhp with 50 horsepower over a 1,000 rpm spread. 'The trouble was that we only had one engine,' Barrie explains. 'We were trying to race it at weekends and do development work in the week. And we were just working men, with jobs to do in the day. I suppose if we were trying to develop it today, we'd get some outside sponsorship to help.'

With the arrival of the 350 Yamaha the writing for the part-time Scott effort was on the wall. Even British ingenuity couldn't match such might.

Barrie Scully showing the Scott's style at Oulton Park in 1964. 'The bike showed great promise and was very easy to ride and drift round corners,' he recalls.

1958 the dynamo gave way to an alternator and from then on there was little change, but some experiments did emerge for the world to see after production ended in 1978.

Scott specialist Ian Pearce has an impeccable background with the marque. His late father bought his first Scott in 1926 and had one until his death 52 years later; Sam Pearce's enthusiasm encouraged Ian to enter vintage racing, where home-tuned Scotts won him numerous championships. His own road bikes include a Birmingham-built 'Flying Squirrel' with Velocette gearbox, Piranha electronic ignition and Suzuki front forks and disc brake. Next to the Squirrel is his 500cc 'Swift', one of the experimental models that didn't make it to the production line, and one of only six built.

'Matt Holder told me that a Squirrel produced 32 bhp at 5,000 rpm, and it also gave 16 bhp at 2,500 rpm,' Ian remembers. 'At 2,500 rpm a Velocette 500 is only giving 8 bhp, which I suppose explains the appeal of the Scott. But I doubt that top figure; I would guess a good Scott gives about 23 bhp at the back wheel.

'What you can do with them is bumble along at 65 mph all day. The problem is that they'll build up to that on a quarter throttle and if you're using petroil mixture you're not getting enough oil through. What you have to do is roll the throttle back now and again and then give it a handful to get a good cool charge through the engine.'

Bob Stephens is one of a band of Scott fanatics who help Ian Pearce in his Bridgnorth workshop when spare time allows. Bob's bike is another example of Matt Holder's experiments, using a lighter frame with revised rear subframe and a longer steering head than the standard product. Built for him by the late Sam Pearce, it was originally fitted with Norton forks and front wheel, but demands of modern traffic have seen a swap to Suzuki front end and the benefits of disc braking. 'Matt Holder gave Sam the frame to rebuild his bike after it was wrecked by a learner driver,' maintenance electrician Bob explains. 'I swapped it to the Suzuki GT500 front end after I'd seen it work so well on Ian Pearce's own bike. The

BIRMINGHAM SCOTTS

Engine: Water-cooled parallel two-stroke twin. 73mm bore × 71.4mm stroke, 596cc, giving a claimed 26 bhp at 5,000 rpm. **Transmission:** Three-speed Scott gearbox, with primary and secondary transmission by chain. Multi-plate dry clutch inboard of final drive sprocket.
Cycle parts: Dowty oleo-pneumatic telescopic forks on earlier model, later modified to spring damping. Lugged frame with rigid rear end and until 1956, when all-welded duplex cradle frame with swinging-arm rear suspension introduced. Two 6-inch drum brakes at front, 8-inch single at rear until 1956, then twin 7-inch drum at front and single 8-inch at rear.
Dimensions: Wheelbase – 56 in. Saddle height – 29 in (rigid frame), Ground clearance – $5^1/2$ in; Tank capacity – $3^1/2$ gallons; Weight – 390 lbs (1954), 395 lbs (1956 sprung frame model) or 405 lbs (1956 rigid).
Owners' Club: Active. Secretary – H. Beal, 2 White Shott, Basildon, Essex SS16 5HF.
Sources of help: Advice – Owners' Club. Spares – Owners' Club scheme; Sam Pearce Motorcycles, Unit 5, Stanley Lane, Bridgnorth, Shropshire WV16 4SF; Markhouse Motorcycles, 1099 Markhouse Road, Walthamstow, London E17 3DG. Restoration – Sam Pearce Motorcycles.

purists wouldn't like this, because as well as having the wrong forks it runs on petroil mixture, which does away with the old Pilgrim pump, which wasn't really very good. It's got a Piranha ignition unit mounted on the crankcase door where the old pump was, and that does make it feel better. It's a bit sharper, and with nothing to get out of adjustment, the electronic ignition is a definite benefit.'

Bob's riding since 1955 has included BSA's A7 twin and a Velocette Viper which he later fitted with a KSS overhead camshaft engine. But since buying a 1929 Scott under Sam Pearce's guidance in the 1960s, he has always had one of the stroker twins in his garage. 'I paid £6 for that 1929 bike,' he recalls with a grin. 'Now I've got another Birmingham Scott to keep this one company – that's fitted with Norton Roadholder forks. It was originally registered by the Scott Company in 1960.

'I'm prejudiced, but I reckon the Scott is second to none on handling,' claims Bob. 'The centre of gravity is so low you always feel safe on it.'

Expert Ian Pearce sums up the loyalty to the marque: 'I know the Scott's faults, but I love them all the same.'

BSA BANTAM

The lightweight for the world

Below *The Bantam started its model life as a three-speed 123cc economy model with a plunger-sprung rear frame available as an optional extra. This spotless restoration was by Staffordshire enthusiast Bob Parry for his wife Janet.*

Until the Earls Court Show of 1948, the mighty Birmingham Small Arms company was recognized as the home of solid, well-made four-strokes to suit most tastes. Even the simple pedal-assisted autocycles that found favour with many for their economy and simple controls were never offered by BSA, even though they did make them under the New Hudson name until the mid-'fifties! But to the man in the street with an itch to beat the bus queues, BSA was the maker whose range started at 250cc. Then came the Bantam.

The bike was one of the surprises of the Show, even though there had been hints when the press revealed that the factory had produced a batch of 125cc engines for a Swedish contract. That same engine was the Bantam's, acclaimed as a major move by BSA to provide the transport-hungry people with an affordable mount. Nobody mentioned that it was, in fact, the German DKW RT125, a design offered to Britain as part of Germany's reparations after the 1939-45 war.

The author can remember being told by a man who knew his bikes about a 1930s DKW whose owner had no trouble with spares in the 1950s – he simply bought them from his local BSA dealer!

The Bantam came with a three-speed gearbox in unit with the engine, undamped telescopic front forks that would flex visibly if you hit a bump in a corner, Wico-Pacy six-volt lighting that equalled anything other lightweights could offer, and an ability to take punishment and keep coming back for more. Its power output of 4 bhp at 5,000 rpm confirmed that the engine was intentionally built with a low state of tune, which made 50 mph appear on the semi-circular speedometer only if the rider really got down to it, and probably kept a lot of novices out of trouble. Popular as a training machine and the natural choice for learners, it sold in thousands.

The D1 125 model was developed to the 150cc Bantam Major, still with just three speeds in the gearbox but offering 5.3 bhp at

5,000 rpm. But at the Motor Industries Research Association test track, development tester Jack Gough lapped the speed bowl at an average of 66 mph, on a version tuned at the Redditch factory where the model was built until 1967. In 1958 came the D5 Super, the first of the 175cc versions that lasted until the end of the model's life in 1971. But the Super still had only three speeds, and it was not until the D10 Sports was introduced in 1966 that a Bantam was available with four speeds. At that time, Suzuki was offering its six-speed 'Super Six' 250 for the sporty types, but the simple little Bantam's appeal was to the traditionalist who shunned complication.

Its easy control and maintenance made it an obvious choice for the General Post Office to issue to the lads who delivered telegrams to the door in the days when a telephone was a relative luxury. Finished in the bright red of all Post Office vehicles of the period, thousands of little Bantams carried urgent news, good and bad, from telegraph offices to

the public. The Post Office bought many thousands of Bantams, a testimony to the model's reputation for reliability.

The Bantam could be tuned for almost any competition, and from the very first 125cc TT in 1951 there was a Bantam amongst the British entries. The great Brian Stonebridge spent time at the Redditch factory during his brief spell as a BSA scrambles team member, working on a Bantam with tuning wizard Herman Meier. The little bike, its lanky rider dwarfing it, was looking very promising when Stonebridge quit BSA and went east to the young Greeves factory in Essex, taking with him valuable knowledge on getting the best from a small two-stroke. From its early days, the Bantam was available in trials trim, but keen clubmen who bought the £86.58p D1 Competition model could not have dreamed that the Bantam would rise to be competitive for honours in National trials in later years.

But those were highlights in 23 years of supplying the masses with economical transport. Some half a million Bantams were made and exported around the world, and with the introduction of the 150cc D10

BSA BANTAM

Engine: Air-cooled, two-stroke single with inclined cylinder. Iron cylinder barrel, alloy head. 1948-63 – 52mm bore × 58mm stroke, 123cc, developing 4 bhp at 5,000 rpm; 1954-57 – 57mm × 58mm 148cc version available, developing 5.3 bhp at 5,000 rpm; 1958-71 – 61.5mm x 58mm 173cc version available developing 10 bhp at 6,000 rpm (12.6 bhp at 5,750 rpm in later versions).

Transmission: Gearbox in unit with engine throughout model life. Three-speed gearbox until 1966, when four speeds became available. Primary and secondary transmission by chain. Multi-plate clutch in oil.

Cycle parts: Rigid rear frame and telescopic forks from 1948, with plunger rear suspension optional. Swinging-arm rear suspension on all models from 1958. Single-leading-shoe drum brakes on all models, 5-inch diameter on early 123 and 148cc models, 5½-inch on all others.

Dimensions: Wheelbase – 50 in (D5 173cc, 52 in; D7 173cc, 51.1 in). Dry weight – D1 rigid frame, 153 lbs; D14/4 Bushman, 222 lbs.

Owners' Club: Active, but rather shy about publicity. Secretary – Ian Wallis, 61 Lynden Avenue, Long Eaton, Nottingham.

Sources of help: Spares – C. & D. Autos, 1193-99 Warwick Road, Acocks Green, Birmingham B27 6BY; Bob Joyner & Son, Wolverhampton Road, Warley, West Midlands; Kidderminster Motorcycles, 60-62 Blackwell Street, Kidderminster, Worcs.

Bushman in 1966, the factory was years ahead of today's trendy trail bikes. BSA had a more down to earth market in mind for its off-road model and sold it to sheep farmers in many countries!

Tom Doubtfire appreciates the power the Bushman engine in his 1969 175cc model produces. 'Fully laden – and I do mean fully – it will still do over 70 mph on the speedo,' he claims. 'We use it for BSA Club rallies, and with two of us and our camping gear it's pulling a bit of weight.'

Tom is the bike's third owner, and bought it 'in a sadly neglected state – everything was on the point of going. I suppose that's why it was so cheap.' 450 hours of spare-time work went into the little two-stroke's revival course, and as a field sales manager in the fur trade, Tom has very little time for anything else. 'No wonder the house painting doesn't get done,' he grins.

The engine was fitted with new bearings and seals, while the cylinder barrel was given its first rebore in nearly 20 years. Wear in the four-speed gearbox surprised him: 'I found the dogs on the third pinion worn,' he recalls. 'That's very unusual, because third gear is normally the most reliable. No trouble with parts, though – you can get bits so easily for Bantams.'

With a handlebar fairing to keep the worst of British weather at bay and a top box that supplements panniers to carry weekend luggage, the cheeky little Bantam is a familiar sight at BSA Owners' Club events. 'The club is a great source of help and information,' says Tom. 'There are some very good specialist dealers and enough knowledge to help you with any problem. And I reckon we must have more information in our library than any other club.'

Even a Bantam can get its owner into trouble if he rides it enthusiastically, as Tom found one day when he was stopped for speeding. 'I suppose I was quite flattered when I realized what I'd actually been stopped for,' he grins. 'But when I took my helmet off and the copper saw my face, he just said "You're old enough to know better" and let me off !'

Dave Rowlands and the D10

The Bantam was used in competitions from road racing to trials, with some remarkable successes to its credit. Perhaps the greatest was towards the end of the model's production life when the four-speed 175cc D10 came in for some special attention from the Competition Shop. Manager Brian Martin decided to develop a trials version, using the Bushman frame with C15 forks and special Girling rear dampers.

Lancashire lad Dave Rowlands first rode the 175 in the 1967 Bemrose Trial and was not impressed. 'It had a standard engine and I thought it was awful,' he recalls. 'It went back to the firm. Michael Martin breathed on it and after that it went like a bomb!'

Michael Martin, brother of Brian, was chief development engineer at BSA's Redditch factory, where he had co-operated with Dr Gordon Blair of Queen's University, Belfast, on gas dynamics and exhaust systems. Michael recalls the motor: 'We got about 14 bhp from it at 5,500 rpm, with good torque through the range,' he says, 'then lopped the power off the top to give more at mid range.' With a special set of wide-ratio gears, the D10 unit went back into its frame in time to be taken north for Dave Rowlands to ride in the gruelling Scottish Six Days trial.

Rowlands was known to be a good lad, but nobody expected him to be second to the great Sammy Miller at the end of the first day. The game little BSA served Dave well for the next five days, and he never dropped out of the top three before clinching second place at the finish. This was one instance when the old saying that no one remembers who finishes second proved untrue, and Rowlands was a hero to all British bike enthusiasts.

From that historic ride, he went on to win outright in the Alan Jeffries and Mitchell national events, but at the end of the season BSA decided to quit trials. It was a pity, because back at Redditch Michael Martin had been experimenting with a 200cc version that was never announced. Dave Rowlands took up an offer of a Spanish Bultaco when BSA withdrew, and moving from Bantam to Bulto enables him to make a direct comparison between what was and what might have been. 'As it stood, the BSA was as good as the Bultaco. It was a super little machine,' he remembers. 'It was a great pity they never developed it.'

The factory gave Dave the Bantam when they parted and it passed through many owners until Dave's son Scott traced it to a Scottish (how appropriate that is!) hotel and brought it back home to the man who gave it its greatest moment. The hero is home to stay.

Dave Rowland's ride to second place in the 1967 Scottish Six Days Trial was a heroic effort, beaten only by maestro Sammy Miller. Dave later won the Alan Jeffries and Mitchell trials on the 175cc Bantam and thought it a potential competitor to the Spanish Bultaco he rode in 1968. The bike is now owned by Dave, seen here giving away a precious mark on German Camp's tricky rocks.

BSA PRE-UNIT SINGLES

Old Gold Stars never die . . .

Below *Ian Perkins' immaculate 1961 DBD34 Gold Star reflects the fashion of the '60s, with alloy tank and special Taylor-Dow parts to aid the process of going fast.*

BSA's sturdy 350 and 500cc singles were amongst the best made and most reliable machines available when the British industry was at its 1950s peak. The modest 350cc B31 and its 500cc B33 brother were destined to live in the shadows of their more glamorous Gold Star cousins, but they were mechanically close enough to gather a little of the aura of success that the sporting versions brought to the factory.

BSA was wary of going racing at International level, but where bikes which the public could see were based on its roadsters could succeed, it put its considerable industrial weight behind the effort. Competitions Manager Bert Perrigo recruited the best men for trials and scrambles, with Irish ace Billy Nicholson applying a fertile imagi-

nation in the workshop to help young hopefuls like David Tye, Brian Martin and a man persuaded to come over from the Norton trials team, Jeff Smith. For the Clubman's races that grew in popularity in the '50s, the Gold Star became the obvious choice, with the fastest men in practice for the Clubman's TT supplied with parts that looked standard to the casual observer, but were not! When Shrewsbury's Ron Jones beat the lap record in practice for the 1952 350cc Clubman's TT, he was offered a tank that looked standard but held extra fuel, and the BSA representative offered to have the works mechanics 'just give your engine a look over before the race'. In fact, a promising Scot won the race for them, one Bob McIntyre. By 1956 the Clubman's TT was such a predictable event

RIAL. 1952.

Left *Early trials teams had their Goldies rigid at the rear, believing it gave them better feel in muddy conditions. In 1952, David Tye (centre) was second in the Scottish Six Days on this 350. Brian Martin (left) went on to become BSA Competitions Manager, and Peter Hammond (right) was a star of the Triumph team who remains firm friends with David Tye.*

Right *A youthful Arthur Lampkin, a top BSA contender in both trials and scrambles, picks a path for his 350 Goldie.*

Right *Not all Gold Stars were kept shining by proud owners. When the works scrambles team found the going muddy, they just kept going!*

Below *At the factory, experiments with the 500cc Gold Star got output as high as 50 bhp in racing trim, but the Goldie is remembered as the definitive British performance single.*

that the Auto Cycle Union dropped it from the programme, and the Gold Star was a victim of its own success.

Skilled men took the Beesa to trials success, with 'Billy Nick' winning the ACU Trials Drivers' Star in 1951 and '52, while Harold Tozer and Jack Wilkes were the most successful sidecar trials crew in the first half of that decade. Works riders were expected to ride in both trials and scrambles, with Bert Perrigo keeping a stern but fatherly eye on them. David Tye remembers being called into Bert's office to be told that he was falling off too often, and he should try riding at his own pace for a while before building up speed and trying to win. David did as he was told and went on to win against the men he had been unable to catch, beating Brian

Stonebridge on the works 500cc Matchless more than once.

The Gold Star engines were hand built in a shop quite separate from the production line where the similar but humbler B31 and 33 were assembled. In charge of the Goldie shop was renowned racer and tuner Roland

Pike, and one of the men promoted to work with him was Barry Johnston, who today is Technical Sales Manager of Amal Carburettors. 'We had nine dynos in the shop to run the engines on so that we could issue the certificate of power output to each customer,' Barry remembers. 'Then the

1952 350cc Clubman's TT

The Gold Star used plunger rear springing until the 1953 range was announced and swinging-arm comfort took over. Not that the plunger frame was being left behind in the 350cc Clubman's TT, where it dominated the finishers choice. In 1952 Eric Houseley, from Clay Cross in Derbyshire, upped the race record by 3¹/₂ mph to beat that of the great Bob McIntyre on yet another Goldie.

Eric was entered by Eric Bowers of Chapel-en-le-Frith, a Derbyshire town better known as the home of Ferodo brake linings, and the two went down to Small Heath in Birmingham to collect the brand new Goldie, which Eric then used for a little fast touring across the country to run the motor in. 'It wasn't anything special, as I remember,' he says. 'I don't think we ever had to touch the bike, it went so well.

'It couldn't have been so quick, because I remember following a lad from Governor's Bridge and I couldn't get past him until the bottom of Bray Hill. I just kept it flat out and the valves were floating, but it picked up again as we went up the hill towards Quarter Bridge and it was all right. It was a beautiful bike, it handled well and the brakes were no problem.'

Eric got a hint that he was a tip for success when BSA competition manager Bert Perrigo posed for a photo with the young rider and his sponsor before the race began. The team supporting him was like a Who's Who of racing: 1950 350cc World Champion Bob Foster loaned a telephone connection to the Sulby signalling station, where a young John Hartle passed on the information, while in the pits to help out was multiple Manx Grand Prix victor Don Crossley. And friend David Tye, then working for the rival Douglas factory, told Eric: 'Douglas have got problems – and the main one is you!'

Practice form came true with Eric's first lap, 2¹/₂ mph faster than the class record! Bob McIntyre was second, but lost a place on lap 2

as Ken James (Norton) closed within a second of Eric, only to drop back when Eric upped the record on lap 3. Bob Mac made a supreme effort on the final lap and lifted the record over 80 mph, but the consistent Houseley was too far ahead to be caught. His four laps average was 78.9 mph, pulverizing the old record of 75.4.

Now a successful solus dealer for Kawasaki, Eric still smiles when he tells what happened to his Beesa. 'Eric Bowers sold it to Reg Dearden of Manchester and we didn't know where it went. Then one day Stan Dibben of Nortons told me the valve timing, the power output and all the details. We didn't realize it, but Reg Dearden had really bought it for Nortons to examine!'

Eric Houseley didn't waste a second as he kept the pace all the way in the 1952 Clubman's 350 TT. Consistent effort was enough to keep even Bob McIntyre at bay!

management put in a special high-speed dyno for the four-valve MC1 250 racer they were developing. Roland Pike got fed up with having to give time to the MC1 instead of his own Gold Stars, and he built a special short-stroke 250 version of the Goldie. He ran it on the special dyno and it didn't take long before it was giving nearly as much power as the MC1! But he didn't pursue the idea, he'd made his point.' The MC1 was destined never to race, despite enthusiastic reports from top racer Geoff Duke after tests at Oulton Park; the cautious approach to pure racing took over, and when designer Doug Hele could not guarantee a win first time out, the project was quietly put away. If the high-revving 250 with cantilever rear suspension had gone ahead in the early '50s, the Gold Star story might be very different . . .

The Goldie was a prime example of how a well-designed but simple engine could excel at almost anything. Apart from the complete domination of the production machine Clubman's TT, it won almost every National trial at some time, it was a major power in British scrambling and European moto-cross, including John Draper's 1955 victory in the first European championship, and it broke world speed records. On the road, it was the fast man's ultimate choice if he wanted to look the part of a racing hero.

Ian Perkins covered some 50,000 miles on five Gold Stars owned in the late 1960s, including competing in moto-cross, and the memory of those thundering big singles has drawn him back. Now he has a 1961 DBD34 500 in Clubman's trim, but has plans to modify it in the way all the fast café racers of the '60s did. 'Almost all the bikes left are back to standard trim,' he explains. 'I'm looking for all the Taylor Dow bits to put on this one.'

Taylor Dow was the specialist Goldie shop started by Clubman's TT winner and ISDT Gold Medallist Eddie Dow, with support from veteran tuner and entrant Arthur Taylor. Under their 'Superleggera' name they provided refinements like a two-way fork damping conversion to smooth out progress over bumpy roads and a handsome

---

BSA PRE-UNIT SINGLES

Engine: Air-cooled, four-stroke single cylinder, with two pushrod-operated valves. Early versions had iron cylinder head and barrel, later versions alloy for road and racing specification. 500cc engine, 85mm bore × 88mm stroke; 350cc, 71mm × 88mm. Power output varied according to specification ordered; DBD34 gave about 42 bhp at 7,000 rpm in racing trim.

Transmission: Four-speed gearbox, with integral footchange. Primary and secondary transmission by chain. Multi-plate clutch in oil.

Cycle parts: 1949 – plunger-sprung frame, telescopic forks; rigid frame optional for trials versions, 1953 – Swinging-arm frame introduced, with Girling hydraulic damper units. Seven-inch single-leading-shoe drum brakes front and rear, with 8-inch front brake optional for racing models.

Dimensions: Wheelbase – 56 in. Dry weight – Trials model, 335 lbs; 350cc, 325 lbs; scrambles and racing models, 350 lbs; touring and Clubman's models, 380 lbs.

Owners' Club: Active in most aspects of riding. Secretary – B. Standley, 7 Austcliff Close, Hunt End, Redditch, Worcs B97 5NZ.

Sources of help: Spares – Britain's Gold Star Service, 50 Church Street, Moxley, Wednesbury, West Midlands; George Prew, Mill House, Barkway, Royston, Herts. Information – Owners' Club specialists.

---

five-gallon fuel that gleamed naked and unashamed in polished alloy. Never mind that the DBD34 Goldie was the most expensive bike in BSA's range – it needed TD bits to make it complete.

Perkins' experience on the road has left him with enthusiasm but no false illusions: 'The ammeter shakes itself to pieces, then one of the clocks,' he admits. 'The biggest problem is the electrics, and it's a problem finding the right Lucas parts today. Even when I was first riding them, you wouldn't go off on a holiday without bits stuffed in your pockets. With the RRT2 close ratio gearbox you have a 60 mph first gear. Once you're on the open road it's a superb bike, but around town it's a pig.'

Spares come easier with membership of the Gold Star Owners' Club, which buys up old stocks for its members. 'The aims of the Club are excellent,' says member Perkins. 'They want to keep the bikes on the road and ridden as they originally were.'

The Gold Star line ended in 1963, and despite critics describing them as '100 mph road drills to ride' they still attract great loyalty from owners. In Ian Perkins' words: 'In terms of going back to real motorcycling, this is it. Even with its faults.'

BSA UNIT SINGLES

From Commuter to World Champion

Right *Proving that competition success improves road models, Arthur Lampkin shows off the successful duplex cradle moto-cross frame that was adapted for the later road models and earned a good reputation for handling.*

Far right *Brian Martin was the manager of the BSA's Competition Shop and the driving force behind a huge list of successes in a variety of sporting spheres. Here he picks a careful path on a works C15T, the first competition version of the unit-construction single.*

Below right *Worcestershire engineer Ian Wallis bought his B25 Trial in 1982 and says it has taught him how to use a set of spanners. Up to 500 miles in a weekend trip to European rallies and regular commuting have shown him its good and bad points, but he will never part with the bike.*

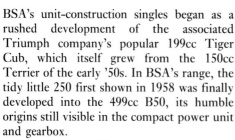

BSA's unit-construction singles began as a rushed development of the associated Triumph company's popular 199cc Tiger Cub, which itself grew from the 150cc Terrier of the early '50s. In BSA's range, the tidy little 250 first shown in 1958 was finally developed into the 499cc B50, its humble origins still visible in the compact power unit and gearbox.

The BSA C15 was announced in September, priced at £172 and one of the sensations of the Earls Court Show. Its compact build looked promising for adaptation to trials use, and before the year was out Brian Martin had won the Southern Experts Trial on a prototype of the coming C15T trials model. Brian was appointed Competition Shop manager in 1958, and went on to see the unit singles succeed in trials, moto-cross and road racing, ridden by world-famous names like Jeff Smith, Arthur Lampkin, John Draper, Bob Heath, John Banks and Dave Nicholl. BSA thought big in the off-road world and its team was big and talented

enough to dominate National trials and moto-cross, even if a certain Sammy Miller insisted on sticking with his obsolete 500cc Ariel, despite being a BSA employee!

The C15 roadster, intended as basic transport, proved ridable and economical. Tested by *Motor Cycling* in 1960, it reached 70 mph and gave 101 miles to the gallon over 500 miles, and even if the early examples proved that the Tiger Club bottom end and kickstart pawl wore out even quicker on a 250 than on a 200, the C15 sold well. In 1964 the roadster had a roller bearing big-end, but when the C25 Barracuda was announced in 1966, it used a shell bearing on its one-piece forged crankshaft to help develop the claimed 25 bhp at 8,250 rpm. The Barracuda used a new frame with duplex bottom cradle and gusseting at vital points. From it came the more flexible 21 bhp Fleetstar, popular with police forces and still able to surprise unsuspecting new owners who expect only C15 levels of performance from a bike with little in its appearance to hint at its potential.

The basic design grew into bigger and bigger capacities, with the 343cc B40 announced in 1960, to be followed by the 441cc (79mm bore × 90mm stroke) B44 and finally the 499cc (84mm × 90mm) B50. The B50T was the world's first 500cc trail bike, but it never reached the levels of success that later developments of the idea from Japan did. The modest B40, a replacement for the long-running B31 350 single, was selected as standard issue for the forces and was produced in thousands, to become an economical first step into British singledom for riders of a later generation who could not afford the more glamorous models.

The faster 250 models developed a reputation for self-dismantling, to the extent that the BSA Owner's Club has a standard joke about the model: 'Wanted to finish a B25 project – a long dual carriageway'!. But Ted Edwards of Frome, Somerset, has laid the rumour to rest with a B25 power unit in a 160 Ducati frame that has won Classic races at National level, defeating some very famous names in the process. In the *Classic Bike* Magazine/Kenning Tyres championship race at Aberdare Park, South Wales, Ted won the 1985 250 race in damp conditions, the BSA unit leaving assorted Ducatis, Suzukis and Yamahas behind. Many defeated opponents attributed the win to Ted's riding ability and having the ideal bike for the tricky conditions; then, in 1986, with the weather warm and dry and the track in perfect condition, Ted and his cheeky little BSA won again.

BSA Owners' Club member Ian Wallis has covered some 25,000 miles on BSA unit singles in five years, and knows their strengths and weaknesses well. Graduating from a Tiger Cub to a B25SS in 1982, and using his bikes as day-to-day transport, leaves him with little sentiment in assessing the models. 'I became an engineer so I could maintain a B25,' he jokes, but it's a bike he will never sell because it was first registered on the day his girlfriend Luan was born. 'The problem with the unit singles is that the ignition advance and retard doesn't get lubricated unless you take the cover off and

actually squirt oil on it,' he explains. 'So the engine can get variable timing while it's running – we've had exhaust valves burn out as a result. Fitting electronic ignition is worthwhile now that prices are going up and you look at the cost of a new advance/retard unit.

'I change the oil every 1,500 miles and the filter every 3,000, but I've got doubts about the circulation with the oil in the frame. I've found the front of the frame hot with the oil after a run, but the back end can be cold. It makes you wonder how much of the oil is really getting around.'

Ian's mileage includes a no-problem 1,200-mile tour of France on a B40 special that gave him 60 miles to the gallon, 10 mpg better than his more sporty B25 250 normally does! And the BSA styling of the '70s puts most of the electrical components in a box under the fuel tank, where rainwater can reach them and a careless owner topping up the oil-in-frame system can drip lubricant on them as well! But he enjoys the taut handling of a frame based on the World Championship-winning Victor and a front brake intended for a much faster machine: 'Provided you've got it set up right, you can squeal the front tyre with that brake,' he claims.

'With the 12-volt system the front light is very good, but the rear one is poor – I wouldn't like to be out in really poor weather on it. To anyone thinking of buying a unit BSA, I'd recommend the Army B40, because the Army wanted a bit of quality in the bottom end and that one's like the 441 Victor.'

For replacement air filter elements, Ian uses a standard Hillman car type that costs less than a pattern BSA part. And he takes great care to see that the engine sprocket retaining nut is tightened to the correct 60 lbs/ft torque figure after losing an alternator from its crankshaft mounting. But living and travelling with BSA's unit singles has left him with enthusiasm still alight. 'I was 17 or 18 when I got my B25, and it certainly taught me what spanners were for,' he says. 'But if you know what you're doing and look after one, it's a decent engine in a very good chassis. Basically it's over-engineered.'

BSA UNIT SINGLES

Engine: Air-cooled, four-stroke single, with two pushrod-operated valves. Early versions had iron cylinder barrel and alloy head, later versions alloy barrels. Capacities – 249cc (67mm bore × 70mm stroke), 343cc (79mm × 70mm), 441cc (79mm × 90mm) and 499cc (84mm × 90mm). 250 C15 produced a claimed 15 bhp at 7,000 rpm; 499cc B50 Victor GP moto-cross engine, 37.2 bhp at 6,000 rpm; 499cc B50 road racer, 45 bhp at 8,000 rpm.

Transmission: Four-speed gearbox with integral footchange in unit with engine. Primary and secondary transmission by chain. Multi-plate clutch.

Cycle parts: Single loop frame on early C15 models, with telescopic front forks and swinging-arm rear suspension. Duplex bottom cradle with oil in frame introduced for road models from 1966. Seven-inch single-leading-shoe drum brakes until optional 8-inch twin-leading-shoe brake offered from 1970.

Dimensions: Wheelbase – 54 in; Dry weight – C15, 280 lbs; B40, 300 lbs; B50SS, 325 lbs.

Owners' Club: Active. Secretary – Ian Wallis, 61 Lynden Avenue, Long Eaton, Nottingham.

Sources of help: Spares – OTJ, The Bullyard, r/o 83 High Street, Edenbridge, Kent; Anglo-Moto, Unit 34, Harriers Trading Estate, Hoo Road, Kidderminster, Worcs DY10 1NJ; Eric Gibbs (York) Ltd, 19a Fetter Lane, York; FBS Motorcycles, Clifford Street, Glascote, Tamworth, Staffs. Technical advice – OTJ and Owners' Club specialists.

1964 500cc Moto-Cross World Championship

BSA's Competition Shop, managed by trials ace Brian Martin, produced a long list of winners, from Arthur Lampkin's Scottish Six Days Trial winner of 1963 to the British Championship race winners like the 500cc single that Bob Heath rode so well. But if a factory wants publicity from competition it aims for the top – a World Championship.

Jeff Smith brought them two titles as World 500cc Moto-cross Champion in 1964 and '65, riding bikes developed from the humble C15 roadster engine. In fact, in the first half of his world-title season, his engine used standard crankcases from the B40 350cc road model that were stretched to the limit in Jeff's 420cc special. The crankcases had to be changed every two meetings! Only for the Belgian Grand Prix at the ancient city of Namur did the engine have special sand-cast cases to give greater strength, and that was the tenth of 14 rounds for the title. Jeff arrived in Belgium four points behind great rival Rolf Tibblin of Sweden on a Husqvarna, but the BSA won the day while the Husqvarna did not finish. That left Jeff with 52 points from his best seven results, to Tibblin's 54.

Neither rider improved his score in West Germany, but Jeff won again in East Germany and the scores were 54 points each with the final round to go! It was scorching in Spain for that final clash, where Smith arrived early to acclimatize after racing in Italy the previous weekend. Tibblin arrived late on Friday, showing the effects of the 1,200-mile drive from a local meeting in his native country. Perhaps reflecting the strain that Jeff Smith's late-season effort imposed, Tibblin sent his mechanic back to France on Sunday morning to buy fuel for the race and ensure good quality. But the mechanic was sent with the bike's tank, not the obvious can, and arrived back to find the meeting delayed for Tibblin to get his bike back in one piece!

Smith, the canny thinker who normally started a race slowly and built up to a storming finish, added to Tibblin's problems with a good start. From the first lap the BSA man was a clear threat, closing on the hard-riding Swede and pushing him to ride on the ragged edge. It was too much for Tibblin, who overdid his efforts, damaged the rear wheel of the Husqvarna and had to retire, leaving a jubilant Smith to bring his BSA home to win the first of two legs of the Grand Prix. All Jeff had to do was finish the second and the world title was his.

In fact, the sporting Tibblin deliberately slowed and tried to get Smithy in front for the final flag, acknowledging the skill and determination of the Briton who had taken his world crown. It confirmed Jeff Smith as the world's number one moto-cross rider, and the BSA as a winning machine.

Jeff Smith's remorseless press-on style kept BSA's name ahead in moto-cross for years. Here he leaves the rest in his dust at the 1963 Moto-Cross des Nations, during the build-up to his 1964 World Championship effort.

BSA PRE-UNIT TWINS

The A10 was A1

One history of the Battle of Waterloo, by Sergeant Cotton, tells how the Duke of Wellington heard many of his infantrymen say as the fight was near: 'Let's give 'em Brummagum' (sic). They were referring to their bayonets, made in the heart of England, where the finest armourers were. Birmingham had the reputation for producing solid and reliable products, and when the Birmingham Small Arms company made its first motorcycle in 1911 it was noted for the same qualities. Likewise their models through the years until the Small Heath factory finally closed, and none upheld that reputation better than the A7 and A10 500cc and 650cc twins.

The A7 was announced in September 1946, a design that had started with experiments in the late 30s (when Triumph's Speed Twin was a strong seller) but was delayed in reaching the buying public by the

Second World War. But as soon as civilian production started up again, BSA was ready with a 62mm bore × 82mm stroke 500cc twin, with a four-speed gearbox bolted to the back of the crankcase. Telescopic forms provided comfort at the front, but further back the sprung saddle was all that absorbed the bumps that the rigid frame found in the road. By 1949 there was a plunger rear suspension as a luxury option and in 1950 came the shorter-stroke version, 66mm bore × 72.6mm stroke. That same year came the 650cc A10, known as the Golden Flash and finished in an eye-catching gold colour that stood out from the black, silver and red of its rivals. The Flash became a legend for untiring service.

It grew from the 35 bhp plunger-sprung model that started the line (rigid frame available for sidecar men who preferred traditional contact with the road through the

Far left *Brian Standley's Rocket Gold Star is an example of the ulti-mate A10 development and is used as a standard reference by others. This one came to Brian as a burnt-out wreck, written off by the insurance com-pany and down to an affordable price!*

Left *The Maudes Trophy-winning team of 1952 met again to approve the restoration of Norman Vanhouse's machine for the National Motorcycle Museum. Left to right are Norman himself, Brian Martin and Fred Rist.*

Above *The A10 Golden Flash is best remembered as the plunger-sprung big twin with distinctive gold paintwork.*

Above right *Mike Brogdale bought his A7SS new in 1954 with a very rare alloy cylinder head fitted. After 58,000 miles on the road it was con-sidered sufficiently run-in to use in road racing, sprints and hillclimbs. 'After all, for £242 you should expect a little quality and fitness for purpose,' says the laconic Lancastrian.*

seat of the pants) to become the 41 bhp Super Flash in 1953 and the 40 bhp Road Rocket two years later, when the rear suspension changed to swinging-arm and no options. The A10 progressed through the 42 bhp Super Rocket of 1958 to reach its performance zenith in 1962 as the Rocket Gold Star, offering 46 bhp as standard or 50 Small Heath horses if the owner fitted a Gold Star silencer.

The smaller brother built a greater sporting reputation, including winning the coveted Maudes Trophy, for an outstanding performance by a manufacturer, in 1952. Three of the sporty Star Twins were selected at random from the production line and entered for veteran Fred Rist, the experienced Norman Vanhouse and rising star Brian Martin in the International Six Days Trial. In a blaze of publicity that reflected true faith in the company's product, the trio rode from Birmingham down to Austria. There they completed the Six Days without penalty to all win Gold Medals, then rode the bikes up to Scandinavia before catching the boat home. All under official ACU observation and without mechanical problems in 4,500 miles!

Perhaps the most famous A10 BSA was Fred Rist's very special rigid-framed version, built for the sand racing that attracted big crowds in the 1950s. Running on methanol alcohol fuel, it was said to be capable of 140 mph! But Fred could tame the monster, broadsiding in speedway style to wins all around Britain's coastal race venues.

But most BSA twin owners used them for more humble work, knowing they would keep going through most conditions. Mr R. H. Vallence was working in Bolivia in 1957, and regularly rode his rigid-frame A10 up the Andes to altitudes of 17,000 feet –

1962 Isle of Man Sidecar TT

The mighty BSA name won only a single International TT race, despite its domination of the production machine Clubman's events. And it was no secretly-works-backed special that brought them glory – it was the privately built and tuned sidecar of Chris Vincent, powered by a single carburettor A7 engine. A tester on the strength at Small Heath, Chris could get help from the more sports-minded staff who admired his underdog fight against the BMW twins that dominated sidecar racing in the 1960s, but there was no official blessing of his David and Goliath struggle against the German and Swiss aces with their faster machinery.

Vincent and passenger Eric Bliss started alongside world champion Max Deubel in the 1962 race, and no one was surprised that the German was way ahead at Ballacraine, the first commentary point on the 37³/₄-mile course. Florian Camathias, the bespectacled Swiss ace on another screaming BMW, had made up the 10 seconds' starting interval and was also ahead of the Vincent BSA. With a first lap at 90.7 mph that shattered the record, Deubel looked to be on his way to another victory; but the BSA was going well in third place, behind Camathias, despite a brush with the bank that bent the gear-lever!

Camathias took a closer look at the unforgiving Manx landscape on the second lap, breaking passenger Burkhardt's leg and leaving Vincent in second place as the crowd cheered the BSA hero on. Never mind that he was 4 minutes behind the world champion, here was a British team chasing the world number one.

Sensation came on the third and final lap. Deubel's BMW seized at Ballig Bridge, 9 miles from the start, and the humble BSA twin was leading the Sidecar TT! Avoiding banks as he drifted in the manner that made *The Motor Cycle* describe him as 'The High Priest of the Prayer Mat', Chris had no chance to take it easy. Otto Kolle on another BMW was less than a minute behind, and any slight mistake on the twists and turns of the Mountain road could wipe that precious lead away and allow yet another foreign win.

But Chris Vincent was always made of championship quality stuff, and the Beesa droned on, cheered by crowds as they realized that Deubel was out and there was a British bike leading. With not a tyre tread off the correct racing line on that tense final lap, Chris brought the BSA home to take the chequered flag and a place in history. His average speed of 83.57 mph for 113 demanding miles was too much for the other survivors of the contest, and final proof of what a strong engine the A7 BSA was.

The Vincent BSA in full flight, and Chris takes on the German BMWs while heading for an historic victory in the 1962 Sidecar TT, with passenger Derek Bliss putting his weight in the right place.

higher than Mont Blanc! And when Chris and Marion Collier were married in 1954, their transport to their Scottish honeymoon was Chris's faithful A10, which threw a fit of sulks at the new woman in its owner's life and burned out an exhaust valve at Biggleswade on the journey north. When a less-than-friendly local dealer refused to help them, Chris asked if he could borrow the tools to do the job himself, only to be told: 'You've got one cylinder working, why don't you go on that?' So they did, the A10 carrying the happy couple and their luggage to Perth, where a more hospitable dealer put the matter right and gave them a quicker journey home.

Brian Standley has built a healthy respect for BSA's pre-unit construction twin in a long association with the model in various forms. From days on an A10 that did 20,000 miles a year as his only transport, the technical engineering manager has risen to the ultimate development of the 650, a Rocket Gold Star that is used as a benchmark for other restorations. 'If you use them properly and look after them, the twins last a long time,' he says. 'I had a friend in the Army who had an A7 and he used to ride it home from Germany on leave and think nothing of it. He came over for the Dragon Rally one winter, then rode back to Germany when it was over.

'I have seen a chap with a pair of Stillsons trying to undo the mainshaft nut and getting nowhere because he was trying to turn it the wrong way. That was a case of "If all else fails, try reading the handbook".'

Brian's own 1963 RGS was bought as a burnt-out wreck in 1969, when the insurance company accepted £25 for the remains they had written off. It was a model Brian had always dreamed about, but could not afford: 'I can remember looking in dealers' windows and wondering how anyone could find £300 to pay for a motorbike,' he recalls. Since it came into Brian's hands, the Rocket Gold Star has been completely rebuilt three times, the first time with an individual but non-original purple and white paint job! 'You can't really say how long a rebuild takes, because you never stop,' he says. 'Spares

aren't much of a problem, because they used so many Gold Star parts and you can get those from the Gold Star Service. The plug-in headlamp unit is hard to find today, even though they were used on trials bikes as well. And wiring harnesses with the correct plug for the headlamp are a problem, too.

'The timing side bush is the weak point and I don't trust some of the pattern parts for work like that. But if you have the needle-roller conversion with positive oil feed through the end of the crank, they can go on for ages. I've had a Gold Star on the road but I prefer the twins – they're less temperamental and more reliable.'

What the world expected of a BSA, in fact.

BSA PRE-UNIT CONSTRUCTION TWINS

Engine (all models): Four-stroke parallel twin, with single gear-driven camshaft behind cylinder axis operating two valves per cylinder via pushrods. Early 500cc A7 fitted with iron cylinder head and barrel, 62mm bore × 82mm stroke; 1949 – 650cc A10 introduced, 70mm × 84mm; 1951 – A7 revised, new dimensions 66mm × 72.6mm. Power output grew from 26 bhp at 6,000 rpm (1946 A7) to claimed 46 bhp at 6,250 rpm (1963 650cc Rocket Gold Star).

Transmission (all models): Four-speed gearbox, with integral footchange. Primary and secondary transmission by chain. Multi-plate clutch in oil.

Cycle parts: 1946 – rigid frame with telescopic forks, 7-inch drum brakes front and rear. Plunger rear springing available from 1949 season on A7; A10 either rigid or plunger rear sprung from introduction for 1950 season, with 8-inch front and 7-inch rear drum brakes. Swinging-arm frame available as an option from 1954.

Dimensions: Wheelbase – 1946 A7, 54.5 in; A10 and A7 plunger-spring frame, 55 in; all models with swinging-arm frame 56 in. Dry weight – A7 rigid frame, 365 lbs; plunger-sprung, 400 lbs; swinging-arm frame, 425 lbs. A10 rigid frame, 380 lbs; plunger-sprung, 408 lbs; swinging-arm frame, 430 lbs.

Owners' Club: Active; 24 UK branches. Secretary – Ian Wallis, 359 Radford Road, Hyson Green, Nottingham.

Sources of help: Spares – C & D Autos, 1193-99 Warwick Road, Acocks Green, Birmingham B11 1AW; Brie-Tie, 1 Armstrong Street, Swindon, Wilts; Vale-Onslow Motorcycles, 104-116 Stratford Road, Birmingham. Restoration – Brian Carter, 76 Malvern Road, Swindon, Wilts. Information – Owners' Club specialists.

Above *BSA's famous 190mm front brake in twin-leading-shoe form is needed with a top speed approaching 110 mph. Twin carburettors meant twin cables in BSA language.*

Right *The best-known unit construction BSA twin is the A65 Lightning used in Central TV's popular* **Boon** *series, where it stars as the mount of Michael Elphick – but the riding is done by a stand-in. The condition of the bike reflects the hard life it leads on a film set.*

BSA's final range of twins was announced at the beginning of 1962, when the front cover of *The Motor Cycle* magazine honoured their arrival with a front cover mention. 'Thrilling new big twins from famous factory' it told readers, who turned inside to find that Britain's leading manufacturer had launched 500cc and 654cc twins that made the entire range unit construction.

The A65 Star weighed 40 lbs less than the faithful old A10 Golden Flash that it replaced, but BSA's handwriting was obvious in the use of a single camshaft behind the cylinder block and a forged crankshaft with a central flywheel bolted on. The A65 engine, destined to become a legend in sidecar racing at National level, was 'oversquare' with 75mm bore and 74mm stroke, while the A50

had the same stroke but a smaller 65.5 mm bore. The new model had been developed under the careful eye of Len Crisp, experimental shop chief at Small Heath and a BSA man since 1935. Perhaps his traditional thinking was reflected in the seat height of 31 inches that allowed riders of medium build to reach the ground comfortably, and in the recommendation that the primary chain tension could be checked by inserting a thin rod (such as a knitting needle) through the hole drilled in the adjusting bolt!

BSA's twins had become a legend for reliable performance, a reflection on the high-quality standards in the Small Heath factory where the giant of the British industry carried out all the work and did not have to depend on sub-contractors. The company's

BSA UNIT TWINS

Small Heath's swansong

Below *Dave Clarke's 1968 A65 Lightning has won numerous concours awards for its proud Nottingham owner, the third of this model he has owned. Not a man to waste money when he has a willing engine available, Dave has ridden the BSA to every show where it has gained an award.*

experiments included a machine to build spoked wheels automatically, feeding the spokes from an overhead hopper and building the rim on to the hub with none of the traditional hand labour; the machine worked, but not reliably enough to be trusted with every wheel, so the wheelbuilders stayed on the payroll.

The 'unit twins' had their teething troubles, with numbers of them going back to the factory for gearbox and piston problems, but the handling of the new frame and the flexible performance of the 654cc big brother of the family made it a good enough ride for Beesa traditionalists to tolerate the trouble. 'You must expect a new model to have some small teething troubles,' said one A65 owner of a bike that had been back to the

factory twice – BSA had a very loyal following!

Doubters were silenced with a growing list of racing successes by British sidecar crews, the fiery Chris Vincent on his unofficially factory-backed outfit the outstanding example with five British Sidecar Racing Championships won with A65 power. Fellow BSA employee Peter Brown won the title in 1968, and when the 750cc Sidecar TT was introduced that same year, Terry Vinicombe and passenger John Flaxman led a BSA A65 1-2-3 domination of the leaderboard.

Solo racing was never as successful as on three wheels, even though the factory tried very hard with specially developed 500cc A50s to repeat its victory in the 1954 American Daytona 100. That win went to a

Star twin ridden by Bobby Hill, but when BSA went back in 1966 with six entries, they all retired and the factory was not at all happy. For 1968, the Daytona A50s were said to develop 56 bhp at 8,200 rpm and things looked promising, but all they had to show in the final results was second place in the Amateur 100 Miles race. No more twins went to Daytona.

The A50 in standard trim was supplied with a 7-inch front brake, and was not a favourite with riders, while the 8-inch unit in the A65 got good reports every time. *The Motor Cycle* could beat the 30-feet mark when stopping the A65 from 30 mph, but the smaller bike took another 30 inches to come to a halt – enough to make the difference between missing or hitting a careless car driver. But once the early piston problems were overcome and riders got used to a rather slow gearchange, the 'unit twins' went on to add to BSA's reputation for reliable, ridable bikes.

Dave Clark of Nottingham, an amateur restorer whose ability has won him many prizes, has liked the A65 in sporty Lightning form since he first owned one in the late 1960s which thrilled him with a speedo needle that got very friendly with the 120 mph mark. 'I've had three A65s and had no problems,'

he reports. 'I think owner maintenance was the real trouble. People would run them on dirty oil and if you did that, you could kiss the nearside conrod goodbye!'

Dave's 1986 A65S Spitfire was priced at £398.37 new, and is the most powerful of the variations on the A65 theme with a claimed 56.5 bhp at 7,250 rpm. The power is still there, but to buy such a pristine example today would cost a lot more than £398! The talented engineer has done most of the restoration work himself, but finding correct parts for the rarer versions of big Beesa twins can be difficult and explains the prices that accurate restorations command. What Dave's work offers to other enthusiasts is a reminder that a small budget after redundancy doesn't stop persistent searching and long hours in a small lock-up producing a bike good enough to win prizes yet still be an enjoyable weekend mount. 'I reckon the Beesa is my favourite of the bikes I've restored so far,' he says. 'It's a good bike to ride, with enough steam to get you there when you're in a hurry. But even though this is the most powerful version, with 32mm carburettors, I can get 45 miles to the gallon.'

BSA twins began to fade from the range in 1971 when the A50 was dropped. For the export market only there was the A70, with the 75mm bore of the A65 and a stroke lengthened to 85mm, but it was listed for 1971 only. For 1972, with the BSA Group in trouble financially, the range of 654cc twins numbered only two, the Thunderbolt and the Lightning. They came with a new frame, designed at the Umberslade Hall group design centre – know to the down-to-earth workers as 'Slumbersglade' – and a seat height of 33 inches that few could sit on in any comfort. Testers at Umberslade had the old stable block for accommodation, and found the attitude of some of the staff in their offices less than understanding, like Dave Vaughan: 'I was testing a new frame at MIRA and it broke underneath me – just held together by the cables. I 'phoned Umberslade and told them, and they just said "Impossible, that can't happen"!' In 1972, with the once mighty BSA in its death throes, the BSA twin faded away.

BSA UNIT TWINS

Engine: Air-cooled, four-stroke parallel twin, with two pushrod-operated valves per cylinder. Iron cylinder barrels, alloy heads. A65, 75mm bore × 74mm stroke, claimed output 38 bhp at 5,800 rpm; A50, 65.5mm × 74mm, 28.5 at 6,000. Highest claimed power, A65S Spitfire IV, 56.5 bhp at 7,250 rpm (A50C Cyclone, 38.5 at 6,750). Engine in unit with gearbox on all models.

Transmission (all models): Four-speed gearbox with integral footchange. Primary and secondary transmission by chain; primary enclosed, optional enclosure for rear chain. Multi-plate clutch in oil.

Cycle parts: All-welded duplex cradle frame, telescopic forks, swinging-arm rear suspension. Eight-inch front brakes on all except early A50 (7-inch) and A65S IV (190mm). All models fitted with 7-inch rear brake.

Dimensions: Wheelbase – 54.1 in; 1970, 57 in. Dry weight – A65, 390 lbs; A50, 385 lbs; A65 Spitfire IV, 408 lbs.

Owners' Club: Active, with sections throughout UK and Europe. Secretary – Ian Wallis, 61 Lynden Avenue, Long Eaton, Nottingham.

Sources of help: Spares – C. & D. Autos, 1193-99 Warwick Road, Acocks Green, Birmingham B27 6BY; Bri-Tie Motorcycles, 1 Armstrong Street, Swindon, Wilts

1965 Hutchinson 100

For its Hutchinson 100 meeting at Silverstone in August 1965, the British Motor Cycle Racing Club announced the revival of the production machine race. The 'Hutch' was the premier National meeting in the calendar and the factory whose machine won the production race could claim to have the best.

Triumph entered World Champion Phil Read and factory ace Percy Tait on 650cc Bonnevilles, while South African Paddy Driver on a 745cc G15 Matchless was thought by some to be a likely prospect. Representing the BSA name were Tony Smith on a factory-entered A65LC Lightning, in support of a similar model entered by Hornchurch, Essex, dealer Tom Kirby for a name seldom seen in production events – Mike Hailwood.

Rain teemed down for the race, and caught quick-starting Tony Smith out when he ran out of road – and out of contention – at Stowe Corner. Percy Tait, always a man to go well in the wet, took the lead on the Triumph and stayed there for four laps, with Read and Hailwood riding in his spray and looking for any slight slip that would let them past. The Matchless challenge from Driver was fast slipping back, the bike bouncing around on a suspension that appeared out of harmony and giving Paddy no chance of staying with the flying trio at the head of the field.

Hailwood was taking on two men with a long record of success in production races, Read as a Norton 650SS rider for Syd Lawton's super-successful team and Percy Tait as the factory's leading tester and regular contender in such events. Hailwood the Grand Prix star was considered by many to be successful because his regular 500cc mount, the Italian MV-Agusta, had little serious opposition. To win the race on the unfancied BSA would take all his racing guile.

Read slipped past Tait to lead for four laps, but the BSA Lightning was speeding up and Hailwood moved up to second place and then went ahead on lap 8. Hailwood's great natural ability showed as he speeded up and opened a gap on the Triumph riders, lapping at 85.8 mph despite the awful conditions, and lapping slower riders in the process. Tait tried to make a break past Read, but found his line blocked by his team-mate and he had to settle for third. Read was second, but the convincing winner on BSA's new Lightning model was Mike Hailwood, averaging over 83 mph on a soaking track to show just how well a Beesa twin could go in solo trim – with the best man in the saddle.

Below Dreadful conditions and fierce competition were not enough to keep maestro Mike Hailwood and Tom Kirby's BSA out of first place. In pouring rain that would have postponed many modern races, the mighty BSA put up a bow wave of victory.

Above Few riders could get a bike to corner as well as Mike Hailwood, as the flattened silencers of Tom Kirby's A65 Lightning and Mike's own peekaboo boots showed at Silverstone.

DOT

Made in Manchester

H. Reed and Co, 38 Ellesmere Street, Hulme, Manchester, was formed by Harry Reed in 1903 to produce Dot motorcycles. In 1926 Dot Motors moved to Arundel Street, off Ellesmere Street, and they are still there in the 1990s.

Harry Reed was a racing man, and victory in the twin-cylinder class of the 1908 TT Races helped to establish his machines as a sporting breed. Then second place in the 1924 Sidecar TT on a 349cc JAP-powered outfit started a giant-killing habit that was to be reborn long after the Manchester works had stopped making motorcycles in the early 1930s.

The Dot came back to the two-wheeled market in 1949 with one 197cc Villiers-powered model that developed into a range of seven variations for the 1952 season, with an optional 250cc side-valve roadster with power by Brockhouse Indian that lasted in production for only two years! But the 197cc Dot went on to become a scrambles legend, with Lancashire lad Bill Barugh leading the way in shaming the 500cc four-stroke

thumpers that traditionally ruled off-road racing. Bill had proved to be a winner on big BSAs, but took to the nimble little Dot like a duck to a millpond.

1952 was Bill's greatest year and he was almost unbeaten on his 125 and 197cc

Above *Bob McGloughlin and son Godfrey show off their 197cc Mancunian roadsters. Bob made the headlamp nacelle on his own 1957 model but Godfrey's 1956 has the factory part.*

Left *The factory's official picture of the 1957 Mancunian shows how faithfully the McGloughlin family's bikes have copied the maker's details.*

Right *Scramblers used the 197cc Villiers engine in a bike that was closely related to the road models, and later a Vale Onslow 250cc conversion was tried as well as the Villiers 2T twin power unit. Both were superceded by Villiers' own 250cc 31A single.*

cheeky little Dot was fourth in the ACU Scramble Drivers' Star competition – the British championship of the day – and had scored points in eight of the 13 rounds. To end the season on a real high note, he was sixth in the very first International Moto-Cross Grand Prix of Great Britain, based on the Cotswold Scramble; every bike ahead of the 197cc Dot was a 500cc model!

Eric Watson joined Dot in 1954, soon after he left school, and worked in the three-storey factory in Arundel Street until 1966. He remembers the labour force numbering about 20, with everyone expected to take on any job that came his way. Having studied welding, he served in the frame-building department on the ground floor until moving up a little to the assembly shop on the first floor. He had to work hard on the piece-rate pay scheme to get a full wage packet at the end of each week.

'We were paid ten shillings (50p) for the first six bikes, then we were on ten shillings a bike after that,' he recalls. 'We could make about eight pounds a week in the 1950s and early '60s, which wasn't bad money then. I liked the scramblers best, because if you had road bikes there was so much more to do. The only trouble was when you ran out of parts and they didn't have any stock!'

The factory's sporting achievements included winning the Manufacturers' Team Prize in the first 125cc TT, in 1951. Frames

bikes. Of eleven National events where there was a race for his little 197, he won six, and when there was no separate race at the Cumberland Grand National he finished second in the 350cc race and went on to win the 1000cc event! At the end of the season, the

The Pulman 250cc sidecar outfit

Arthur and Lyn Pulman saw the 1960s in as the top sidecar trials team in the country; with their 500cc Matchless outfit, they had won the ACU Star in 1960 and '61. But Arthur was looking for a greater challenge, and with a decision that rocked the established idea that only big bangers could pull a sidecar, he signed to ride a 250cc Dot for 1962.

He had discussed the possibility of using the 250 Matchless, a recent arrival, but Associated Motor Cycles' competition manager Hugh Viney would not hear of it. 'I didn't realize at the time that it was such a disaster,' Arthur recalls. 'And they didn't want to let me loose on one with a chair.'

'I was working as a representative with Doherty at the time, and we supplied levers to a lot of the manufacturers, including Dot. I spoke to Bernard Scott-Wade and his works manager at the 1961 Motor Cycle Show and we went out to dinner that night and made the deal.'

The 250 trials version was supplied as a standard model, and the only notable modification Arthur made was to reduce the fork trail for lighter steering. A Wessex trials sidecar was fitted at first: 'It was a monster, far too heavy, so I got on and made my own,' says Arthur.

Switching to a mere 250 two-stroke when all his major rivals had 500cc four-strokes to tackle big hills with the weight of two people brought Arthur plenty of criticism: 'Ralph Venables said I'd thrown my career away and was just wasting my time.' He still smiles at the memory. *The Motor Cycle* headlined an article on the new outfit 'Just what are you trying to prove?', as Bob Currie detailed the revolution.

Announced in December 1961, the little 250 took some getting used to after the weight and power of the 500 Matchless. 'The technique was totally different,' Arthur remembers. 'With the 500 you had to use lots of speed to get through, but with the Dot you had a tremendous amount of grip, so it was more like a solo, driving it all the time.'

The sidecars-only D. K. Mansell trial in March brought all the three-wheel stars together, for one of the toughest events in its history. And when the many marks lost in the Gloucestershire mud were added up, a clear 16 ahead of the field were Arthur and Lyn Pulman, silencing critics and showing what was to come in the years ahead. Modestly, Arthur suggests it was an easy ride: 'I had so much grip I couldn't believe it. In sections where the big bikes were struggling, I just pootled through.' Like so many who made their mark in motorcycling, Arthur was an individual who ignored others who were telling him he was attempting the impossible. He 'pootled' into a place in the history books.

History in the making in March 1962, as Arthur and Lyn Pulman guide their little 250 Dot to victory in the sidecars-only D. K. Mansell trials. The minimal but effective sidecar was Arthur's own home-made job.

of square-section tubing carried the rubber-mounted fuel tanks slung below the top tube, and the swinging-fork rear end was controlled by modified Newton car hydraulic dampers. Power was by laid-down Villiers, the cylinder barrel some 20 degrees above horizontal to keep the height down. Eric Hardy of Birmingham finished the race in seventh place, the best-placed British machine and leading team mates Newman and Horn home in a demonstration of reliability if not great speed!

Competition models dominated the Dot range and in 1954 there was not one roadster in the catalogue. In 1955 the Mancunian was announced, a stylish 200cc Villiers-powered model with deeply valanced mudguards, headlamp nacelle and enclosure of the battery box to blend with the rest of the bike. Colour options were red or green. The front forks were another Dot breakaway from conventional teles, with leading links damped by Armstrong units between wheel spindle and bottom steering head yoke.

Birmingham enthusiasts Bob McGloughlin and his son Godfrey have 1957 and 1956 Mancunians respectively. Bob's model came as a bent frame with front forks and hub, swapped for an ancient Honda that he couldn't sell. With scarce parts like the headlamp nacelle and side panels almost impossible to find, the motor engineer made his own, using a photocopy of an old catalogue as a guide. 'I'm the first to admit they may not be quite like the originals,' he admits. When dome-headed nuts couldn't be found, Bob welded two nuts together, with a halfpenny piece to blank one end off, then profiled each on his lathe before nickel plating in his own small Dynic plant.

The engine is a collection of sundry parts. Crankcases are from an invalid carriage motor and the cylinder barrel from an old go-kart motor that reminds Bob of his class win in a nine-hour kart marathon with Villiers power. In all, seven different units have contributed something to build Bob's finished job. He estimates that 1,000 hours went into the conversion of those sorry remains into the complete bike, and he built his own grit blaster and a beading machine to handle some of the work.

Godfrey's 1957 version was bought complete but showing its age: 'Virtually a heap of rusting junk,' is his description. But with few components to find before restoration could begin, the Mancunian took only a year to restore to full health, with stainless steel nuts used wherever possible – much easier than Bob's painstaking production of domed nuts in the garage workshop. His experience helped when the front fork damper covers were found to be too far gone to restore; another set was made from brass tubing and plated to look like the originals.

Another deviation from standard specification was the painting of the backing plates of the twin 6-inch front drum brakes to match the red of Bob's bike and the green of Godfrey's, 'Much better to look at than the original grotty silver paint they used to come with,' says Bob. 'My bike cost £169.85 when it was new; I wish it only cost that to restore! I reckon I spent £730 on it, including buying the nickel-plating kit. Godfrey's cost about £650.' And his son is happy with the result: 'The performance is really good,' he reports. 'It will hold 60 mph uphill, two up. That's enough for me.'

DOT

Engine: 1951 200 DST trials – Air-cooled single cylinder two-stroke with iron cylinder barrel (alloy in 1962) and alloy head. 59mm bore × 72mm stroke, 197cc, with 8:1 compression ratio, developing a claimed 8.2 bhp at 4,000 rpm. 1962 Demon International Scrambler – 68mm × 68mm, 246cc, 12:1, 25 bhp at 6,500 rpm.
Transmission (both models): Primary and secondary drive by chain, through multi-plate dry clutch. 1951, three speeds; 1962, four speeds.
Cycle parts: 1951 – single-loop lugged and brazed frame with MP telescopic forks and rigid rear end; 1962 – single-loop welded square-section frame with leading link front forks and swinging-fork rear suspension, 1951 – 5-inch drum front brake, 6-inch rear; 1962 6-inch brakes front and rear.
Dimensions: 1951 200 DST trials: Wheelbase – 52.4 in (1962 Demon International scrambler: 54 in); ground clearance 5.5 in (9.5 in); dry weight 200 lbs (220 lbs); seat height 27 in (31 in).
Owners' Club: Active (combines with Greeves RA in competitive events) with regular newsletter. Club secretary – Eric Watson, 31 Propps Hall Drive, Failsworth, Manchester M35 OWD.
Sources of help: Owners' Club (possess some factory records). Spares – Dot Cycle and Motor Manufacturing Company Ltd, Arundel Street, Hulme, Manchester.

DOUGLAS

Bristol's best

The Douglas flat twin was first advertised for sale in 1907, when most makers were offering vibratory singles or smoother V-twin engines. But the Bristol makers were never to be slaves to convention, remaining loyal to the flat twin layout until motorcycle production ended 50 years later.

The final phase of Douglas production was based around the 60.8mm x 60mm stroke 348cc flat twin, with a four-speed gearbox bolted to it and driven through a single-plate clutch. Any similarity to the long-standing BMW twin ended there, as Douglas opted for chain final drive, with bevel gears turning the output through 90 degrees and incorporating a cam-type transmission shock absorber. A British flat twin mounted across the frame was novel in 1945, but at a time when many makers had rushed back into civilian production with rigid frames and girder forks, the Douglas rolling chassis was revolutionary.

The rear wheel sat in a box-section swinging-arm with movement controlled by torsion bars contained in the lower frame tubes. And the front boasted 'Radiadraulic' leading-link forks with combined spring and oil damping; with 6 inches of movement claimed for the new forks, Douglas offered comfort of a new standard. Their advertisements at one time mentioned factory testers riding up and down kerbs at 30 mph with no problems!

Early models were the T35, later developed by ex-racing star Freddie Dixon and renamed the Mark Three. But the T35 sold all over the world, and a page from the 1947 dispatch records shows them going to Canada, Switzerland, Belgium, Santiago and even Russia! One of those has recently been rebuilt by Canadian enthusiast George Cameron, starting with a box of parts. 'After a strip, clean and rebuild, all original parts being used except rings, the engine started

Above *The last of the Douglas twins was the Dragonfly, using a beefed-up version of the established 350cc engine in an arc-welded duplex cradle frame with Girling dampers. The front forks were a Reynolds-Earles development, based on the type that Ernie Earles had proved on a number of successful racing machines.*

on the first kick. Just proof that it is a Duggie!' he wrote in the Owners' Club magazine.

In 1948 *Motor Cycling* tested the Mark Three and at 78 mph top speed set a new standard for 350cc production bikes. That made the bike a natural choice for the production-based Clubman's TT and in 1949 Ferenc Pados, a Hungarian who was to campaign the twins on numerous British tracks,

was the best Duggie rider in 16th place. Encouraged, the factory announced the 28 bhp 90 Plus for 1950, with the 80 Plus, its slightly slower 25 bhp brother. The 90 Plus looked every inch a racer and John Clark gave the factory its best post-war TT result with 4th in the 1950 Clubman's 350cc Junior race, and C. E. Robinson of Louth finished 5th. That was the factory's best result in the Clubman's series, but the 90 Plus had clearly shown enough speed to worry the likes of BSA. When Ron Jones was contesting the Clubman's and getting some unofficial 'help' with his Gold Star, he was specifically asked to pace one of the Bristol twins and report back to the BSA depot. In fact, he found the Douglas no serious threat to the highly

Above right *The lean and purposeful 90 Plus was developed from the roadster and offered a claimed 28 bhp and a weight of 350 lbs in this racing form. This example is from the Sammy Miller museum in New Milton, Hampshire, and the unusual high mounting of the rev-counter drive on the special timing cover may come from an experimental engine.*

Right *Bob Dix (left) shows off the rare 80 Plus sportster that was a close brother to the 90 Plus racing model. Trevor Howell's 1950 Mark Four touring model was what most Douggie enthusiasts could afford.*

developed BSA, and in the 1951 350cc race there were eight BSAs and four Nortons in the first dozen.

Douglas could not afford development on the scale of the giant BSA factory for their competition ambitions, but they made sure that their flagship models were seen by the trade as much as possible. When David Tye joined the company as a sales representative, with his weekends committed to riding in the trials team, he was given either an 80 or 90 Plus to take him to meet customers. He was one of the team entered in the International Six Days Trial in 1949, when the event was held in Wales. 'They went to a lot of trouble to build a good bike,' he remembers. 'And they would have been good if the compression ratio hadn't been too high. It was up to about 10 to 1 and the team all retired with burnt pistons.'

One notable success was Don Chapman's 350 Clubman's race win at the prestigious Silverstone Saturday meeting in 1950. Not on a 90 Plus, but a very rapid Mark Three Sports that had reputedly revved to 10,000 rpm. Winning clearly with a 19-second margin, Chapman was also awarded the *Motor Cycling* £50 for the most meritorious performance in the Clubman's races.

But by 1953 sales were not good and the range was cut to the Mark Five tourer and

the 90 Plus, and both were reduced in price for 1954. Later that year came the final form of the twin, the 'Dragonfly', with a strengthened development of the 60.8 x 60mm unit in an all-welded duplex cradle frame. Conventional swinging-arm at the rear and Earles-type forks were Girling damped. It wasn't fast, but it handled well and stood out from the single-cylinder crowd. But not for long. A change of ownership in 1956 saw a new company direction and the final stocks were cleared in 1957 as the Douglas twin came to an end.

When Bob Dix bought his first Douglas in 1954, London dealers Brackpool's tried hard to dissuade him. 'They told me I could have a 500 Triumph for only £10 more,' recalls the Staffordshire bookkeeper. 'And when I insisted, they told me I'd have trouble with it. It did about 100,000 miles in 12 years and I've still got it in bits waiting for restoration – but their shop isn't there any more!

'The only real problem was when it ran out of oil; that was my fault for not checking it. I did sell it to a local lad, and later it was offered back for a fiver so I bought it again – but that was years ago.'

Bob's long experience of bikes has seen him happy to settle with a Douglas in pride of place. It's a rare 1951 80 Plus sports model, with alloy five-gallon fuel tank and the impressive 9-inch front brake the model shared with the 90 Plus racer. 'I don't get to use it much,' he admits. 'Being self-employed, I don't get much time to get it out in the garage to work on it. I'm going to restore it when I retire, so we can go on some of the local vintage runs around the lanes. These bikes are no good on main roads today, but round the lanes you can enjoy their handling – the weight is all low down on the Douglas and they're really good on the corners.'

Bob's enthusiasm is catching, and friend Trevor Howell has restored a 1950 Mark 4 tourer in the distinctive polychromatic blue to complement the sporty 80 Plus. Together they form an enclave of enthusiasm for the Bristol-built twins close to the Staffordshire base where Nortons are made today!

DOUGLAS

In 1954, the Mark V roadster and 90 Plus were the only motorcycles in the Douglas range.

Engine: Air-cooled four-stroke horizontally opposed twin, with two pushrod-operated valves per cylinder. Cast iron cylinder heads and barrels. 60.8mm × 60mm stroke, 348cc. Compression ratio, 7.25 to 1 (90 Plus – 8.25), claimed power output, 18 bhp at 6,000 rpm (90 Plus – 32 at 7,000).

Transmission: Four-speed gearbox in unit with engine, with integral foot change. Single-plate car-type clutch. Final drive by chain.

Cycle parts: Duplex cradle frame with Douglas 'Radiadraulic' leading link front forks and torsion-bar-controlled swinging-arm rear, Seven-inch drum brakes front and rear (90 Plus – 9-inch front).

Dimensions: Wheelbase – 55 in (90 Plus – 54½), Dry weight 340 lbs (393), Ground clearance 6¼ in (5¼), Saddle height 30 in (both).

Owners' Club: Active. Six UK sections, spares scheme. Secretary – M. Meinertzhagen, 20 Bradhurst Road, Wigmore, Gillingham, Kent ME8 OPF.

Sources of help: Spares – Owners' Club scheme; G. D. Brown, 12 Meadrow, Godalming, Surrey GU7 3HN. Advice – Owners' Club specialists.

David Tye and the 1949-50 season

David Tye was a likely lad from Derbyshire, riding his own BSA to good places in trials, when rider Ted Breffitt approached him with the offer of a 'works' bike for Douglas in the 1949-50 season. During that single season on the Bristol twin, David brought them more results than any other trials rider, including a Special First Class award and the Nevis Trophy in the 1950 Scottish Six Days Trial, a First Class in the testing time-and-observation Scott Trial and the 350cc Cup in the Mitchell Trial.

A flat twin may seem an unlikely choice for a trials mount, but David found width no problem. 'If you look at the average riders's feet on the rests, the cylinders don't stick out a lot more than they did,' he explains. 'We did have occasional problems with the carburettors. It was known for us to have one knocked off in the middle of a section, but if it was level you had a chance of keeping going as a 175 with lots of clutch slip!'

The Competition model was based on the standard roadster, with the rear frame a rigid unit while the leading-link forks were standard. Upswept exhaust pipes were naturally fitted, while lower gearing and compression ratio were the only major power unit changes.

Those vulnerable carburettors meant that the works team carried a spare carburettor body in their pockets, ready with the same jets to replace one damaged on rocks. 'It took me about five minutes to change one,' Tye says, 'after I was used to it. It was just a matter of getting the damaged carburettor off and swapping the cables and slide into the spare body, then carrying on.'

He remembers the Douglas Competition, which turned the scales at a claimed 300 lbs, with affection. 'It was excellent on rocks. The low centre of gravity was good, and the tank was low too, so you could grip it below your knees and throw the bike around.

'It was all right in flat mud sections, but diabolical in a rut if you had to knock it off and open it up again. Then it would try to climb up out of the rut with the torque reaction.'

David completed his year with Douglas despite an approach from BSA, even though he had no formal contract and no paid retainer. Then he moved on to the giant of the industry and greater challenges, while Douglas dropped the Competition model from its range in 1951 and faded from the trials scene in a very short time. T. H. Wortley brought them some success in 1951, including losing the Bemrose Trial on the Special test after dropping no marks on observation, but by 1952 the name had disappeared from the major wards and into trials history.

A works Douglas rider at the age of 20, David Tye shows off the paces of the Competition model near his Derbyshire home. The up-and-over exhaust pipes were sometimes changed for others passing under the cylinder barrels and sweeping up towards the pillion seat.

FRANCIS BARNETT

The Coventry commuter models

Right *Ernie Smith joined Barnett from another Midlands Villiers-powered maker, DMW. Working from a shed in the grounds of the factory he masterminded the trials team and handled experimental work, sometimes working through the night to complete a project away from prying eyes and interruptions. A very good trials rider in his own right, here he heads for another award in the 1955 Mitcham Vase trial.*

Below *a 1958 Light Cruiser, with 175cc AMC power, poses for a publicity shot by the gentle Avon. Cynics said the extensive panelling was designed to rattle and drown out the mechanical chorus from the unloved engine!*

Francis Barnett was founded in 1919 by Gordon Francis and Arthur Barnett, and from the beginning the company was using Villiers two–stroke power to offer simple bikes of good quality. In the 1920s and '30s the name was kept in the public eye by the exploits of, Tommy Meeten, who showed that it was possible to complete really hard events like the Scottish Six Days Trial on a humble 'stroker', even if most riders thought a big four-stroke was essential.

The company was taken over by Associated Motor Cycles in 1947, after its ability to handle a variety of servicing work was proved in the Second World War, when the factory, in Coventry's Lower Ford Street, was a Transport Workshop handling a variety of bikes. Amongst the dispatch rider mounts they restored to active service was the 350cc Matchless G3L, and AMC's Managing Director Donald Heather had them on his list when he began a programme of expansion into the old-established Midlands factories. Francis and Barnett stayed on, and the company ran profitably until AMC politics dictated a move to unite with old rivals James in their Birmingham factory.

war, was made Service Manager. It was a job that brought him into contact with customers throughout the country and leading figures in the industry and the sporting sphere. Having happy customers brought its own benefit to factory personnel, and Joe remembers ex-World Champion Freddie Frith calling in for bikes and spares, bringing a parcel of fresh fish from his Grimsby home town. When it was shared amongst the testers, they made sure that the next trip on the eight-mile check given to every machine took them past their own front doors.

Francis Barnett led the lightweight field with telescopic forks on their 1949 122cc and 197cc models. And in 1952 the 197cc 'Falcon 58' was available with optional swinging-arm rear suspension, a luxury to be coveted in days when lesser makes offered only saddle springs between an owners's

Don Lawley's 1962 Fulmar features leading-link forks and a spine frame hidden beneath sleek bodywork. It's a very different bike from the 125 he rode in trials and scrambles in the early '50s, then rode to work every weekday.

The Coventry works was watched over by foreman Alf Pickering, who had a small but skilled workforce producing frames and other cycle parts, with Cosletising (a chemical coating of parts to prevent rusting) and stove enamelling plants within the factory. Francis and Barnett also owned the nearby Clarendon Pressing and Welding Company, where presswork like tanks, mudguards and chainguards was produced; chrome plating was handled next door by the Sherburn Plating Works.

Joe Goddard joined the company in 1924 and, after managing the factory during the body and the potholes. Design was in the capable hands of Bill King, who joined the firm to work on the assembly line and moved on to the design side as his ability matured and was recognized.

Success in trials was still the best way of proving small-capacity bikes in the early '50s, when the results sheets had been dominated by big bangers from the likes of AJS, BSA and Norton. Francis Barnett recruited the talented Ernie Smith from DMW Motorcycles of Dudley and put him in charge of experimental work and the Competition Department – a very grand title for a shed in the yard of the old Triumph factory in Coventry's Priory Street, which

George Fisher and Francis Barnett

Francis Barnetts may be seen as typical low-cost transport within the reach of everyone, but their sporting background includes some major surprises. Like the streamlined 125 which Jack Scott rode to a speed of 85.6 mph in 1957, to set new 125 and 250cc records for Western Australia.

The factory did well in its choice of trials riders, thanks to Ernie Smith's astute eye. When BSA's new competition Bantam began to win 'tiddler' class awards at the beginning of the 1950s, Francis Barnett answered with the loan of a 122cc Villiers-engined bike to new-comer Brian Martin, who set about putting the Coventry make firmly in the public eye with form that had *Motor Cycling* describing him as '. . . one of the brightest young men in a season notable for new stars.' In 28 National trials in the 1951 season that included a small bike award, Brian Martin won 14 of them! 'Brian was a blood and thunder rider,' remembers service manager Joe Goddard. 'He would use all the power he could get.' Not enough from the humble 122 Villiers, it seemed, and for 1952 Brian joined the BSA team to begin a career that took him finally to be their Competitions Manager.

Brian's place was taken by Bristol's George Fisher from the end of April. It was not officially a trade, but BSA's 125 successes dropped when George changed from Bantam to Fanny Bee; it was BSA's loss.

'There was definitely no blood and thunder with George,' Joe Goddard recalls. 'He used his loaf like Hugh Viney did. If Brian Martin used all the power he could get, George used as little as possible. He had superb throttle control.'

Fisher's first ride for Francis Barnett was at the Mitchell Trial, where he established a firm control of the new mount with the 125cc cup.

From then on he was almost unbeatable, taking the class award in seven of the 16 National trials that offered one. The little Villiers power unit was prepared by competitions manager Ernie Smith with 'a bit of touching up, but they weren't far from standard', according to Joe Goddard.

1953 saw George Fisher still on top form, winning 15 of the 27 National trial 125 or 150 class awards. And in the Kickham Trial he made history with the first ever overall victory by a 125 in a trade-supported trial, beating the accepted trials irons of 350 and 500cc capacity in a strong field that included Johnny Brittain on a Royal Enfield and the official team of John Draper, David Tye and Bill Nicholson. Giant-killing George later went to ride a Tiger Cub for the Triumph factory and was also a good speedway rider, but his unique place in history was carved on that humble 125 Francis Barnett.

No man did more to get small two-strokes recognized in 1950s trials than George Fisher, the top rider for the Francis Barnett team. Here he picks a careful path up Kinlochrannoch in the 1953 Scottish Six Days Trial.

Francis Barnett had taken over after Triumph moved to its famous Meriden address. Smith recruited the man who did most to put the 125cc trials bike on the map, George Fisher, and he teamed with another youngster who went on to greater things – Brian Martin.

Smith and Fisher worked in the experimental department to hone the basically standard trials models into winners. When George Fisher wanted to try a steeper steering head angle he modified his bike the quickest way possible by riding it gently into a wall! His point was proved, and from 1954 the head angle on the roadster frames was altered from 28° to 26.5°. It is unlikely that the customers who benefited from the revised geometry ever knew quite how rudimentary the experimental work had been!

A happy working relationship with engine suppliers Villiers was put under strain when the parent AMC Group decided to produce its own two-stroke units; Joe Goddard suggests that this was a reaction to Villiers' rejection of AMC's approaches for takeover talks. Goddard recalls Group Managing Director Donald Heather visiting Coventry when Eric Barnett was away ill, and telling the assembled senior staff that they were to place an order for 2,000 AMC 250 power units and cancel the development of a Villiers 2T twin-cylinder 250 model. 'It was the demise of Francis Barnett when AMC made that engine,' is Goddard's opinion. He was in a good position to judge, watching the 250 AMC unit cost the group heavy losses and then tasting a bitter pill after taking on the post of Service Manager to both FB and James, when AMC closed the Coventry factory and moved operations to the James factory in Birmingham's Greet area,

In Greet, the James factory's own chrome-plating plant stood unused as the company could not afford to buy the necessary anodes. And the last straw for Joe Goddard came when he ordered 2,000 prop-stand legs, to be used on both the two-stroke ranges and Norton's 250 Jubilee; the contractor wanted to see the money before taking the order, which was enough to convince Joe he should move on. In 1964 he left, to finish

---

FRANCIS BARNETT

1950 – range comprised 98cc single-speed 'Powerbike' with girder front forks, rigid frame and pedal starting; 122cc three-speed 'Merlin' with tele forks and rigid frame; 197cc three-speed 'Falcon' with tele forks and rigid frame. Legshields on 'Merlin' and 'Falcon' £2.75 extra. All with Villiers power units. 1951 – swinging-arm frame optional on 'Merlin' and 'Falcon'. 1953 – 225cc four-speed 'Cruiser' introduced. 1954 – 150cc version of 'Kestrel' introduced. 1957 – 250cc AMC-engined 'Cruiser 80' introduced. 1958 – 250cc AMC-engined 'Cruiser 82' Scrambler introduced. 171cc AMC-engined 'Light Cruiser' introduced in May. 250cc AMC-engined 'Cruiser 84' added in November, with full rear enclosure. 1961 – all models now powered by AMC engines. 1962 – 250cc Cruiser Twin 89' introduced, with Villiers 2T power unit. 'Fulmar 88' introduced, with spine frame and leading link forks; 150cc AMC power. 1964 – 150cc three-speed 'Plover' introduced, with AMC power unit. 1966 – Production ceased.
Owners' Club: Secretary – Mrs Cher Gardner, 58 Knowle Road, Totterdown, Bristol BS4 2ED. Also the British Twostroke Club. Secretary – Alan Abrahams, 38 Charles Drive, Cuxton, Rochester, Kent ME2 1DR.
Sources of help: Spares – DMW Motorcycles, Valley Road Works, Sedgley, Dudley, West Midlands; Alf Snell, 17 Drysdale Avenue, Chingford, London E4; Autocycle, 50 Church Street, Moxley, Wednesbury, West Midlands; Metten and Ward Ltd, 360 Kingston Road, Ewell, Surrey. Technical advice – Owners' Clubs.

---

his working life at the Reliant motor works.

Don Lawley, whose racing career includes TT Silver replicas, recaptures memories of youth with his 150cc Fulmar. As a young man, he began his competition career on a 122cc Fanny-B, used to ride to work and to whatever event he was contesting at the weekend, trial, scramble or grasstrack. 'Just a simple lightweight and not as good as the Dot I also had,' he says. Now Don keeps the Fulmar he shares with son Shaun to display at local charity shows where classic British machinery attracts attention. 'I bought it restored with just two owners before us, and I've got another one that we've taken bits off to get this complete. It's an interesting little bike, a bit different from what all the others were making, with those front forks and the tank tucked away under the seat.

'I support local shows and like to have a bike to use for them, because it's good for motorcycling. I used to take my 50cc Honda racer, but as it's so small the kids climb on it – it got more damage from shows than when I raced it. With the Francis Barnett I don't have to worry so much.'

The small factory in Church Road, Thundersley, not far off the A13 from London to Southend-on-Sea, was where Bert Greeves produced the bikes that carried his name to success all over the world. It started as the Invacar works, and the telephone was still answered with that name after the Greeves title was familiar to motorcyclists all over the world! Bert Greeves was an original thinker, and when his first production bike was shown to the world in 1953 it used a cast alloy front down-section from steering head to the front engine mounting, while suspension at both ends was via rubber in torsion, with friction adjustment. Engines were two-stroke units, single cylinders by Villiers and twin by British Anzani in the 25D 'Fleetwing', top of the range at £178.80 including the Purchase Tax that was cursed in the 1950s just as VAT is today.

The suspension soon changed to a more conventional rear swinging-arm with Girling dampers, and the front forks were standardized with a development of the leading-link type, using Girling dampers up the inside of the main fork leg to supplement the rubber bush at the link pivot. It proved to be a very strong structure and the development of competition versions was quite natural, especially when Brian Stonebridge joined the

GREEVES

A small firm, a big reputation

Left *The Greeves Sports of 1959 used Villiers single-cylinder power that whispered through an adaptation of the trials silencer. On the road, the handling was capable of taking much more than 197cc of the Villiers could produce.*

Below *Martin Studer on Selwyn Mallet's 1967 250 'Silverstone', showing determination at Cadwell Park. In 1988 Martin won the 'Classic Bike' Championship in the 250 class, the highest honour in British classic racing.*

firm in 1956. One of the greats of moto-cross, the lanky Stonebridge had starred on 500cc Matchless singles until joining BSA and riding the humble 125cc Bantam at speeds few others could match. Stonebridge brought to Thundersley precious knowledge of the then rare art of two-stroke tuning, and soon had the Villiers 197cc scrambler flying, to beat the established 500cc singles on demanding courses like the hilly Hawkstone Park. It was there in April 1957 that Stonebridge beat the four-strokes in the 350cc final and came home runner-up in the 500cc final, with the BSA and Matchless works teams in opposition. This established the Greeves name

beyond any reasonable doubt, even if old prejudice against two-strokes was slow to die.

Bert Greeves had an astute eye for riding talent, and amongst the young riders he supported were Ipswich lad Dave Bickers and a Yorkshire trials rider, Bill Wilkinson. Wilkinson hit the headlines for Greeves when he won the British experts Trial in 1960, the first stroker to take the title. The fact that his 250cc Greeves wore L-plates at the time made even more headlines for the little Essex factory, of course. Bickers stepped into the gap left by Brian Stonebridge's death in a car accident, and took British lightweight motorcycles to new heights of success in moto-cross riding.

Bert Greeves himself was an active rider, riding competition models on whatever ground the factory had available for tests, including the Salvation Army ground at nearby Hadleigh! His collection of veteran and vintage models included a 1912 Triumph registered OLD 1, which must have been one of the most photographed machines in the factory. In his office he sat in a chair built to his own design, using a Girling damper to control rocking movement.

1962 Trophée des Nations

Dave Bickers won so many honours in a long career that picking out a highlight is almost impossible. His victories in the 1960 and '61 European 250cc Moto-Cross Championships did immense good for Greeves's prestige, but in September 1962 Dave led a British team of 250s to a victory that they badly needed.

In the Moto-Cross des Nations earlier that summer, the winning Swedish team had won the international 500cc competition with its team members taking the chequered flag line abreast for the first four places in the final and a sweeping victory. The 250cc competition, the Trophée des Nations, was held at Shrublands Park, near Bickers' home town of Ipswich, and the home team was out to avenge defeat in Switzerland. There were to be two races for points, in the normal continental manner, with scores totalled for each team to decide the winners.

In the first leg, Bickers on the Greeves and Jeff Smith (BSA) headed the field, with Dave pulling away for a clear win after 15 laps of his local circuit. Smithy was second and with Arthur Lampkin (BSA) fifth, the British team had a 20-point lead. Then team manager Harold Taylor called the squad together, as Dave Bickers remembers well. 'We decided to stage a really good finish if we could and finish with all five in a line. There were no real team orders, but if it was possible we'd do it.'

Bickers led the 39-man charge off the line with Finnish ace Erola close behind on his Husqvarna. After one lap Dave was still ahead, Jeff Smith was third, Lampkin fourth, Don Rickman sixth on his Metisse and Alan Clough catching up from tenth. After five laps the British squad of five dominated the race, with only the persistent Erola still with them in third; Clough had ridden through to fourth place and as he put pressure on the lone Finn the Husqvarna seized and the Brits filled places one to five.

At the front Bickers and Smith, on the slower BSA, were neck and neck, lapping the opposition up to the eighth man, but eased their meteoric pace as a British domination was confirmed by Harold Taylor's delighted signals. At the final corner, Bickers and Smith waited and were joined by Clough, then Rickman and Lampkin rode up to join them in a victory cruise to the line with the whole British team led by the day's highest scorer – Dave Bickers and the Greeves. The Swedes in Switzerland had got four out of five team men together, but the British went one better and got the entire five-man squad lined up in a demonstration of superiority. The timekeepers gave the official first place to Dave, making his a maximum score in a famous victory.

Knees gripping the tank, his high and wide handlebars making him look taller than he was, Dave Bickers on the 250 Greeves was almost unbeatable in the early 1960s.

A great Greeves factory character was Derry Preston-Cobb, the sales director whose physical handicap gave him credibility in discussing the virtues of the Invacar products. But Derry's own invalid carriage was far from standard, with a development motor sometimes hidden under the innocent-looking covers; the tales of expensive cars being overtaken on the Southend road by an invalid carriage still live on. Derry and cousin Bert Greeves were strong believers in competition benefiting road machines, as well as selling trials and moto-cross models in greater numbers.

The factory spread its interests further with the introduction of the 'Silverstone' road racer. With a clear victory in the 1964 250cc Manx Grand Prix, Gordon Keith took the Greeves round for the fastest lap of the race at 87.6 mph, the best speed ever by a production British 250, to finish ahead of a field dominated by foreign bikes. It was all part of building a reputation for sports machinery that could outshine good road models, with power units from 197cc Villiers singles to 325cc twins, also with the Villiers power that took over from Anzani soon after production started. The road bikes used the same alloy front beam frame and attracted some discerning customers, including police forces for the radio-equipped version of the bigger twin.

The alloy beam finally gave way to a more conventional tubular frame and the distinctive Greeves leading link forks to conventional teles, but the sporting outlook remained. At the end of the Greeves motorcycle name, the factory was producing competition models only, but they live on firmly in the public eye because of that. In any sphere of competition for classic bikes, the Greeves name is active, the Moorland Blue colour a reminder of success from as long ago as 1953.

One example of the long active life for Thundersley's finest is the 1967 'Silverstone' RES that Martin Studer borrowed from Selwyn Mallet for his racing debut. At his first meeting, the former kart racer was second and next time out he won twice; he and the Greeves have become a force in Classic

GREEVES

Engine: 1954 Model 20 – air-cooled two-stroke single cylinder, 54mm × 72mm, 197cc, claimed 8.4 bhp at 4,000 rpm. Optioal tuning for scrambles (20S) and roadster (20D). 1964 34DC – air-cooled two-stroke twin cylinder, 57mm × 63.5mm, claimed 18.5 bhp at 5,200 rpm.

Transmission: 1954 Model 20 – three or four-speed gearbox. 1964 32DC – four-speed gearbox. All models with integral footchange. Primary and secondary transmission by chain. Multi-plate clutch in oil.

Cycle parts (all models): Welded tubular rear frame, with alloy beam front down member. Leading link front forks, with rubber in torsion and damper. Swinging-arm frame. Six-inch drum brakes front and rear.

Dimensions: Wheelbase – 1954 Model 20, 52 in; 1964 32DC, 54 in. Dry weight – 1954 Model 20, 240 lbs (4-speed road); 1964 32DC, about 275 lbs.

Owners's Club: Active and growing. Membership secretary of the Greeves Riders' Association – P. Smith, 6 St George's Road, Winsford, Cheshire SW7 1DA.

Sources of help: Spares – Terry Silvester Motorcycles, Spring Lane Mills, Woodhead Road, Holmfirth, Huddersfield, Yorkshire HD7 1PR; Smoothline Motorcycle Components, Tyffynon, Crickhowell, Powys NP81 1RU; Frank Conley, 13 El Cuenco, Carmel Valley, California, USA 93924. Advice – Riders's Association specialists.

racing since then. 'It's a super bike,' enthuses Martin. 'It's given me a good grounding in racing and it's only let me down once – when a main bearing sleeve worked its way off and went through the Motoplat ignition unit. Apart from that it's finished every race in the last four years.

'The handling is very soft and forgiving, and it's so good in the wet that we've never been beaten when it rains! The front forks make you think the brakes aren't too good because the front doesn't dip at all, but I've come in and said the brakes weren't feeling good when I've had the back wheel in the air, they're working so well! It's very deceptive.

'We've got two motors, and they've been no real trouble. We do squirt a mixture of oil down the inlet after a meeting to help the main bearings, because the outer rollers get very little lubrication. And we change the right-hand crank oil seal after each day's racing – on Saturday night in the paddock at a two-day meeting. I reckon it must have given me 35 wins in the four years I've raced, and in 1987 it had 11 wins in 19 races. A lovely little bike, really.'

JAMES

Little Jimmy was everyone's friend

The James Cycle Company was renowned through the 1950s and the '60s as a maker of good-value two-strokes. But the roots of the James dynasty went back to the beginning of the century, and included a reputation as a quality manufacturer of sporting V-twins in the 1920s. Its product range in those far-off days included the only V-twin Speedway model ever catalogued by a British factory!

The James factory was a well-equipped and independent unit, boasting that it could produce most of the parts it used, apart from obvious bought-in items like tyres, electrical parts and sparking plugs. Chrome plating was done in the factory's own plating shop, still there in the post-1939-45 war era when Villiers-powered two-strokes were all that were offered, the four-strokes of yesteryear long forgotten as the factory concentrated on economical assembly of low-priced bikes for the masses.

With the arrival of the 1950s, the range varied from the single-speed 98cc 'Superlux' Autocycle to the three-speed 197cc 'Captain de luxe'. But the sporting heritage was not forgotten, with promising young riders being entered on the trials version of the Captain; Johnny Brittain made his mark with class wins on a 125cc James before Royal Enfield snapped him up in 1950 and put him on a 350cc four-stroke and the road to fame! In 1951, Bill Lomas was James Captain-mounted and rocked the established world of big-banger trials men with a win in the trade-supported Travers; he then capped a season of class wins with victory in the Northern Experts Trial. James was the company that really started the two-stroke takeover of trials, and its successful riders also included ten times TT winner Stanley Woods and a young Irish lad by the name of Sammy Miller . . .

An old trials hand working in the factory was Bert Kershaw, but by the 1950s he was showing the James paces in another way. Hitching a Watsonian sidecar to a Captain for his 1951 holiday, he covered over 4,000 miles in four weeks, including taking the three-speed 197cc outfit over the 9,040-feet-high Stelvio Pass as he visited Italy, Austria and Switzerland. Pass-storming with only 8.2 bhp to haul an all-up weight of 7 cwt (387 kg)

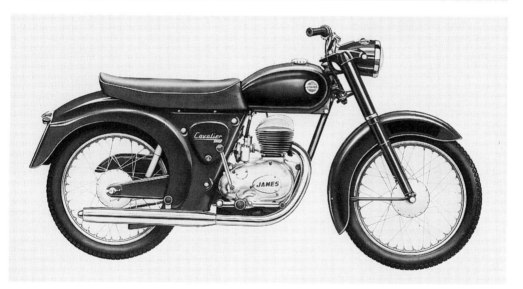

may sound impossible, but Bert completed the trip with an average fuel consumption of 83 mpg to prove that even on a severely restricted foreign travel allowance a James could take you a long way.

The company was sold out to the London-based Associated Motor Cycles in the early '50s, long-serving F. A. Kimberley continuing as Managing Director until his retirement in 1955, when he was succeeded by Charles Somerton. The James factory under AMC ownership started to lose its way as the group began to hit problems, in some cases selling machines abroad at less than cost in an effort to keep out the threat from other manufacturers – particularly those in Japan. When AMC decided it would produce its own two-stroke power unit rather than depend on the Villiers company, it proved a bad move. The members of the group could be bullied into ordering the AMC engine instead of a Villiers unit, but the result was a flood of problems and irate customers who expected better from a name they had learned to trust. First seen in 1958, the unloved AMC singles were being replaced by the trusty Villiers again by 1962, when the 250cc twin Super-swift appeared, with a 2T Villiers motor.

But the damage to the name had been done, and Japanese machines were making inroads around the world. In 1964, AMC Director Alan Sugar admitted to a colleague as he showed him five gleaming Suzukis in the AMC boardroom: 'This is what we're going to sell. We can't make them, and we can't beat them, so we're going to join them.' AMC was importing Suzukis into Britain, using the James factory as its base. Production of James bikes ended in 1966, as those in higher places gave up!

But the name lives on today, with enthusiasts delighting in their simple and sturdy build. Secretary of the British Two Stroke Club, Alan Abrahams, counts no fewer than 17 of the marque in his collection, and reckons his 1951 98cc Comet is ideal for long weekends, covering up to 300 miles in a day at 100 miles to the gallon.

George and Margaret Browning have a smaller collection of the marque, and find it easy to keep them all in use. George's love of two-strokes spread to Margaret when she got a present of a box of bits and a promise that aircraft design engineer George would restore the heap of bits into a complete bike. When it was done, Margaret used it to pass her bike test. 'It was snowing,' she remembers. 'I think the fact that the examiner used to have a James himself may have helped a bit!'

Next James in the Browning house was a 150cc Cadet that was kept behind the TV set after restoration, until the summer arrived. Now used for daily commuting to her job with the local police force, it rewards Margaret with easy 45 mph cruising and the proven ability to do 60 mph two-up. This example came complete, but if cycle parts are missing George finds the only answer is to scour the small ads and autojumble stalls.

A Cotswold scrambler dating from 1957 is George's own bike, now registered for the road and used for riding the green lanes of East Anglia at weekends. The Cotswold model may have been listed as a scrambler, but its roadster heritage shows in the pillion footrest lugs still on the frame. Chrome-plated rims were an expensive luxury for an economy competition bike in the '50s, and the Cotswold wears typical silver-painted rims. Conventional swinging-arm suspension at the rear combines with James' own slim telescopic forks that keep their working areas covered with dirt-excluding gaiters.

All the Brownings' James bikes are finished in the traditional maroon that was the factory's livery until a change to dark grey with royal blue tank panels for the 1957 season. Various colours were on offer from then, until the Greet factory accommodated the Francis Barnett range after the latter's Coventry works was closed, and some colours became common to both names. For most followers of 'The Famous James', as the company logo called it, maroon paint and a reputation for quality at an affordable price were what the name meant.

JAMES

Model range: 1950 – from 98cc single-speed Autocycle, with girder forks and rigid frame, single speed, pedal start, and 98cc two-speed Comet, through 122cc three-speed Cadet to 197cc three-speed Captain, the latter two available in trials trim at extra cost. All models used Villiers engines.
1957 – AMC single cylinder engine introduced in the 250cc L25 Commodore.
1958 – Cavalier introduced with 175cc AMC engine. Commando L25 with 250cc AMC engine available in trials or scrambles trim.
1962 – Villiers 2T-powered 250cc Superswift twin introduced. Francis Barnett machines built in James factory from this time on.
1963 – Trials and scrambles models now Villiers powered. AMC engine now assembled by Villiers factory at Wolverhampton.
1966 – the final year range was 150cc M16 Cadet, 200cc Captain and Sports Captain, 250cc Commando Trials, 250cc Cotswold Scrambler and 250 Sports Superswift twin.
Owners' Clubs: There is no separate James OC, but they are catered for by the James section of the Vintage MCC (Secretary – Ian Telford, 70 Park Hill Road, Wallington, Surrey) and the British Two-Stroke Club (Secretary – Alan Abrahams, 38 Charles Drive, Cuxton, Rochester, Kent ME2 1DR).
Sources of help: Spares – DMW Motorcycle, Valley Road Works, Sedgley, Dudley West Midlands; Alf Snell, 17 Drysdale Avenue, Chingford, London E4; Autocycle, 50 Church Street, Moxley, Wednesbury, West Midlands; Meeten and Ward Ltd, 360 Kingston Road, Ewell Surrey. Technical advice – Owners' Clubs.

1965 – three National trials wins in three weekends

Pre-'65 trials flourish today, and that date was selected to recall the time before Sammy Miller and his Spanish Bultaco set about changing trials for ever. But 1965 wasn't only about the invading Armada beating everything out of sight – the British did fight back.

Mick Andrews, the Derbyshire lad who had been riding a factory 350 AJS for three years, was presented with a 250 James 'Commando Trials' for 1965, sent with a Cotswold scrambles model by James competition manager Ernie Wiffen. 'A lovely little bike,' Mick recalls. 'It had a beautiful little alloy tank and a very low seat. I remember people used to laugh at that, but it's like they build today! It had a Villiers engine with a Parkinson barrel, and I know I geared it right down – it would only do a bit more than 30 flat out in top, but I liked my bikes like that.'

'M. Andrews (James)' began to make a mark in trials, but in October the combination showed the British were far from dead. On 2 October Mick was in Devon for the West of England trial, and after a storming day he was just one mark behind Sammy Miller at Buckeridge, the last section. Mick cleaned it and Miller dropped a boot and one mark – it was a tie with 34 marks lost by each rider. But when the results sheets were checked, Andrews

had cleaned more sections on the James than Miller on the Bultaco and the British team man was declared the winner – his first National trial win on a James.

Mick was in the east on 9 October for the Suffolk Mardle Trial. With his confidence in the lightweight James growing, he finished the time-and-observation event 12 marks ahead of local lad Dave Bickers on a works Greeves. BSA-mounted John Banks was back in third place, another moto-cross rider finding that he needed trials skills as well as speed for this outing.

One week later the James was in action again, facing Sammy Miller's Bultaco in the Welsh One Day Trial. Mick was in determined mood and not thinking of giving anyone an easy victory – not even the legendary Miller! When the observers' scorecards were totalled at the end of the day, the nail-biting ended with the announcement that Mick Andrews on the James had lost 34 marks, with Sammy Miller three marks behind in second. The James had won three National trials in as many weekends! As a delighted factory ordered adverts shouting about the success of their 'tough, powerful trials winner', Mick Andrews was on his way to a scramble, to win on his other 250.

He remembers his James with affection: 'Reliable, a cracking little bike. And getting off a 350 AJS on to that, it felt so light. Wish I had it now!'

Mick Andrews and his 250 James were a formidable combination in 1965, the Derbyshire star revelling in the light weight of the Villiers-engined Commando.

MATCHLESS TWINS

Racing was in their background

The Matchless 'Super Clubman' twin was announced in 1948, as the big Associated Motor Cycles group moved to keep up with the trend started by Triumph's 'Speed Twin'. The solid singles were selling well, but the sporting rider was looking for something with a little glamour – and the megaphone-shaped silencers and a deep roaring exhaust note provided it.

Sales Manager Jock West told the *British Trade Journal* in 1949 that the Philip Walker-designed twin had been given a 200,000-mile test programme, including thrashing over the tank testing ground at Bagshot Heath to see how it would take to the rough stuff in overseas markets. The established 'Teledraulic' telescopic front forks were matched with a swinging-arm frame using 'Teledraulic' damper units that became affectionately known as 'candlesticks' from their slim appearance.

Walker's design for a twin-cylinder engine

Above left Rob Pearce's 1958 500cc G9 wears a two-into-one exhaust system to give better access to the primary transmission and a Citroen oil filter to keep its lubricant clean. Rob is a keen green lanes rider— on an AJS two-stroke 370.

broke away from established convention with a three-bearing crank, a plain bearing supporting the centre of the shaft and roller bearings at the outer ends. Iron cylinder barrels were separate and contained 7.8 to 1 wire-wound pistons, putting out a claimed 26 bhp from the 66mm bore × 72.8mm stroke unit. Tappet adjustment of the twin was an easier task than most similar models, with the rockers mounted on an eccentric and easily tightened at the correct setting with a clamp bolt. The bike was not the fastest of its type, with a realistic top speed estimate of 85 mph, but it earned a good name for pulling well from low revs and smooth running so long as it wasn't revved

Matchless twins are still active today, as the winning team in the 1987 BMF National Rally confirms. Left to right, Lol Reeday (650 G12), Kevin Coxon (600 G11) and Bob Boaden (500 G9) were the best team in the premier road riding event of the year, against bikes of all ages. Lol was also the Best Individual.

too hard – then the rigid three-bearing crank passed on a clear message that two pistons jumping up and down in unison can develop vibration, whatever the advertisements might claim!

But the G9, as the Super Clubman was called in factory parlance, would reward sensible riding with long, faithful mileage. John Drudge, president of the AJS and Matchless Owners' Club, covered over 100,000 miles on his 1959 example with a single rebore and crankshaft regrind. When rumours of a 750cc version circulated, John, a regular visitor to the factory, enquired about it of Service Manager Fred Neill, 'Stick with your G9, it'll do you better,' was the honest answer.

The essential simplicity of British bikes came home to John when he was in Italy on one of his regular European touring holidays. A short in the wiring saw the system burned out, but a local shop took it in at nine in the morning and made up and fitted a new wiring harness working from the factory manual by the time John called back at midday. Factory manuals were always the work of Fred Neill, whose intimate knowledge of the bikes made his written words law if an owner was to keep his Matchless in top trim.

In 1956 the 592cc G11 was introduced, the engine enlarged by simply taking the bore out to 72mm. Many experienced riders reckoned the 600cc version the sweetest of all the AMC twins, a view backed up by journalist Vic Willoughby, who took a G11CSR sport model round the Motor In-

1952 Manx Grand Prix

The Matchless Super Clubman twin appeared in an unusual form for the 1951 500cc Manx Grand, with a twin-carburettor version of the engine in an AJS 7R frame. Ridden by Robin Sherry, who went on to a full works team ride with the AJS factory, it averaged 83.7 mph to finish fourth amongst the Manx Nortons which were then the only racing 500 available for the private owner.

The bike was a natural development for a factory which was selling a lot of the popular 7R AJS 350s and which wanted to provide customers with a 500 to keep the Plumstead flag flying. Maurice Brierley, a man with a racing background that included competing on a 7R before losing a leg in a road accident, took up the offer of a job 'to help develop our new multi-cylinder racing machine'. He was disappointed to find that he was working on an uprated roadster engine, but saw how the claimed 48 bhp at 7,200 rpm was obtained: 'The engine was running on methanol, and the power wasn't a constant figure, it was a snatch reading to keep the Board of Directors happy.'

Whatever the true power output of the G45 Matchless racer, it was enough for the promising 23-year-old Derek Farrant, from St Leonards in Sussex, who had the works devel-opment bike for the 1952 Manx Grand Prix. It was not going to be an easy race for Derek, who faced opposition from Bob McIntyre, on a works 7R AJS, and past winners on the TT course like Denis Parkinson and Eric Houseley, both on 500cc Manx Nortons. But Farrant had celebrated his 23rd birthday two days earlier with third place in the 350cc Junior race behind with McIntyre and Harold Clark to complete an AJS 1-2-3, and in the big race he was out for nothing less than victory.

Derek beat the lap record on four of the race's six laps – the standing start first and a stop for fuel kept the other two laps slower than his meteoric normal pace. Behind him, McIntyre, the never-give-up Scot, was battling his 350 ahead of 500cc Nortons, but no one could get near Flying Farrant at the head of the field and on his way to establish the G45 Matchless as a racer to be reckoned with. He won by almost 2 minutes, setting a new race record for the 227-mile race and the lap record at a new high of 89.64 mph. The G45 went on offer to racers for the 1953 season at £376.94, which made it £50 cheaper than the 500cc Manx Norton, and it was a popular choice in the days when the average wage was around £8 a week. But it never won as big a race as that 1952 Manx Grand Prix, the ultimate test for the private owner and a convincing demonstration of the G45's urge.

Derek Farrant keeps his eyes on the road ahead as the rear tyre takes a pounding at the bottom of Bray Hill. His race average of 88.65 mph was a new record and would have taken him to sixth place in that year's Senior TT.

dustry Research Association track one lunch hour in 1958 to cover 103 miles in 60 minutes at 35 miles to the gallon.

The 650cc G12 came in 1959, with 72mm bore and 78.3mm stroke; it built a reputation for lusty pulling power and a lot of vibration if the sporting performance was used. There was also a 750cc version of the three-bearing crank engine made in small numbers, but towards the end of the AMC group's life in 1964, a blend of Matchless frame with Norton forks and wheels and the 750cc Norton Atlas engine was offered; this never had a chance to get over its identity crisis before the Plumstead factory finally closed and the Matchless twin line came to an end.

But the bikes are still very much alive. The very active Owners' Club entered a trio from its Nottingham and Derby Section as Team Matchless in the 1987 BMF National Rally, Bob Boaden on a 500, Kevin Coxon on a 600 and Lol Reeday on a 650. Riding 100 miles to the Goole, Humberside, starting point, they planned to cover 500 miles and visit 23 checks around the country in the next 24 hours.

The only problem was the borrowed magneto on Kevin's 600, fitted as a precaution because the original was waiting for overhaul. The replacement broke down in the night and the three friends spent a frantic quarter of an hour fitting the original back on, which completed the Rally with not one trace of a misfire. Competing with over a thousand riders, many on the latest hi-tech superbikes, Team Matchless was consistent enough to take the Team Award in the biggest road riding event of the year.

And in the final test, ties were decided by attempting to average 24.8 mph over a course in the grounds of the National Exhibition Centre. Only one competitor managed to hit the target time spot on – and Lol Reeday went home as overall winner of the Rally. He dismisses the win with a modest 'Biggest stroke of luck in history' to describe his efforts, but riders of much more expensive and luxurious bikes must have wished for a little of that luck.

A man who lives with Matchless twins most of his riding day is Rob Pearce, a shop-fitter from the West Midlands area who has 18 years of the model behind him. Rob acts as Technical Adviser for the Owners' Club and his own well-used 1958 GP 500 is an example of keeping the breed in use with 30 years under its wheels.

Rob's bike uses a Citroen 2CV car oil filter in the return line to keep the lubricant clean, as he doesn't trust the original felt filter located in the crankcase to keep the oil really clean. 'There is no weak point with the twin, so long as you don't work it too hard,' he explains. 'Motorways kill them, but they're fine on normal roads.

Rob's bike was rebuilt after he bought it in boxes of bits, and part of the personalized specification is an old Mossley airseat, its perished inner tube now replaced with a comfortable blend of foam. He says pistons are the most difficult part to find, and his engine runs on 8.5 to 1 types with an extra gasket under the barrel to reduce the true ratio to about 8 to 1. With an engine sprocket one tooth bigger than standard, 50 mph cruising gives an economical 70 miles to the gallon. Rob got the Matchless habit after moving up to a 600cc G11 from a BSA Bantam, and 30,000 trouble-free miles on that twin convinced him to stick with the bike that has given him many happy years.

MATCHLESS TWIN

Engine: Air-cooled, four-stroke parallel twin, with two pushrod-operated valves per cylinder. Separate iron cylinder barrels with alloy heads; three-bearing crank, G9 500cc – 66mm × 72.8mm, claimed output 26 bhp at 6,300 rpm; G11 592cc – 73mm × 72.8mm, claimed output 34 bhp at 5,800 rpm. (Sports version 39.5 bhp at 6,000 rpm); G12 646cc – 72mm × 78.3mm, claimed output 46 bhp at 6,500 rpm;
Transmission (all models) : Four-speed gearbox with integral footchange. Primary and secondary transmission by chain. Multi-plate clutch in oil.
Cycle parts: Swinging-arm frame with 'Teledraulic' telescopic front forks until Norton forks were used from 1964 to 1966 end of production. Seven-inch single-leading-shoe drum brakes front and rear.
Dimensions: Wheelbase – 55¼ in. Dry weight – G9, 397 lbs; G12, 430 lbs.
Owners' Clubs: Very active; 26 UK sections. Secretary – Mrs L. Reeday, 263 Leicester Road, Mount Sorrel, Leicestershire LE12 7DD.
Sources of help: Spares – AJS & Matchless OC Spares Scheme; Russell Motors, 125-7 Falcon Road, Battersea, London SW1 2PE; Hamrax Motors Ltd, 328 Ladbroke Grove, North Kensington, London W10. Advice – Owners' Club specialists.

NORTON SIDE-VALVE SINGLES

Plodding through the ages

Below *Hardly luxurious conditions in which to service essential transport, but Chris Collier gets down to some maintenance in the Egyptian sunshine in 1945. Glass replaced a shroud in the headlight in areas where aerial detection at night was not a threat.*

Norton built its reputation in the early years of the company on solid simple side-valve singles. As early as 1912 James Norton introduced the 79mm bore × 100 stroke 490cc engine and those dimensions for the 16H stayed the same until its final year of production in 1954. Its bigger brother was the Big Four, a model renowned for its pulling power from the 82mm × 113mm 633cc engine and said to be 'Pa' Norton's favourite; he was certainly seen on one at many events, with large sidecar attached, and he even made a tour of South Africa on such an outfit to assess the market for his products.

Side-valve engines inevitably gave way to faster overhead valve models as technology made the newer type more reliable, but the old sloggers still had a faithful following. And when the Mechanical Warfare Experimental Establishment reported on a series of tests in 1935, it concluded '. . . of the 500cc machines, the best is the Norton.' By December 1936 it referred to the 16H as '. . . the WD-pattern Norton solo motor cycle' and the factory in Bracebridge Street, Birmingham, was working hard to meet the military's demand. They wanted a rugged machine, simple enough for raw recruits with no riding experience to be trained to ride and maintain. The 16H provided just that, and some 100,000 of them were made during the 1939-45 War.

The output dictated a change in the factory layout. The old method of lifting the frame from bench to bench as the bike was assembled was far too slow and the factory floor was fitted out with wooden tracks, along which simple wooden trolleys were

Above *The 79mm bore × 100mm stroke measurements of the 16H date from 1912 and lasted to the final year of production in 1954.*

Left *Stripped of lights and mudguards, the 16H was readily adaptable for informal trials in the Egyptian desert. Riding in shorts brought its own particular hazards, as one rider found when a hornet flew up his leg!*

Below *Chris Collier on the 16H Norton he restored from a rusty derelict to a faithful replica of his mount when he served in the 18th Air Formation of the Royal Corps of Signals. Many thousands of miles in Egypt included a single puncture and one mechanical breakdown.*

pushed as the bike grew from bare frame to complete machine. The same layout was used right through to the 1960s, so the 16H can claim to have altered Norton's method of production during its long life.

The Big Four did its bit for King and Country, too. Fitted with a sidecar that carried a Bren gun, it drove the sidecar wheel via a shaft from a dog clutch on the adapted rear wheel spindle, engaged or disengaged by a lever behind the driver's left leg. The dog clutch was protected by a leather gaiter that had to be removed every week for the grease in it to be replenished. All three wheels were interchangeable, with a spare carried on the sidecar.

The Big Four outfit was finally replaced by the American-built jeep, which could carry bigger loads across country faster. The

service department didn't mourn its passing, and fitter Michael Usher remembers dreading the return of a Big Four outfit for overhaul. When they were sold off after the war was over, the sidecar wheel drive was cut off before they were released to a civilian population that couldn't be trusted to use the extra drive which could be a hazardous busi-

Bill Bennett's Big Four

In the popular field of pre-'65 trials, one of the sidecar outfits that competitors fear is the 1951 Big Four Norton owned by agricultural engineer Bill Bennett of Chipping Sodbury, near Bristol. Built by Bill with ports gas-flowed and polished, the Norton is fitted with a modern sidecar adapted to the traditional look with alloy panelling, complete with Norton Owners' Club badge on the nose.

Bill has handed the outfit over to Roger Tuck to drive, with brother David in the sidecar. A top-line enduro sidecar driver on modern machinery, former British champion Roger has made the Norton the leading outfit in its field, with wins in the 1988 Talmag trial and at the international British Bike Bonanza in Gloucestershire. 'It's a brilliant bike,' says Roger of the 633cc Big Four with its cast iron cylinder barrel and head. 'The best I've ever ridden for pulling power from nothing. But it's bloody heavy, especially if you've got to push it!'

Strict rules mean that the Norton uses its original frame and major cycle parts, which means heavy cast iron hubs to which modern alloy rims have been laced. The gearbox is still the slow-changing Norton-Burman type of the early '50s, but as Roger normally uses only first or second gear, rapid changes aren't important. 'I have to stay with first or second in sections,' he says. It leaps around a bit if I use anything higher.'

In six years' use, the Big Four has never let Roger down as he has learned to use its enormous low-down power to best effect and ridden it to a growing tally of wins. Regular rides in modern events leave him little time to get out and enjoy the strong, lazy power of the Norton, but he has no doubts about his preference. 'I love it,' he says. 'It's the best bike I've ever had and I'd rather ride it than the moderns. Just marvellous for steering, because it's set up so well. In the wet it's no good at all, but in the dry it's unbeatable. The way it pulls makes it so easy to ride and it gets you out of trouble.'

Bill Bennett, who does less competitive riding as his interest in mountaineering grows, is not likely to sell the faithful old side-valver. But if he ever does come back from a trip to the Himalayas in a light-headed mood and decides to part with it, Roger already has his promise of first refusal. 'If ever Bill wanted to get rid of it, I'd have to have it,' he states firmly. 'It's such a brilliant old bike.'

Owner and rider together – Roger Tuck at the controls and owner Bill Bennett keeping the sidecar down and an eye on his award-winning Norton outfit as the two drop down a leafy slope.

ness, and the military didn't want claims coming in from civilians with damaged bikes and persons.

The 16H carried on as one of the standard War Department models right through into the 1950s. It was simply very difficult to wear out, as Chris Collier recalls from his own days with the Royal Corps of Signals during the war. Chris wasn't officially a rider, but when one of the dispatch riders was hurt in a road crash during the Normandy landings in 1944, the Commanding Officer turned to him and said: 'You can ride a motorbike, Collier, so you can take it over.' He carried on riding Army bikes until he returned to civilian life in 1947, and then carried on riding his own. Most of his miliary miles were on a Norton 16H, including patrol work and desert training rides in Egypt, an area where a breakdown could be very serious.

'I can only remember having one puncture and one mechanical breakdown,' Chris recalls. 'The puncture was when six of us were out in the desert and no one had a puncture repair outfit. The others left me and went back to camp and I lay there under what shelter I could make for four hours until they came back with a jeep.

'When we were on a training exercise in the desert once, there were about 70 or 80 bikes, all riding abreast. I hit a rock and broke the main fork spring, so the bike came back on a jeep again.' In general, the Nortons proved very reliable, with each rider responsible for the maintenance of his own machine in accordance with the official Booklet 406. 'The separate gear selector mechanism was the most trouble,' Collier remembers. 'There were a few cases of the timing plug blowing out of the top of the cylinder head, but you could put that down to poor maintenance. There were no air-cleaners on the bikes in our unit, and I remember getting new carburettor parts from the stores. Part of the kit was a 6-inch nail with sawcuts that we used down the timing plug hole to get the ignition timing right!'

Years of official duties on the 16H and unofficial trials and sand racing left an enduring memory, and when Chris was look-

NORTON SIDE-VALVE SINGLES

Engine: Air-cooled, four-stroke single, with upright cylinder, two side-valves operated by cam follower acting on cam. Iron cylinder barrel and head (late 16H versions with alloy head). 16H – 79mm × 100mm, 490cc, developing claimed 13.5 bhp at 4,800 rpm (1954 model). Big Four – 82mm × 113mm, 633cc, 15.5 bhp at 4,000 rpm.

Transmission: All post-war models – four-speed gearbox separate from engine, with footchange. Primary and secondary transmission by chain. Multi-plate clutch in oil.

Cycle parts: Rigid frame and girder forks in early post-war models, telescopic forks from about 1947. Seven-inch brakes front and rear.

Dimensions: Wheelbase – 54¹/₂ in. Dry weight –16H, 367 lbs; Big Four, 373 lbs. Ground clearance 5¹/₂ in, fuel tank capacity 2³/₄ gallons.

Owners' Club: Very active, 21 UK branches and 12 overseas. Secretary – Dave Fenner, 18 Wren Crescent, Addlestone, Surrey KT15 2JR.

Sources of help: Spares – A. Gagg, 106 Alfreton Road, Nottingham; Mail Spares, The Firs, Othery, Somerset; Russell Motors, 125-7 Falcon Road, Battersea, London SW11 2PE; RGM Motors, Haile Bank Farm, Beckermet, Cumbria CA21 2XB.

ing for a bike to restore in 1979, he was happy to find a rusty, dented 16H at an affordable price. Sold into civilian life through Cope's chain of bike shops in the West Midlands, it was in traditional Norton black and silver and restoration to correct military trim included repainting in regulation khaki colour. Parts came from autojumbles and friends in the old-bike movement, with much work needed to repair the ravages of many years and different owners. 'The rear mudguard was like a collander where it had had different pillion seats fitted to it at some time, but it had the basis of what I wanted,' says the retired Customs and Excise officer.

The final personal touch on the restoration was to put the official number of his original Army 16H on the tank, but without the Arabic version used on bikes serving in Egypt when he was there. Military bikes normally had the prefix C before their numbers, standing for Cycle. 'Our Commanding Officer wouldn't have that,' smiles Chris. 'He said that if you couldn't tell a motorcycle from a car you shouldn't be in his regiment, so we never painted them on!' It is typical of the solid old 16H that this particular departure from standard did not affect its ability to keep going.

NORTON OVERHEAD VALVE SINGLES

Living in the shadow of the Manx

Norton's pushrod overhead valve singles stayed in the range, apart from the Second World War, from 1922 to 1966. The final years from 1964 to '66 saw a mix-and-match of AMC components, with a Norton badge on the AJS or Matchless singles. The *real* Norton ohv line, with its sturdy 79mm bore and 100mm stroke, ended in 1963 as an economical tourer with legendary Featherbed frame handling and effective braking from the 8-inch unit at the front. There was a 350cc version until the 1963 end of the line, but it always lived in the shadow of the bigger ES2. The author had one, and cannot argue with the description given to it by a more experienced rider: 'The safest motorbike in the world. The best frame, the best brakes and the slowest engine.' The other

variation from the dominant 500cc theme was the short-lived Model 19, its 600cc engine intended primarily for sidecar work. The 19's post-war span was from 1954 to '58, when the factory recognized that small family cars were an affordable and comfortable alternative to the sidecar, and the Model 19 was dropped from the range.

As soon as civilian production started again, the side-valve 16H was joined by the overhead valve Model 18 and six were prepared for trials work by the factory and sent to selected dealers, TT winner Harold Daniell amongst them. One is known to survive, rescued from a special school where a sidecar had been welded on and the bike driven around the grounds by the pupils; its survival is a tribute to the quality of the

Far left *Father and son Brian and Neil Smith enjoy Norton single power on the road. Brian's is a rare 597cc 19S of 1957 in a swinging-arm lugged frame, and Neil's 490cc ES2 is one of the last of the 'Wideline' Featherbed models from 1958.*

Left *Norton 500T at play. Roger Allen's 1950 example has been used for most forms of vintage sport, and here gives racing passenger Sue Darbyshire an absorbing introduction to the gentle art of finding grip on a mixture of tree roots and leaf mould.*

Above *Waiting to go out and serve. Ron Watson (left) of Watsonian Sidecars and Bert Hopwood (bareheaded) of Norton have a final look at 16 ES2- Watsonian outfits awaiting delivery to the RAC.*

materials that went into it!

Development of a true trials iron resulted in the 500T being offered for 1949, its frame based on the 16H and the engine an alloy-barrelled ES2 with a lower compression ratio. It stayed in the range until the end of 1954, and was ridden by such talented trials men as Rex Young, Geoff Duke, Jeff Smith, Johnny Draper, Rex Clayton and Australian champion Bill Young, who worked in the Bracebridge Street competition department in the early '50s and rode his own ex-works 500T well enough to beat all the factory men and win the 1950 Cambrian trial. Always sold in the rigid frame form, the 500T lives on today in vintage sidecar trials ridden by Roger Allen, after a busy life that has included grass track racing, road racing and

family transport on holiday. It is nothing if not versatile!

The ES2 roadster was always a simple workhorse, and a natural choice for the RAC patrols, who hitched a box sidecar up and drove them through winter and summer. In 1958, the final year of the lugged and brazed frame, Norton's advertisement claimed over 95 million miles covered by the RAC men in ten years. From then on, the 350cc Model 50 and the ES2 used the welded Featherbed frame, which the factory did not recommend for sidecar use, regardless of the racing men who bolted racing platforms to Featherbed Manxes and got on with it.

The ES2 and its brother Model 18 – dropped from the range in 1954 – mainly appealed to the ride-to-work market in

Britain, but in Japan the police chose ES2s and Model 7 Dominator twins to preserve the law of Tokyo.

Norton singles have a character that encourages loyalty. Brian Smith, a retired ship's Chief Engineer living in Suffolk, has had five and admits his addiction: 'I think I've always had a Norton, and for the last 20 years I've been a single cylinder nut. I've had others – I rescued a Velocette Viper when I was in Ghana on a trip and I'm doing that up – but when you know a bike really well you tend to stay with it.'

Brian's Norton single habit has been passed on to son Neil, who rides the 1959 ES2 that Smith Snr owned for six years. The last of the 'Wideline' Featherbeds, the '59 'EasyTwo' served Brian well, but its performance on the road was limited by the big singles' inherent vibration at speed, as Brian recalls: 'You can cruise at 60 to 65 mph, but after that the old long-stroke motor makes itself felt, and 70 mph was too uncomfortable to hold for a long stretch. But it would do about 70 miles to the gallon on a journey if you didn't ride too hard.'

Today, Brian has opted for his rare 1957

19S, the sprung frame, long-stroke model whose 82mm bore × 113mm stroke engine dimensions date back to 1933. 'I know it was essentially designed as a sidecar bike,' he says, 'but for an old man like me it's ideal. You can just put it into top gear and it'll cruise all day at 50 to 55 mph. I took it down to a Norton Owners' Club rally at Bristol and it gave me about 60 to the gallon, cruising between 50 and 60 mph. I've a mate who's got a 350cc Model 50 and he gets 75 to the gallon regularly.'

The rare singles do not attract the spares service that the twins riders enjoy. 'They can be a problem,' says Brian. 'I'm lucky, because I've got a collection of parts and if I haven't got it, one of my mates in the Owners' Club has. If not, we can make it – one of the lads is a toolmaker and I've got a fair workshop, so we can help each other.'

The staid image of the pushrod singles has been dented in the 1980s by racing successes in Vintage MCC events, where the Model 50 and ES2 have proved capable of beating many of their exotic Manx brethren. Having watched them in action, Brian Smith's fifth Norton single will be rather special: 'It won't please the purists, but it will be interesting,' he grins. 'I'm building something special, using all sorts of bits I've picked up over the years. It will have a Featherbed frame, of course, and one of the old lay-down gearboxes. The trouble with the old singles if you start to push them hard is the big-end bearing, and the heavy flywheels don't help – they're cast iron. So I've managed to turn up some ES2 flywheels from EN24 and we'll use a Gold Star big-end. I've had a lot of help from John Hudson, who worked at the factory and knows the singles well – he's helped with the best balance factor. We're hoping for a 90 mph ES2, something for an old man to play with!'

Unexciting the ohv Norton singles may have been, but they were a tangible link with the models that built the company's name in the 1920s. When the 79 × 100 model was replaced by an amalgam of AMC parts with a Norton badge, it made hardly a ripple on the sales charts. Nortons have to be real Nortons, it seems.

NORTON OHV SINGLES

(1963 ES2, with 1950 ratings in brackets)

Engine: (1963 ES2) Air-cooled single cylinder, with two pushrod-operated valves. Iron cylinder barrel, alloy head (iron to 1955). 79mm × 100mm, 7.3 to 1 compression ratio (1950, 6.45 to 1), developing 25 bhp at 5,300 rpm (1950, 21 at 5,000 rpm)

Transmission: (1963 ES2) Four-speed separate gearbox with integral foot change. Primary and secondary transmission by chain, with optional enclosure of rear chain from 1955 to '61. Multi-plate clutch in oil.

Cycle parts: (1963 ES2) Twin loop welded cradle frame (lugged, single down tube, duplex cradle) with telescopic front forks and swing-arm rear suspension (plunger). Eight-inch drum front brake (7-inch to 1954) and 7-inch rear drum brake.

Dimensions: (1963 ES2) Wheelbase – 55 1/2 in (1950, 54 1/2); Dry weight – 384 lbs (1950-56, 379, then 389); Ground clearance – 6.2 in (1950, 6.5); Seat height 31in.

Owners' Club: Very active, 21 UK branches and 9 overseas. Secretary – Dave Fenner, 18 Wren Crescent, Addlestone, Surrey KT15 2JR.

Sources of help: Spares – RGM Motors, Haile Bank Farm, Beckermet, Cumbria CA21 2XB; A. Gagg and Sons, 106 Alfreton Road, Nottingham NG7 3NS; RJ Motorcycles, 10 Hotel Street, Coalville, Leics; Russell Motors, 125 Falcon Road, Battersea, London

Geoff Duke and Norton

Geoff Duke rose to stardom as a multi world champion on road racing, but his competition career began in trials. After catching Norton's eye with his ability on a 350 BSA, he was recruited into the Bracebridge Street trials team, working in the Competitions Department during the week and competing in scrambles or trials at the weekend. 'Not that the department was much,' he remembers. 'It could only have been about ten feet by ten, and I built up the competition bikes in there.'

In Geoff's first season he showed his versatility as a member of the British team in the Moto Cross des Nations, finishing fourth on a rigid-framed 500. With the introduction of the 500T came growing trials success, even though he was the rising star in the road racing squad. In 1950, the year he set new race and lap records to win his first Senior TT race and went on to finish runner-up in the 350 and 500cc world championships, he was still justifying his place in the trials team with a string of awards in National trials.

1950 brought Geoff what he still thinks was the outstanding ride of his trials career. In the clinging Shropshire mud around the hilly Church Stretton area, the only rider in a star-studded field to finish with no marks lost was G. E. Duke (500 Norton). Even the great Hugh Viney dropped one mark, while Jimmy Alves, who went on to win the newly introduced ACU Trials Drivers' Star, was third overall with two marks gone.

Geoff is still generous in his praise of Viney: 'He was simply brilliant, with such precise throttle control,' he says. 'I remember riding in a moto-cross meeting on the continent where Hugh was entered. It was extremely wet and there was a field with a bad adverse camber that we had to cross. His experience as a trials rider showed there and I think he lapped everybody to win.

'I found trials good practice for road racing. It was throttle control of a different sort, but obviously as important, because although you're going slowly in trials, things do tend to happen quickly. I found it sharpened up my reactions, and was better practice for racing than scrambles ever were.

'A favourite event of mine was the Scottish Six Days, which would get you in really good shape for the start of the racing season. But when I began to win races, Gilbert Smith put a stop to that and wouldn't let me ride in the Scottish, because he didn't want me breaking an ankle with the TT coming up.'

Geoff remained in the trials team until 1952, and even when he won both 350 and 500cc road race world titles in 1951, he showed his form off-road with ten first-class awards in National trials. All on the rigid-framed 500T.

Geoff Duke is best remembered as one of Britain's greatest road racers, but he first joined Norton as a member of the trials team. The full length greatcoat looks cumbersome to modern eyes, but could prevent the observer seeing the occasional probing foot!

The Norton company celebrated its Diamond Jubilee in 1958 and the natural name for a brand new model announced that year was the Jubilee. Coming from a factory renowned for its big singles and twins, the 250cc Jubilee was a complete break with Norton tradition.

The four-speed gearbox was in unit with the short-stroke 60mm bore x 44mm stroke engine that offered a claimed 16 bhp at 7,750 rpm. Hard miles across Welsh hills by factory testers had shown the little twin was fast for its engine size, but needed to be revved hard to make real progress. It was a modern design from a traditional factory, and those who bought it expecting an undemanding engine that would pull strongly from low revs were disappointed.

Above left *Chris Keohane's 1983 Christmas present was very different from the average offering like a Marks and Spencer voucher. He came back on leave to find this restored Navigator waiting for him.*

Above right *Norman Coulson's 1967-registered 250cc Jubilee is the standard model with no rear enclosure. This example was restored when Norman was recovering from open-heart surgery.*

Cycle parts reflected the parentage of Norton at the time, with Associated Motor Cycles dictating that the frame, forks and wheels seen on the James and Francis Barnett 250s should be used. Only when the 350cc Navigator was announced in 1960 did the famous Norton Roadholder forks and 8-inch front drum brake come to the lightweight twins, but the frame remained the same serve-all-makes compromise, with a stiffened

NORTON LIGHTWEIGHT TWINS

A break with tradition

Below *The 350cc Navigator was announced in 1960, with typical upmarket pictures taken in Hampton-in-Arden, a Warwickshire village not too far from the Birmingham factory. The use of Roadholder forks and the 8-inch front brake from the bigger models won approval.*

front down-member its only concession to increased power, 22 claimed bhp at 7,000 rpm.

The Navigator was road tested with a top speed well into the 80s, but a hint of its potential came when factory sales representative Bob Collier persuaded dealer Harold Daniell – winner of three Senior TT races for the factory in earlier years – to enter one in a 1,000-kilometre production bike race at Silverstone. 'It was standard apart from boring the carburettor out by an eighth of an inch and jetting it up a bit,' recalls Collier. 'It was fitted with a rev-counter and we reckoned it was doing 101 mph on the big straight. It was a good little bike.

The Navigator was aimed at the non-sporting rider and came with deeply valanced mudguards and a fairing over the rear wheel to keep road muck away from rider's and passenger's legs. In 1961 the factory announced a range of extras for the touring rider, colour-matched to the standard finish. For an extra £23.10 a Navigator owner could buy a matching handlebar fairing and screen, legshields and panniers to fit his £229.75 350. Naturally, the units would fit the smaller Jubilee as well.

In 1963 came the final development of the type, with the 63mm bore × 56mm stroke Navigator motor bored out to 66mm to give the Electra 400 a capacity of 383cc. This was a bike intended to take on the sophisticated specifications offered from Japan, with 12-volt electrics, direction indicators and a Lucas M3 electric starter. But Associated Motor Cycles were in deep financial trouble

1960 Scottish Six Days Trial

The Jubilee 250 has a place in history for its achievement in the 1960 Scottish Six Days Trial. Bob Collier, ever ready to attempt what less determined men would not even consider, rode a standard Jubilee and sidecar through the trial to show its durability.

'I suggested the idea to Bert Hopwood,' Collier recalls. 'He gave the idea the OK so long as we used a standard sidecar. That was a bit of a problem, but after I'd looked at what was available we decided that the little Watsonian Bambini would be the best bet. It was meant to be fitted to a scooter and had a single tube chassis with a flange to mount it to the scooter, and I had to produce a mounting on the bike to take it.

'The trouble was that the mounting made it wider than usual, and we wanted it as narrow as possible to have a chance of getting through the sections. So I reduced the chassis width and moved the body right up against the bike; that meant we had to cut a section out of the body so I could get my leg on the footrest. But whatever we did it was quite a handicap – we had an outfit twice as heavy as any other, with a power output of about 16 bhp!'

That lack of power didn't deter Collier and regular passenger Gordon Wild. They struggled through the six days, climbing Scottish paths and passes in slow time, even Collier's renowned point-and-blast tendency dampened by the lack of urge. 'Gordon Wild always refers to that trial as "My push around Scotland",' he smiles when telling the story. 'By the Wednesday we were both fed up and tired, we'd got the publicity we wanted for the bike, and no one could complain if we didn't finish after all that effort. So I said to Gordon "I'll break the bloody thing and we'll retire".

'I thrashed it through the gears and slipped the clutch until the rubbers in the centre shock absorber broke up. The clutch started to slip and we had to collect grit from the roadside and put it in to make it grip so we could get back that evening. But the engine never stopped – never missed a beat! We even towed Peter Roydhouse on his 500 Norton outfit 23 miles into Fort William when his magneto packed up, and the bike still took it.'

Whatever Bob Collier threw at the willing little Jubilee, it kept going with its heavy load and finished the trial. There was no trophy to bring back to the factory, but if achieving the seemingly impossible was reward in itself, Collier, Wild and the Jubilee were rewarded.

Bob Collier and passenger Gordon Wild must have walked more miles than any other competitors in the 1960 Scottish Six Days Trial. But the game little Jubilee kept going and finished the week intact.

nd not in any condition to meet the compe-tion head-on; in 1966 they closed the doors f the Plumstead factory and Norton's maller twins came to an end.

Living in the shadow of their more lamorous Featherbed-framed big brothers, he lightweight twins have never commanded he premium prices asked for collector's ems like the 650SS Dominator. The result as been a low-profile growth of enthusiasts ho could afford bikes that few people anted. With the Norton Owners' Club list-ng a specialist in the models and holding a ood stock of parts in their own spares cheme, the Jubilee, Navigator and ES400 re affordable classics with a back-up.

Norman Coulson found his late model ubilee more than an interesting hobby. ecovering from open-heart surgery and onfined to bed in the early days of convalesc-nce, Norman's idea of therapy was to sit up nd get on with rubbing down parts of his ubilee ready for painting! 'It really gave me n interest, something to aim for,' remem-ers the gritty Yorkshireman who shares a ollection of British classics with his son. My Norton gave me something to live for – wasn't going to go with that still to be inished!' An active member of the astleford and District British Motorcycle lub, Norman rides to local shows and rallies nd confesses that he finds the Jubilee easier o start than the family Velocette Venom.

Chris Keohane got his 1961 Navigator as Christmas present, coming home on leave rom a tour of duty as an aircraft mechanic ith the Royal Navy to find that his wife Jan ad been scouring the small ads. She wanted o find the more modern bike that Chris ad been talking about, to supplement his unbeam S8 twin, and a smart Norton at an ffordable price seemed to fit the bill.

'It was in excellent condition,' recalls hris. 'It just needed setting up properly, he timing doing and the chains adjusted, hat sort of thing.' Used for commuting to is Royal Navy base, it proved reliable and ewarded regular maintenance: 'I used to pend two or three hours at the weekend, ightening things and checking the timing,' e says. 'If the timing gets out at all, it

vibrates awfully.'

Chris found the clutch the only problem area, with the central retaining nut loosening off despite his efforts to lock it into place. 'It wasn't a reflection of the previous owner's rebuild, I think. It was just the design that wasn't too good,' is Chris's opinion.

Fuel consumption has increased since he started to use the performance a little more after bigger Nortons came past the cruising Navigator at a fair rate of knots. 'If you use it gently, you can get 65 to 70 mpg,' he estimates. 'But now I'm using it a bit more and having more fun, it does about 50 to 55.'

The Navigator gave up commuting duties when Chris left the Royal Navy and started work as a Maintenance engineer at a Dorset dairy. Now used solely for pleasure riding, it could prove too tempting in its shining blue and dove grey livery if left all day in a works car park. Parking it inside a Royal Navy yard was a lot more secure, of course.

Would Chris part with his Christmas pres-ent, even if it is not the most glamorous of Norton's twins? 'I wouldn't dare to and I wouldn't want to,' is the answer. 'It's such a nice bike to ride and enjoy.'

NORTON LIGHTWEIGHT TWINS

Engine: Air-cooled parallel twin cylinders, with two pushrod-operated valves per cylinder. 249cc Jubilee – 60mm bore × 44mm stroke developing claimed 16 bhp at 7,750 rpm; 349cc Navigator – 63mm × 56mm developing claimed 22 bhp at 7,000 rpm; 383cc ES400 – 66mm × 56mm developing claimed 24 bhp at 7,000 rpm.

Transmission: Primary and secondary drive by chain, through multi-plate clutch. Four-speed gearbox in unit with engine on all models.

Cycle parts: Cradle frame with pressed steel front down-member and seat tube combined with tubes. Telescopic front forks and swinging-fork rear suspension on all models. 6-inch front brake on Jubilee model, 8-inch on Navigator and ES400; 6-inch rear brake on Jubilee and Navigator, 7-inch on ES400.

Dimensions: Wheelbase – Jubilee, 53.5, others 51.5. Dry weight – Jubilee, 330 lbs; Navigator, 335 lbs; ES400, 338. Ground clearance – all models, 5.5 in. Seat height – all models, 29 in.

Owners' Club: Very active, with 21 UK branches, 12 over-seas and lightweight twins specialist to advise. Secretary – Dave Jenner, 18 Wren Crescent, Addlestone, Surrey KT15 2JR.

Sources of help: Owners' Club model specialist and spares scheme.

NORTON DOMINATOR

A twin built to take corners

Norton naturally followed the trend to twin-cylinder engines in the 1940s. Designer Edgar Franks suggested an in-line version that the Board of Directors thought too radical, so Edgar was back at his drawing-board putting the finishing touches to a more conventional engine when Bert Hopwood joined the company in 1947. The latter laid down the design that was announced at the 1948 Earls Court Show and which stayed in production as the basis of the 828cc engine 30 years later.

Hopwood's design featured a single camshaft ahead of the cylinder axis and driven by chains. In the early versions the inlet manifold for the single carburettor was cast into the iron cylinder head, but this was soon changed for a more conventional separate manifold. The three-piece crank featured a cast iron flywheel 7 inches in diameter with two bearings, roller on the drive side and ball on the timing side.

The engine was mounted in a conventional lugged frame, with plunger rear suspension and Roadholder tele forks. Brakes were 7-inch single-leading-shoe drum type, adequate in their day but quite a frightener if

an unwary rider moves from modern machines to try such a bike today! The Model 7 Dominator was first sold only for export, then came on to the home market late in 1949, proving to be a smooth and lively bike which hinted that there were more oil-tight ways of getting along than the more sporting International single, which needed felt around the exposed hairpin valve springs if the rider wanted to keep oil off his knees!

Hints of good things to come began with an experimental Dominator with a Featherbed frame, first spotted in Holland in 1951. The Featherbed was the legendary frame that kept the Norton racing team ahead of much faster rivals from 1950 until Geoff Duke quit and went to ride for the Italian Gilera team. The Dominator De Luxe, as it was known, was shown at the 1951 Show and if you were lucky you got one in 1952. Priced at £226 it was £27 more than the Model 7 and weighed 33 lbs less. It was the start of a long line that proved so popular that the rest of the range stopped selling. In the 1952 season the factory had great problems selling anything but the Featherbed Dominator, and as the

Bracebridge Street factory relied upon Reynolds Tubing to make the all-welded frame, there was a limit to how many it could

produce. A frantic weekend session by development engineer Bob Collier resulted in the old lugged frame being converted to swinging-arm, and the 1954 Model 7 looked much more up-to-date than the plunger-sprung offering of the previous year. In 1954 the Featherbed version got the benefit of an 8-inch front brake.

For 1955 the 597cc Dominator 99 was announced, a logical development of the 500 on which Bob Collier can remember putting 70 miles into an hour's riding on the A5 in the days before motorways made overtaking heavy traffic simple. Even driven that hard, the single-carburettor engine would return 65 miles to the gallon. For the sidecar brigade, the Model 77 of 1956 used the 600cc engine in the old lugged frame that the factory insisted was the only choice for hitching a third wheel to; braver owners ignored this advice and successfully used Featherbed models with a sidecar, even if the warranty on a new bike was invalidated by such ingenuity.

In 1960 the Featherbed frame was altered, its top rails closer together to narrow the tank and give riders more comfort with what

Above left *The final form of the 500cc Dominator 88 was the SS version, with twin down-draught carburettors and a 110 mph potential.*

Above *Long-time Norton owner Phil Mayo has this 750cc Atlas (left) and 600cc Dominator 99 as the pride of his collection.*

Right *The British and French tastes never were the same! The French police had their Nortons supplied in black livery with whitewall tyres.*

1961 Senior TT

The late Tom Phillis showed what the Norton twin could do as a racing model in the 1961 Senior TT. Offered the ride on the works development of the 500cc Model 88 after Phil Read dropped it at Creg-ny-Baa during a practice session, Phillis jumped at the chance to show what an ambitious young star from down under could do with the right bike.

The Domiracer represented the ultimate development of Bert Hopwood's original design for a 500cc roadster, thanks to devoted effort by Doug Hele and the skilled men of the Race Shop. A stiffer crankshaft carried shorter conrods, with 11 to 1 compression pistons each carrying one Dykes ring and a single oil control ring. Lightened valve gear, that essential ingredient for high revs and increased power, opened standard-size valves of nimonic steel. The frame was naturally a Featherbed, but a lower version of the established type used for the Manx racers and dubbed the 'Lowboy' by the press. The Domiracer weighed 35 lbs less than a 500cc Manx and Phillis quickly adapted to his new mount.

1961 was in the era of the four-cylinder MV-Agusta, with the lucky works riders enjoying a huge performance advantage over the private owners on single-cylinder Manx Nortons and G50 Matchlesses. So no one was surprised when Gary Hocking was 15 seconds ahead of Mike Hailwood at the end of the first lap, but the firm fifth place for Phillis on a mere

pushrod model amongst the pure racing machinery came as a real surprise. But that opening lap at an average of 98.93 mph was a hint of what was to come, as the lightweight Phillis moved into fourth place on the second lap with a lap at over the 'ton' – 100.36 mph. At the end of the fourth lap he was just over a second ahead of the great Bob McIntyre in third spot, and though Bob Mac fought back and passed the twin which was slowed by valve clearances slightly errant after a missed gear had a piston gently kissing a valve, Tom kept his hard-won third place. Gary Hocking's MV had stopped, Mike Hailwood was riding to an historic third TT win in a week and the bike that some had dismissed as a no-hoper came in third in its first TT race.

Phillis's second lap was the first time a pushrod engine had lapped the 37¾ mile TT course at over 100 mph, and it retained that record until Malcolm Uphill beat it eight years later on a 650cc Triumph. The proposal to develop the Domiracer as an economical replacement for the Manx racer that was so labour intensive to build seemed sound until the financial troubles of Norton's AMC owners brought development to a halt and the parts were sold off. That remarkable ride by Tom Phillis remains as a reminder of what might have been.

Tom Phillis gets the fairing very close to the Creg-ny-Baa kerb as he takes the works Domiracer to a sensational third place in the 1961 Senior TT to make Norton's domination of the leaderboard complete.

became known as the Slimline Featherbed. And two years later the Slimline was wrapped around a strengthened 650cc engine to form the 650SS model, regarded by many as the best of the Dominator line and capable of an honest 110 mph with its twin-carburettor engine pumping out a claimed 49 bhp at 6,800 rpm. Finished in the traditional Norton racing colours of silver tank with black cycle parts complemented by the chrome mudguards, it was a handsome bike that went as fast as it looked. Southampton dealer Syd Lawton, himself a Norton team rider in the early '50s, entered one for the factory in the *Motor Cycle* 500-mile race for production bikes and it won three in a row, from 1962 to '64.

The Dominator line was in its final decade when the 750cc Atlas was introduced in 1962, its 73mm × 89mm engine offering no more power than the more glamorous 650SS but with a spread of beefy power from just above tickover to the 6,800 rpm maximum that was used only if the rider could stand the experience of a vibro-massage at high speed. The Atlas officially lasted until 1968, surviving the crash of the parent Associated Motor Cycles group and continuing in production when the Norton name moved to Andover. It was phased out when the Commando was announced in 1967, but delays in production of the new model saw a panic measure to keep something available, and the single-carburettor 650cc Mercury supplemented the Commando until it was dropped in 1970, the very last of the famous Featherbed Dominators.

A rare 1969 Mercury has been a faithful friend to Heather MacGregor, taking her all over Europe to rallies and covering 30,000 miles in three years before it was rebuilt by boyfriend Paul Mullis with over 50,000 miles covered since new. At that mileage it needed new main and big-end bearings, only the second set in its life; the biggest problem with parts was finding piston rings of the correct 'plus 40' size, which eventually turned up in a London dealer's stock. In regular use since that 1979 rebuild, when a jack plug was fitted to provide power for a camping light and a pump for an inflatable mattress on continen-

tal rallies, the Mercury has proved economical, giving 70 miles to the gallon at a cruising speed of 65 mph. If Heather is in a hurry to get to a rally site in distant Europe, a steady 80 mph drops the fuel thirst to 65 mpg.

The Mercury shares garage space with a Brough Superior and a 750cc Matchless G15 with a Norton Atlas engine. Although she covers long distances in her committee work with the Women's International Motorcycle Association, Heather has not been tempted by modern conveniences and fashion, preferring to apply her modest weight to a British kickstarter rather than press a foreign starter button. 'When my sort of bike lets me down, maybe I'll look at something modern,' she explains. 'So far, that hasn't seemed likely at all.'

NORTON DOMINATOR

Engine: Air-cooled four-stroke parallel twin, with two valves per cylinder operated by pushrods from a single chain-driven camshaft. Cast iron cylinder head and barrel on early models, alloy cylinder head introduced in 1954 on Model 7, on Model 88 in 1955. 500cc – 66mm bore x 72.6mm stroke, developing claimed 29 bhp at 6,000 rpm (36 bhp at 7,000 rpm on twin-carb 88SS); 600cc – 68mm x 82mm, developing 31 bhp at 5,750 rpm in 1956 (44 bhp at 6,750 rpm on twin-carb 99SS); 650cc – 68mm x 89mm, developing 49 bhp at 6,800 rpm in 650SS twin-carb form; 750cc – 73mm x 89mm, developing 49 bhp at 6,800 rpm.

Transmission (all models): Four-speed gearbox with integral footchange. Primary and secondary transmission by chain. Multi-plate clutch in oil.

Cycle parts: Model 7 – lugged frame, plunger rear suspension 1948-53, swinging-arm rear 1954-56. All Featherbed models welded duplex cradle frame, swinging-arm rear, Roadholder telescopic forks. Seven-inch drum brakes to 1953 on Model 7; 8-inch brakes on Featherbed models from 1955.

Dimensions: Wheelbase – Model 7, 56 in (54.5 in from 1953); all Featherbed models, 55.5 in (except 88SS and 99SS, 55.2 in). Dry weight – Model 7, 314 lbs; 88, 380 lbs (to 1955), 390 lbs (1956 on); 99, 390 lbs; 650SS, 434 lbs; Atlas, 433 lbs (1966 model).

Owners' Clubs: Norton Owners' Club – very active, 20 UK branches. Secretary – Peter Thistle, 30 Rosehill Avenue, Sutton, Surrey SM1 3HG. Worldwide Norton Riders' Club – little formal structure, no local sections, devoted to the use of machines. Secretary – Emlyn Stayte, 2 Daffodil Walk, Etching Hill, Rugeley, Staffordshire WS15 2PF.

Sources of help: Spares – Fairspares, The Corner Garage, Cannock Road, Chase Terrace, Burntwood, Staffordshire WS7 8JP; Mick Hemmings Motorcycles, 36-42 Wellington Street, Northampton; Russell Motors, 125-7 Falcon Road, Battersea, London SW11 2PE; RGM Motors, Haile Bank Farm, Beckermet, Cumbria CA21 2XB. Technical advice – Les Emery at Fairspares (address above) or Owners' Clubs specialists.

Norton's Commando hit the top when it first hit the streets, winning the *Motor Cycle News* Machine of the Year award five times in a row, from 1968 to 1972. First shown to the public at the 1967 Earls Court Show, it blended old with new. The long-standing parallel twin in 745cc form was the old, while rubber mounting of the engine, transmission and rear fork to isolate the rider from vibration was the new. The product of a design team headed by ex-Rolls Royce boffin Dr Stefan Bauer, with most of the work handled by Bernard Hooper and Bob Trigg, it made headlines with its first public appearance.

The model grew from 745 to 828cc in its ten years of production, and proved a great favourite with those who appreciated flexible power with a frame that handled as well as any of its contemporaries. By clever mixing and matching of components, designer Trigg offered a range of styles from the chopper-style Hi Rider to the Interpol police model and the John Player version that aped the official racing machines that the factory entered with support from the famous tobacco company.

Many talented riders and engineers worked in the race shop, with Peter Williams combining the ability to design original concepts and then win races on them, including a start-to-finish victory in the 1973 Formula One TT at a record average of 105.47 mph. Amongst the experiments tried were a cantilever rear suspension and mono-

NORTON COMMANDO

Last of the Big Twins

Left *Peter Williams combined outstanding engineering and riding talents to lead the racing team, his tally including the 1973 Formula 750 TT race. The flattened megaphones say more about Peter's riding than any words could.*
Below *Phil Cox built his 750cc Commando from assorted second-hand and new parts in 1975 and covered 163,000 miles on the original engine, with the big-end shells needing replacement after 96,000.*

coque chassis, but Williams' racing career ended with an Oulton Park crash in 1974 and the team lacked the spark of his unique blend of skills after that.

But the big Norton shone in American flat track racing, particularly after Californian tuner C.R. Axtell called on Norton's modest West Coast office and told sales manager Mike Jackson: 'I'd like to become involved with Norton.' Jackson still smiles at the idea of a legend coming to see such a small operation as his: 'Like Doug Hele going to see Panther,' he says. With Axtell's preparation, and riding talent like Dave Aldana's, the Norton was the bike to beat on US West Coast tracks – and that was where the market was biggest.

Innovation on the road models had little publicity, but when engine production was at the old Villiers factory in Wolverhampton, Bob Hirst was the chief electrical engineer. Recruited from Rolls Royce by Stefan Bauer, he found a happy working atmosphere there in 1974 and enjoyed working on a new ignition system with Texas Instruments. 'It was fitted to six pre-production Mark Three Commandoes and the timing was absolutely spot on,' he recalls. 'The engine would tick over at 300 rpm and you could get 75 miles to the gallon from the 830 engine.' But Bob quit Norton in 1975: 'It was obvious the place was going downhill at a great rate of knots. I think the Government backed the wrong horse by supporting Triumph instead of the Norton which had a lot of miles left in it.'

In 1976 the appropriately named Model 76 was built as an experiment, with twin front disc brakes, cast alloy wheel, dignified black livery and a single SU carburettor. Only two prototypes were built and progressed no further, as Norton fell victim to the malaise that had killed off most of the British industry and closed production down. Designer Bernard Hooper still has a Model 76 and offers Commando owners a conversion kit to fit an SU carburettor if they are looking for greater economy than that offered by the standard twin Amal Concentrics.

The Commando proved a long-term winner in production events. Birmingham development engineer Pete Lovell built his 750cc engine into a Commando chassis in 1980, when changing rules made his old Featherbed-framed mount ineligible. Still using the rubber engine mountings that some 'experts' say detract from the handling, Pete used his Isolastic adjustment of 'Up to tightness, then back off a fraction' to outpace

NORTON COMMANDO

Engine: Air-cooled parallel twin cylinders, with two pushrod-operated valves per cylinder. 750cc version – 73mm bore x 89mm stroke (77 × 80.4 from 1973), developing a claimed 56 bhp at 6,500 rpm (Combat engine, 65 bhp at 6,500); 829cc version – 77mm × 89mm, developing a claimed 60 bhp at 5,900 rpm.
Transmission: Primary and secondary drive by chain, through diaphragm multi-plate dry clutch. Four-speed gearbox on all models.
Cycle parts: Twin cradle welded frame, incorporating rubber mountings for engine and gearbox assembly. 750 model – 8-inch (203mm) twin-leading-shoe front brake until 1972, then 10.7-inch (272mm) disc; 829cc models – disc front brake; all models – 7-inch (178mm) drum rear brake.
Dimensions: Wheelbase – 56³/4 in (850, 57 in). Dry weight – 398 lbs (850, 415 lbs; Electric Start 850, 466 lbs). Ground clearance – 6 in. Seat height – 31 in (850, 32 in).
Owners' Clubs: Very active, 21 UK branches and 12 overseas. Club secretary – Dave Jenner, 18 Wren Crescent, Addlestone, Surrey KT15 2JR.
Sources of help: Owners' Club machine specialists and the club's own spares and services directory. Spares – Fair Spares, 96-98 Cannock Road, Chase Terrace, Burntwood, Staffs WS7 8JP; RGM Motors, Haile Bank Farm, Beckermet, Cumbria CA21 2XB; Mick Hemmings, 36/42 Wellington Street, Northampton NN1 3AS; Norman Hyde, Rigby Close, Heathcote, Warwick CV34 6TL; Carl Rosner Motorcycles, Station Approach, Sanderstead, South Croydon, Surrey; Wilemans Motors, Siddals Road, Derby DE1 2PZ.

four-cylinder opposition and add another five racing championships to his tally. 'I guess it does about 135 to 140 mph,' he says. 'It's certainly faster than a CB900 Honda.'

As a road bike, the Commando has won many friends with its ability to cover big mileages with the rider insulated from the traditional British parallel twin vibration. Phil Cox, who works for British Waterways on the Bridgwater and Taunton Canal, has covered more miles on his 750cc version than most of the narrow boats whose routes he helps to restore today.

Phil built the bike from assorted parts, most of them new, in 1975. 'The John Player Special version was £990 then, and I thought I couldn't afford that,' he remembers. 'But in the end my own bike came out at just over £900, so I didn't exactly save a lot!'

The Cox Commando has been ridden all over Europe and the UK, including one year when, as Chairman of the Norton Owners' Club, Phil covered 23,000 miles on weekend trips to club events. 'The original engine did 163,000 miles,' he quotes from detailed notes of the Norton's history. 'I gave it a decoke every 50,000 and changed the oil every 1,500 miles until I fitted a cartridge oil filter, then it went to 2,000. And I tried never to do a short journey on it; if I had a short trip, I'd take the long way round instead.

'The big-end shells were replaced at 96,000 and it had new pistons at 50,000, 96,000 and 135,000. I changed the engine sprocket from 26 to 28 teeth, and it does 60 plus to the gallon, cruising comfortably at 80 mph.

'With the original Interstate tank, which should hold five gallons but with dents was about 4.85, I could do 300 miles on a tankful on the continent.'

The braking was improved with the fitting of a standard Norton single disc at the front in 1982. 'Once you're used to taking a big handful you can forget it,' says Cox. 'The good point about the Commando is the availability of the spares. I've kept mine going with supplies from the Owners' Club spares scheme and our approved dealers. It has the advantage that it was built to a high standard, because I wanted it right and was prepared to spend a bit of time getting it right.'

1975 Ontario Supernational drag race, Los Angeles

In American drag racing, only the bikes were bigger than the men as double-engined Harley Davidsons dominated the winners' circle in the 1970s. When one 1670cc engine wasn't enough, the habit of putting two into one frame grew, and the opposition was simply overwhelmed – until Tom Christenson, a nine-stone, slow talking bar owner from Kenosha, Wisconsin, rode his Norton past everyone. It was like a Western, with the quiet little man winning the shoot-out against the big, bad outlaws.

Christenson's Norton was built by John Gregory, known as 'Spiderman' from his thin, gangly walk. Few have influenced the technology of the quarter mile more than Spiderman did, taking two 750cc Norton motors, opening them out to 810cc with Paul Dunstall alloy cylinder barrels and fitting them with Hilborn fuel injection adapted from a racing car. Where the bigger machines would spin their rear wheels with an excess of power, Gregory designed and made his own automatic clutch and adapted a Rambler car overdrive unit to build a two-speed gearbox.

It worked beyond anyone's dreams, and in 1975 Christenson beat all comers at the Ontario Supernationals, near Los Angeles in California. Russ Collins used 3300cc and three Honda engines to set the new record at 7.86 seconds, and Joe Smith's 3340cc double Harley hit a new record speed at 182 mph at the end of the standing-start quarter mile. But Christenson, the cool campaigner who relaxed between races

and left the mechanical work in John Gregory's expert hands, showed his class with consistency no other team could match. He made one qualifying run in 7.99 seconds with a finishing speed of 176 mph, making him second to Collins in the eight-bike field. Three brief races was all he had to complete, but every one had to be on a knife-edge of judgement if TC was to win.

He won the first in 7.93 seconds and 175 mph, then the second in an identical time and 176 mph. And in the final he just left a troubled Russ Collins Honda far behind, with a time of 7.95 and another 175 mph. It was the Norton's third consecutive win in the Supernationals, in effect drag racing's world championship, and in 1976 he went back to California and made it four in a row. By then the modest 1620cc Norton – known as 'Hogslayer' for its habit of killing Harley Davidson 'Hogs' so frequently – was showing its age, and was under threat from Japanese four-cylinder technology. A promised three-engined Norton remained uncompleted after John Gregory left the team to develop his career in other directions, but the double-engined version became part of American drag racing legend. A popular American phrase about engine performance is 'You can't beat cubes'. Christenson's Norton could, and very frequently did!

Tom 'TC' Christenson powered his famous 'Hogslayer' with two 750cc Commando engines uprated with Paul Dunstall alloy barrels to 810cc each. With 1620cc of Norton power, TC beat Harleys and Hondas with two or three engines and up to 3340cc.

NORTON MANX

Always a winner

Above *One of the greatest exponents of the Manx was Derek Minter, who rode models prepared by Ray Petty and Steve Lancefield.*

Left *Stan Dibben at speed, testing Perry Chains by continuous high-speed running with engine and gearbox sprockets minus alternate teeth.*

The Norton Manx is a legend that still lives an active life, with many examples racing today as the interest in classic racing has grown. From the debut of the 'Featherbed Manx' in 1950, when Geoff Duke was narrowly beaten into second place in the 350 and 500cc World Championships, the Birmingham-built overhead camshaft single was the mainstay of the bigger classes in Grands Prix until the late 1960s, when Godfrey Nash was third in the title race on a machine built by John Tickle. Tickle took over the Manx name when the Norton company withdrew the faithful old single from production, and Nash valiantly showed how it could still provide a reliable ride when Italian and Japanese factories were dominating the winning.

Geoff Duke was the glamour boy of the early 1950s, a British sporting hero who took on the foreigners and often left them in the dust with a brilliant combination of machine handling and riding skill. But at the end of the 1952 season, he could see that four-cylinder opposition from Italy was going to overwhelm the single-cylinder Manx. He joined Gilera and began a three-year domination of the 500cc World Championship, while the Norton fought a last-ditch battle for the Senior TT – the factory's major target during its racing years. Ray Amm won it for them in 1954, then the factory's owner, Associated Motor Cycles of Plumstead, decided that racing would be confined to developments of the over-the-counter Manx and one-offs would no longer be built. It dropped the Norton name out of contention in the Grands Prix, but it meant the private racer got more development of his machine.

Stan Dibben was a tester for the Experimental Department at the Bracebridge Street works, and recalls how every engine

Above right *Mike Colin's 500cc model is a blend of parts from different years, several of them identified by the late Ray Petty as coming from the machine ridden for him by Derek Minter and John Cooper. The present owner admits that he is still learning to ride the bike properly.*

Below *Throughout the '50s and '60s, the Manx engine dominated the field in 500cc racing, with the lighter G50 Matchless taking over its role in later years.*

was run in and tested on the dynamometer to establish satisfactory power output before being fitted into a frame and sent to the waiting customer. Never one to bite his tongue in the presence of authority, Dibben once told Managing Director Gilbert Smith that he'd 'never known a Managing Director who broke his neck falling off an office chair!' when they were arguing over what the tester should be expected to do. Naturally, the outspoken Dibben didn't last too long and got his cards at the end of 1953.

His experience was put to good use by Perry Chains, who provided him with a 350cc Manx for chain tests at the Motor Industry Research Association's high-speed track near Nuneaton, Warks. Primary chains were tested by machining alternate teeth off the engine and clutch sprockets and averaging 100 mph around the banked track, with a drop down to bottom gear included in every lap. 'It did about 20,000 miles, revving to 6,800 or 7,000 rpm, and apart from 11 conrods it was no problem,' he laughs at the memory of those long days at top speed.

Top riders had little choice except the Norton until Matchless developed its lighter G50, and those who did their own tuning and maintenance found the Birmingham factory ever helpful. Welsh ace Malcolm Uphill remembers trips to get new main bearings

1961 Isle of Man Senior TT

By 1961, few thought the ageing Manx had much chance of beating the four-cylinder opposition from Italy in World Championship events. MV-Agusta had dominated the bigger classes of the TT in recent years, and few would give any other maker a chance of beating them; Rhodesian Gary Hocking was expected to dominate the results in the way that John Surtees had before him.

Doubt set in when the MV failed in the 350cc Junior race, letting Mike Hailwood into a clear lead on his British 7R AJS. But a broken gudgeon pin stopped Mike on the final lap and Phil Read, who had won both 350 and 500 Manx Grands Prix in 1960, brought his Bill Lacey-tuned Manx Norton home to an historic victory. MV, it seemed, would have to be content with Hocking bringing home only the Senior TT trophy.

Few knew about the very special Manx engine that Bill Lacey had built for the promising young Hailwood, and during practice Mike had given no hint of its considerable power, keeping his lap speeds quite moderate. The engine used Lacey's own one-piece crank, with a Jaguar D-Type connecting rod running on a plain main bearing, all fed with oil from a pump that Lacey also made himself. Interviewed years later, he claimed the power output was 66 bhp at 7,900 rpm, figures far beyond what a standard engine could produce.

Hocking was 15 seconds in the lead at the end of the first lap, and was ahead on the road despite starting 10 seconds after Mike. But as Hailwood swooped right at Ballacraine, Hocking was struggling to get the MV back up the slip road, having misjudged his braking and overshot the corner. Was the pressure from this unexpected source getting through?

After four of the race's seven laps, Hocking led Hailwood by a meagre 15 seconds when he stopped for fuel, but lost time as a plug was changed in an attempt to cure an elusive misfire. Hailwood also stopped, but only to fill the tank and take up the chase.

Reports from around the 37¾-mile course were of an ailing MV and a very healthy Norton, as Hocking slipped back and Hailwood headed for his third race win of the TT week. There was no hope for the MV as it called into the pits once more, for the throttle cable to one carburettor had broken; glum-faced Italian mechanics wheeled it away to fight another day.

Hailwood made no mistake, completing seven laps at 100.6 mph to record the highest TT race speed ever by a Manx Norton, with Bob McIntyre the battling Scot in second place on another Manx and Australian Tom Phillis third on the factory's racing development of the Dominator twin. Of the top 12 finishers, only two were not Norton mounted!

The style says more than words. Mike Hailwood on his Bill Stuart-prepared Manx Norton heads for the model's final TT victory in the 1961 Senior race.

fitted in his 350's crankcases: 'They took them in over the counter, then brought them back steaming hot, with the new bearings in. They charged for the bearings, but not the fitting – the factory was inclined to help the boys lower down the field.' With a 100 mph lap of the TT course on Francis Beart's Manx to his credit, Malcolm was hardly one of the boys 'lower down the field', but the Welshman is renowned for his modesty.

Racing and maintaining a Manx Norton today is a task for the truly devoted, who will not be deterred by offers of over £10,000 for a bike that may have been bought years ago before collectors appreciated them. Mike Colin, a self-employed builder who started racing late in life, takes great care to get his historic machine right. Several of the components in the 500 Manx were identified by the late Ray Petty as from the bike he built for Derek Minter to dominate British short circuits with in the late 1950s, and Mike learned a lot about careful preparation from Petty before the tuner's sad death from cancer.

'I build the engine up with the workshop temperature at 80 degrees,' he explains. 'The bevel drive to the camshafts set up with the nominal five thousandths of an inch clearance becomes too loose at working temperature if they're built up in the cold.'

The ex-racing car builder who includes one of Mike Hailwood's old Lola V8s in his track-testing experience, sets his precious Manx up with an eye to mechanical safety: 'I always run the carburation a bit on the rich side. To get the absolute maximum power you would have to run it on the point of detonation, with the maximum compression ratio and ignition advance, and the mixture as lean as possible. Ray told me he used to modify a dope piston to get a compression ratio of 12 to 1 when Derek Minter raced this.

'They were revving them to 8,000 rpm in those days, but changing the bottom end regularly. I use 7,200 rpm, which is about the maximum for absolute safety, because they used to crack the flywheels if they went to maximum revs to get the absolute performance.

'Those big cooling fins on the cylinder head and barrel are there for a reason. When a Manx is working well it's really hot in there, and you need all the cooling you can get; it just amazes me when you pick up barrels that people have cut the fins off. It just doesn't make sense at all.'

Ray Petty's view was that $1^3/8$ inches was the maximum choke size for a carburettor on a 500cc Manx, and he disapproved of the $1^1/2$-inch Amal fitted to Mike's bike since it left his hands. 'That was probably done by Bill Stuart, it was something of a trade mark of his,' Mike explains. 'I find megaphonitis is a bit of a problem and 5,000 is about minimum revs. At 6,000 that's when it really takes off, then you've really only got up to 7,200 rpm.

'The first time I rode it, it was absolute magic. I just couldn't believe it could handle so well. I'm still learning to ride it quickly – very few can ride them really well. You don't really need a bike as strong as this except in the Isle of Man. They really were built from the ground up for the Island.'

What else could a factory call the ultimate TT racer, except Manx?

NORTON MANX

Engine: Air-cooled, four-stroke single cylinder, with two valves operated by single overhead camshaft via rockers (later by twin overhead camshafts). Alloy cylinder head and barrel; magnesium alloy crankcases. To 1953 – 499cc Model 30M, 79.6mm bore × 100mm stroke, developing 35 bhp at 5,750 rpm; 348cc Model 40M, 71mm × 88mm, 28.5 bhp at 6,200 rpm. 1954-62 499cc Model 30M, 86mm × 85.6mm, developing about 48 bhp at 7,500 rpm; 348cc Model 40M, 76mm × 76.7mm, about 36 bhp at 8,000 rpm).

Transmission: Four-speed gearbox with integral footchange. Primary and secondary transmission by chain. Multiplate dry clutch.

Cycle parts: From 1951 – 'Featherbed' duplex cradle frame in Reynolds 531; telescopic forks, swinging-arm rear suspension. Eight-inch twin-leading-shoe front brake in conical hub (7-inch rear). 1951-61 – Twin 7-inch two-leading-shoe front brake in full-width hub for 1962 season.

Dimensions: Wheelbase – 55 in. Dry weight – 292-307 lbs according to model.

Owners' Clubs: None specifically for the model. Norton OC, Vintage MCC Racing Section and Classic Racing MC all cater.

Sources of help: Spares – Summerfield Engineering Ltd, Cotes Park Industrial Estate, Somercotes, near Alfreton, Derbyshire DE55 4NJ; Unity Equipe, 916 Manchester Road, Castleton, Rochdale, Lancashire. Rebuilding and tuning – Andy Savage, 1 Beryl Grove, Hengrove, Bristol.

Panther was the name adopted by the old-established firm of Phelon and Moore for the bikes made in its factory close to the Bradford Road in Cleckheaton, Yorkshire. Before the First World War it had established the basic design feature of the engine forming the front down section of the frame, and its big singles stayed faithful to the concept until the last one left the works in 1966.

Not that the Panther company was stick-in-the-mud when it came to different ideas. In its final 20 years of bike production, it made a range of Villiers-powered two-strokes and the Princess scooter, as well as importing a French-made scooter with preselect gears. But the mighty sloping single is the Panther style recognized all over the world, renowned for its ability to haul huge sidecars and some-times a trailer as well, taking in the steepest of hills as a matter of course. As soon as motorcycle production got under way after the 1939–45 war, the Model 100 single headed the range; the 1939 600cc 87mm bore ×

Above left *The characteristic sloping cylinder of the Panther big single dates from the early years of the century. In its 600cc form, with 87mm bore and 100mm stroke, it is the favourite of the range with today's sidecar men, who prefer its smoother power. The small lever ahead of the gear lever is the half-compression device, to aid lighter riders in kicking over compression when starting. The Model 100 carries its name proudly on the timing cover, but when the Model 120 was introduced the same cover was used and the name ground off – economies were needed.*

Above *Motorcycle journalist Jonathan Jones has owned his Panther since 1976. A 1960 650cc Model 120, it has been fitted with an earlier 600cc Model 100 engine after the original broke its connecting rod. The spare wheel on the genuine Panther sidecar chassis is just visible on its rearward mounting – all three wheels are interchangeable.*

100mm stroke model was made in 1946. Then for 1947 came the luxury of telescopic forks, a special design developed by Panther with the Dowty company, and described as

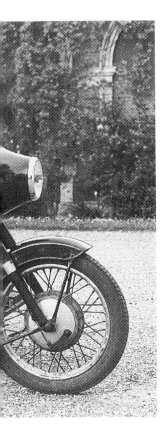

PANTHER

The Yorkshire pussy that could pull a house down

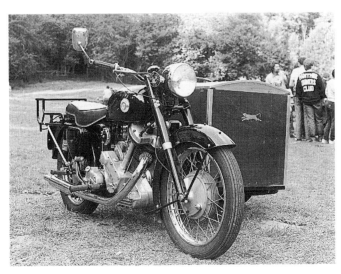

Above *At Panther rallies, spares arrive in Brian Jay's box sidecar, hitched to a 1962 Model 120 fitted with a 600cc Model 100 engine of the middle 1950s.*

oleomatic air type – many years before air forks became fashionable on sports bikes from the East!

As the acknowledged sidecar bike supreme, at a time when family cars were a rare sight, the Panther 100 was offered with a specification that experienced sidecar men thought best for the job. So the rear end remained unsprung until 1954, when changing fashion demanded a little more comfort and the factory offered a swinging-arm rear end to absorb the bumps and potholes. The engine remained the same 600cc unit, with a Burman four-speed gearbox, even when the spring frame was added, but an improvement in the stopping department came with the development of beefy 8-inch diameter drum brakes. Interchangeable between all three points of a sidecar outfit, they are still good enough to be used on sidecar outfits in classic racing events in the 1980s; in the 1950s they were one of the best brakes available.

In 1959 the Panther single was stretched

to its capacity limit with the introduction of the Model 120. Its 650cc 88mm x 106mm engine still driving through the faithful Burman gearbox, it developed a lowly 28 bhp at only 4,500 rpm on a compression ratio of just 6.5 to 1 and was a torquey hauler that could move almost anything – a Panther 120 and sidecar pulling a van out of a muddy field where it had sunk up to its axles is just one example – but it was not such a sweet engine as the smaller Model 100. The 100 stayed in the range until 1959 and the 120's swansong was in 1966, when bike production at Phelon and Moore came to an end and traditionalists mourned the death of the Panther, its appeal to the family man overtaken by the growth of small cars that could beat it easily on performance and keep all the family in the dry.

The Panther Owners' Club keeps the tradition of the biggest British single alive, with members all over the world able to get advice and parts to keep their mounts running. Motorcycle journalist Jonathan Jones is a name known to all of them, as editor of the club's magazine *The Sloper*. Jonathan came to Panthering because he wanted affordable family transport, and in 1976 he bought a sidecar outfit, a 1960 650cc Model 120 fitted with a genuine Panther sidecar chassis topped off with a huge Busmar sidecar body.

The Panther has proved a faithful friend and servant, and when Jonathan was restoring the Cambridge cottage he now lives in, the sidecar body was unbolted and replaced by a strong box. This part-time builder's transport has carried 5 cwt of cement, or even 100 feet of 6-inch floor-boarding from the builder's merchant to the Jones residence-to-be. When the original 650cc engine snapped its conrod and destroyed itself (and left a dent in the frame in doing so!) it was replaced by the smoother 600cc Model 100 unit, a simple matter as both of the wet-sump engines use the same basic mounting

points. Oil consumption of the 600cc unit has proved to be twice as good as the 650.

The Panther sidecar chassis, which has a mounting for a spare wheel that can be swapped for any of the other three, includes a separate stand to make changing the sidecar wheel simple. And the quickly detachable rear wheel is a boon, as Jonathan knows: 'I've timed myself changing a wheel. It took me seven minutes from putting the bike on the stand to change the rear one.'

The Panther sloper has its weak points – just a couple. The electrics show their age and regular riders fit 12-volt alternators to give better lighting and cheap reliability. Jonathan Jones has fitted a car unit he bought for £5, and enjoys the improved view at night, while Club specialist in sloper engines and gearboxes Rod Handover has fitted a Triumph bike alternator on the end of the original Lucas dynamo. Rod acknowledges that the Panther clutch can be a problem if the unit is not assembled very precisely, the splines of the clutch body wearing rapidly if any play develops, as that thumping torque takes its toll. Rod and family use their Model 100 as regular transport, from weekend shopping to covering long distances to Club rallies, when Rod and wife Margaret share the outfit with three children and the cat, while the luggage goes in the camping trailer hitched to the Panther sidecar chassis towing hitch. The factory thought of most things for practical family transport! Cruising at 40 mph, the heavily laden 600cc Model 100 gives 40 miles per gallon, but the 8-inch drum brakes do have to work hard with all that weight to stop.

At Club rallies, specialists give advice and spares are available. They naturally come by sidecar, and cycle parts specialist Brian Jay has used his trained coachbuilder's skills to fabricate a large commercial box to carry a selection of parts. It speaks volumes for the appeal of the biggest thumper made in Britain in the '50s that there is enough interest in them to keep the spares coming – the Owners' Club claims that the only parts it cannot supply are fuel tanks and toolboxes. Panthers were definitely built to last.

PANTHER

Engine: Air-cooled, four-stroke sloping single, with two pushrod-operated valves; iron head and barrel. Model 100 598cc – 87mm bore x 100mm stroke, developing 23 bhp at 5,500 rpm. Model 120 (introduced in 1959) – 88mm bore x106mm stroke, developing 28 bhp at 4,500 rpm.

Transmission (both models): Four-speed Burman gearbox with integral footchange. Primary and secondary transmission by chain. Multi-plate clutch in oil. (Lower overall ratios available for sidecar work as an option, then standard from 1955.)

Cycle parts: 1946 – rigid frame and girder forks. 1947 – Panther Dowty oleomatic air telescopic forks introduced. 1954 – swinging-arm frame and Panther telescopic forks; 8-inch drum brakes. 1958 – improved rear frame, swinging-arm members forged.

Dimensions: Wheelbase – Model 100 rigid frame, 54 in; Models 100 and 120 swinging-arm frame, 56 in. Dry weight – Model 100 rigid, 385 lbs; Model 120 swinging-arm frame, 426 lbs.

Owners' Clubs: Very active; 19 UK sections. Membership secretaries – Angela and Jonathan Jones, Coopers Cottage, Park Lane, Castle Camps, Cambridge CB1 6SR. Club spares scheme, available only to members.

Sources of help: Spares – Autocycle, 40 Church Street, Moxley, Wednesbury, West Midlands; A. Gagg and Sons, 106 Alfreton Road, Nottingham.

1953 Monaco Rally

The solid Panther single may not seem the obvious choice for pass-storming on a rally through Europe to Monte Carlo, but in 1953 'Titch' Allen hitched a Watsonian chair to 600cc of Cleckheaton single to take part in the Monaco Rally. Titch had developed an internally sprung dual seat for the Feridax accessory makers, and wanted to demonstrate it with a long-distance run on a rigid-framed bike; as the Panther only came with the back end rigid, it was the obvious choice. 'It was probably the most vintage-style bike in production,' he recalls. 'And in view of my interest in old bikes, it was the right model.'

Titch and his wife were part of the British contingent that set out from Oxford at midnight, and arrived at Folkestone to find the official control unmanned! After persuading the local police to sign their route cards, they caught a few precious hours of sleep on the ferry before facing the 783 miles to Monaco at an average of 31 mph.

'The Panther would cruise at 60 mph on the main roads, but we were struggling when we got into the hills and I had to come through the gearbox,' Titch remembers. 'I drove like a lunatic and the Panther gradually fell apart, except the engine, which was marvellous.' The British drivers had standard touring oufits, and were surprised to find the Germans on Six Days Trial-style sportsters that would leave

black rubber marks when accelerating away from the time checks. But the Panther kept slogging on, despite hitting a rock in an attempt to miss a wobbling cyclist; a rapid roadside adjustment soon put that behind the Allens, but there was worse to come.

'We were within sight of Monte Carlo, coming down a winding road, with the traffic pulling over to give us a clear run,' Titch says of the final drama. 'This bus went wide on the approach to a hairpin and I thought he was pulling over like the others, so I went up the inside. But he was taking a swing at the corner and came across in front of us and forced us up the bank. But the Panther didn't give up easily – it took three panels out of the side of the bus!'

As the bus driver tried to take details, sporting passengers pushed him aside and sent the Allens on their way, the sidecar wheel squealing in protest and the gear lever jammed in one place. To cheers from the roadside crowds, the faithful Panther plodded to the finish. 'And at the final inspection we lost no marks because everything was working,' grinned Titch. 'It might have been bent, but nothing was broken, not even a bulb!'

A local garage straightened the sidecar, and with just half a pint of oil added, the Panther was driven home. In 2,500 miles the tappets needed no adjusting and the plug was never changed. Titch still remembers the noble old single with respect: 'That engine was unbelievable, so unconcerned.'

Battered but unbowed, Titch Allen's Panther and Watsonian 'Avon' completed the 1953 Monaco Rally despite an argument with a bus. Unlike most outfits in the Rally, the Panther was standard, with extra-strong mudguard stays the only special modification. The 600cc Panther was 91st in the final rally classification.

ROYAL ENFIELD 250

Small, smart and snappy

Right *Plumber Keith Foster uses his bike for both leisure and work, and claims the engine still gives him 70 miles to every gallon, even with well over 100,000 miles covered.*

Below *The compact Crusader Sports was a favourite with learners in days when they could ride a 250, and its smooth engine and 80 mpg thirst pleased more experienced riders looking for economy with good looks. This 1962 example is a restoration by specialist Ron Maund.*

Royal Enfield's neat little 250cc Crusader was announced in 1957, and the short-stroke (70mm bore × 64.5mm stroke) single was destined to stay in the Redditch company's range for ten years. It was the first British 250 single from a notable maker to use unit construction of four-stroke engine and gear-box, and a claimed output of 13 bhp at 5,750 rpm made it the most powerful four-stroke British 250 of its day. BSA was soon to bring out its own C15 unit-construction model, but when the Crusader was announced the world's biggest maker was still offering the uninspiring side-valve C10L or the almost

right for the job, and the Crusader proved a good handler. A top speed of 75 mph and a fuel thirst of only 85 miles to every gallon made it an economical road mount, but the compact build also made it an obvious candidate for conversion to off-road use, and for the 1961 season there was a trials version available. Also in the range by then was the Sports Crusader, boasting 17 bhp and a claimed top speed of 85 mph. If anyone doubted how well the model could go, French rider Bargetzi won the Two-Hour Race at Montlhéry in 1960 to top a list of successes on his Sports model in production machine events.

In 1961 there were headlines for the Redditch-made 250 again, with the announcement of the 'Super 5' with five-speed transmission – another first on a British road model. Leading-link forks were another feature of the new sportster, which came with a compression ratio of 9.75 to 1 and a bigger Amal Monobloc carburettor than previous versions, to give a claimed 20 bhp at 7,500 rpm. Touring types were not forgotten, and the other versions were available with the excellent Airflow front fairing to keep the weather at bay, so the Crusader catered for almost every 250 rider's taste.

And there were experiments behind the scenes as the future needs were considered: in 1962 a Crusader with a bulge in the timing cover was spotted in the Midlands, with a Siba Dynastart to turn the engine over at the press of a button. Commonplace today, it was unheard of on a single-cylinder motorcycle then, and a touch of ingenuity showed in the way the Siba unit generated 12-volt power when the engine was running, feeding four six-volt batteries in the tool box. But when the starting button was pressed, a solenoid switched all four batteries into series and produced a 24-volt current for the best effect to get the piston over compression! However, the model did not get into production. There was also an experimental touring 250 model with enclosure front and rear, and panniers built into the smooth glass-fibre tail, but it never reached the production line, and is now in the collection of a Japanese enthusiast.

equally dull overhead valve C12 for the 250 owner; the success of the good-looking and peppy Royal Enfield was assured from the beginning.

The alloy-cylinder-headed power unit sat in a conventional single top-and-down-tube frame with no bottom cradle that was just

1964 John O'Groats to Lands End

The final development of the Crusader was the sporting Continental GT, a five-speeder with all the glamorous appeal a young rider could ask for. To announce the model, the factory arranged a novel run, with testers from the three weeklies joining in a run from John O'Groats to Lands End. Twenty years after that cold day in 1964, they all remember the little 250 with affection.

Pat Braithwaite had the first official press ride, taking over from factory rider Peter Fletcher at Carlisle and heading down the A6 towards the Midlands. 'It was ahead of its time,' he recalls. 'Easily the most powerful 250 of the day, and relying on components that were already well proven. It was a free-running little engine and had outstanding smoothness at high revs.

'I remember the ignition switch had fractured, but it was taped up and we just carried on. It was cruising at a speedo 80 mph and felt comfortable.' At Wolverhampton, Pat gathered his notes for a report in *Motor Cycle News* while *Motor Cycling*'s Bruce Main-Smith took over. He rode it to Silverstone, where racing star John Cooper put in some high-speed laps, then headed south across the testing hills of the Cotswolds.

'It steered and braked nicely, and it had all the power a 250 of the day should have,' is Bruce's memory of the bike. 'I liked the sculptured tank – you could fit your knees in nicely. But it was rather noisy, and it really barked up some of the hills in the Cotswolds.

'It was a capital bike, but I thought then, and still do, that the five speeds were not necessary. On some hills it was better with five ratios to choose from, but when we did some acceleration tests later, against an ordinary Crusader, the four-speeder was quicker than the five-speed over the standing start quarter mile.'

At Chippenham in Wiltshire came the final swap, with David Dixon of *The Motor Cycle* taking over for the ride to Lands End and still enthusiastic about the memory of 150 miles of bend-swinging. 'I loved it,' he says. 'It was quick and would pull on at well over 70 mph. Beautiful little bike.

'My running average was something like 50 mph, which was not all on main roads, and there were no motorways in the west then. It had very good road holding and the brakes were very good, but it was a bit noisy.

'I really enjoyed the ride down through Devon and Cornwall because it steered so well. But as Geoff Duke was working with Royal Enfield at that time, I suppose you'd expect that. I do remember that when I got down to Lands End the only person there apart from our photographer was Colonel Davenport from the factory!'

Wrapped up against the November cold and enjoying uncrowded West Country roads, David Dixon averaged some 50 mph for the final 150 miles of the end-to-end run. The sporty looks of the Continental GT were matched by its bark!

Bruce Main-Smith was a road tester for the weekly magazine *Motor Cycling* in the early '60s, and recalls a brief ride in a 1,000 kilometre production race at Silverstone. He and Des Craig (son of ex-Norton technical director Joe) were entered by dealer Comerfords of Thames Ditton on a Crusader prepared by the factory. 'I recall that Dunlop made us some 17-inch tyres to fit the standard-size wheels, but in special racing compound,' he says. 'We got past the scrutineer with no problem, but it does show just how genuine the "production machine" description was!

'We were told not to rev the engine over 7,000 or the conrod would break. I found in practice that I could keep with Derek Minter on a 250 Honda until we got to the straight, then he'd naturally walk away with our rev limit keeping our top speed down. In the race itself I never got a ride – the conrod broke at Copse Corner with Craig aboard and that was that.'

In use today, the Crusader's versatility adds to its appeal. Steve Mayhew, Machine Dating Officer of the Royal Enfield Owners' Club, built his example from an assortment of bits and uses it for road and trail riding. 'It's beautiful on the road,' is his report, 'so long as you don't want to go fast. If you don't thrash it, the engine is so smooth.'

For high-mileage experience, plumber Keith Foster's 1960 Sports model beats most 250s. He is the third owner, and bought the bike in 1982 with 100,000 miles on the speedometer, most of them put there by a Shropshire carpenter for whom the little Royal Enfield was sole transport. 'I had a 90cc Honda that I couldn't get rid of, and I swapped it for this,' Keith explains. 'It came with the cylinder head off, but really the problem was the contact breaker points welded together! The old chap worked in Wales and rode it there and back every day, and as he kept some goats at home he'd made a big set of wooden panniers that rested on the pillion footrests, and brought two bags of goatmeal home every night. When I got the bike it was absolutely covered in goatmeal and oil, but mechanically it was well looked after.

'I gave it a complete mechanical check, but not much needed doing – it did need the oil pump drive replacing, and I got one of those from Jack Meredith's shop in Shrewsbury. What I didn't do was replace the crankshaft oil seal, and you should always do that if you strip one of these – the big-end seized and twisted the conrod!'

Keith's Crusader is used for business and pleasure, and can be a good talking point if he meets a customer on a building site with a piece of British motorcycling history as transport. With 28,000 miles since its rebuild, the little single with the crisply thumping exhaust note cruises happily at 55 to 60 mph and returns 70 miles for every gallon of fuel. Showing the model off at local events brought an extra bonus when a spectator offered Keith another Crusader in bits as spares, and it turned out to be the racy Continental GT model, which quickly became the latest Foster rebuild project. But Keith still loves his original Crusader. 'The nicest 250 I've ridden.'

ROYAL ENFIELD 250

Engine: Air-cooled, four-stroke single cylinder, with two valves operated by pushrods from chain-driven camshaft. Alloy cylinder head, iron barrel. All models from 1958 Crusader on with 70mm bore × 64.5mm stroke giving 248cc. Claimed output – 1958 Crusader, 13 bhp at 5,750 rpm; 1967 Continental GT, 20 bhp at 7,500 rpm.

Transmission: Four-speed gearbox in unit with engine on all pre-1962 models; integral footchange. Five-speed gearbox on Super 5 and Continental GT models. Primary and secondary transmission by chain. Multi-plate clutch in oil.

Cycle parts: Welded tubular frame, with swinging-arm rear suspension and telescopic front forks on all models except Super 5 and Olympic, which had leading-link front forks. Seven-inch single-leading-shoe drum breaks front and rear, in full-width alloy hubs.

Dimensions: Wheelbase – 54 in. Dry weight – from 300 lbs (Continental GT) to 325 lbs (1958 Crusader).

Owners' Club: Active, but hard to find! Secretary – John Cherry, Meadow Lodge Farm, Henfield, Coalpit Heath, Avon BS17 2UX.

Sources of help: Spares – Keith Benton, Via Gellia, Kirk Head Road, Grange-over-Sands, Cumbria; Burton Bike Bits, 152a Princess Street, Burton-on-Trent, Staffs DE14 2NT; L. and D. Motors, 367/9 Bath Road, Brislington, Bristol. Machine dating – Steve Mayhew (REOC Dating Officer), 9 Mafeking Drive, Wrockwardine Wood, Telford TF2 7BB.

ROYAL ENFIELD BULLET

The sophisticated single

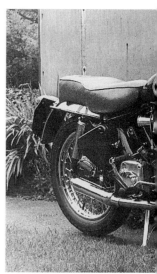

Left *Plain. The 350cc Model G catered for the conservatives who wanted a rigid frame instead of the Bullet's spring-framed comfort; in 1950 it cost £152.40, £25.40 less than the Bullet. It was listed in the 1954 range, but faded away that year.*

The Bullet was the main weapon in the Redditch armoury for many years. The model name dated from the early 1930s, when 250, 350 and 500cc versions of the pushrod single were listed. Little can H. L. Frame have imagined what a long-term trend he was starting when he won the 350 cup in the 1932 West of England Trial on a model that cost him less than £50 brand new. In the years ahead, the Bullet roadsters and their trials cousins remained close members of the family.

The Bullet made its greatest impact at the 1948 announcement of the works trials team, a complete break from convention with swinging-arm rear suspension in an age when all good trials men used rigid frames for greater sensitivity to the bike's movements. It was a very brave move, flying in the face of convention, but a sign of faith in their new 350 Bullet roadster, available only with spring frame. Never afraid to set trends, Royal Enfield could see the day when

riders would want comfort beyond that of the rigid frame. They hedged their bet a little by keeping the 350 Model G in the range, with rigid frame, but the Bullet was one of the Redditch flagships.

The trials team made no fairy tale début, but hard work and astute recruitment built up a strong squad of men. By 1952 they had won four Manufacturer's Team awards of the 18 presented in National Trials; in 1953 they took nine of the 16 team awards offered, dominating with riding strength in depth.

The roadster was clearly very similar to the competition versions, and *Motor Cycling* captioned a picture of the 1952 model: 'Listed with either trials or scramble specification, the 346cc Royal Enfield is a real competition machine differing scarcely at all from those ridden by the works teams'. Not all enthusiasts rated the Bullet highly, and the author can remember Stan Turner of the Sunbeam MCC saying of a trials Bullet that he had recently ridden: 'All I can say is that

Above *Fancy. History in disguise – Tony Lynch's 90 mph 500 café racer, built from Johnny Brittain's 1954 ISDT Gold Medal-winning 350. After 65,000 miles on the road it is being rebuilt to its original form.*

Above *Don McKeand's 1959 Airflow 350 Bullet has covered over 20,000 miles in nine years, including ride-to-work duties. When used on Owners' Club rallies, the original pannier frames prove very useful for carrying provisions.*

Below *The liberal use of alloy tempts restorers to overdo the polishing, and this very nice 1960 Bullet has been attended to with a polishing mop that reaches parts the factory mops never reached.*

Johnny Brittain is a b—— good rider!' But when developments were announced after proving them in the hands of the star riders, the public was probably more willing to accept them, despite the disastrous 1956 ISDT, when new all-welded frames broke. Johnny Brittain was stranded in a remote spot and was woken from his depression by the whistle of a train, looking up to see the crew gesturing him to bring the machine to them. Despite a complete absence of common language, Brittain and his newfound friends got the bike aboard and back to a station accessible to a rescue vehicle!

In 1958 the Airflow version of the Bullet was offered, following a much-publicized development of full streamlining by the staff of *The Motor Cycle* and the associated *British Plastics*. The Airflow represented weather protection affordable by all, and was even fitted to the 125cc two-stroke models. Thirty years later, the styling did not look outdated when compared with BMW's industry-standard R100RS.

The company found markets all over the world and in unlikely places at home. So when Keijo Virtanen bought a 1956 500cc

Bullet Scrambler in his native Finland, his search for restoration parts covered a wide spread, the headlamp bracket coming from America. And a true enthusiast for the marque who wanted to carry spares to the Owners' Club gatherings might find a Pashley-Enfield commercial three-wheeler of the early '60s, powered by a 350 Bullet engine.

Club members are fortunate to have the factory dispatch records available. They were cleared out of the Redditch factory when it was closed and kept in store in a Shropshire warehouse with all the spares, which were sold off at a scrap price of about £35 a ton! The dispatch records were ordered to be burnt, but an anonymous employee with a greater sense of history than the receiver took them, and later sold them to the newly-formed Royal Enfield Owners' Club.

Yorkshire dealer Tony Lynch takes a break from selling and servicing modern bikes by riding his 1954 Bullet, a bike with a history. It was Johnny Brittain's mount for the 1954 ISDT and after John had won his Special Gold medal it was sold to Graham Garner, who later sold it to Tony. Converted to a stylish 500cc café racer – the special 350

motor used a 500 bottom end to take advantage of the revised and stronger bearings due to go into production in 1956 – it covered 65,000 miles on the road. Tony has acknowledged the Bullet's faithful service and has promised to convert it back to ISDT trim.

Don McKeand is the head teacher of a Bedfordshire school, regularly using one of his Enfield collection to ride to work. 'There are a few eyebrows raised when I park the bike in the playground,' he admits. 'But you do make some useful contacts. The chap who delivers the school dinners saw my 125 there and next day he brought me a handbook for it. Apparently he used to have one.' But Don's favourite model is the 350 Bullet and he has a 1956 standard and a 1959 Airflow model to choose from, part of a garageful built up while actively Enfielding since 1973.

'It's such easy motoring, and dead reliable. It gives you relaxed riding, no faster than a decent 250, but so nice to ride,' he enthuses. 'The 1956 model gives me about 60 miles to the gallon, but the Airflow is really economical. I get a regular 80 mpg, cruising around 60 to 65 mph.'

Problems are few, thanks to regular servicing, with the 20/50 oil changed every 1,500 miles. In the gearbox, Don uses EP90 heavyweight lubricant, with automatic transmission fluid in the primary chaincase. 'I've really had little to do except routine maintenance,' he claims. 'The rear brake backplate is not very rigid, so occasionally you get a graunch. It's a little unsettling, but no real problem.

'The rockers wear. They're in split bearings that go rather quickly, and I'm using some from the Indian Enfield at the moment, as they're so easily available. And the alternator rotor works loose occasionally; it frightens you to death, because it sounds like the big-end. Apart from that, they're not really a lot of trouble if you look after them.'

With rallies all over the country since he helped start the Royal Enfield Owners' Club, plus regular visits to Holland on one of his selection from Redditch, Don has enough good experience to keep loyal to the Royal brand.

ROYAL ENFIELD BULLET

The specification is for the 1950 Bullet, as this represents the era when the model was considered a benchmark by which to judge the industry's offerings.

Engine: Air-cooled single cylinder, with two pushrod-operated overhead valves. 70mm bore × 90mm stroke giving 346cc. Compression ratio 6.5 to 1, claimed output 18 bhp at 5,700 rpm.

Transmission: Four-speed separate gearbox, with integral foot change. Primary and secondary transmission by chain, multi-plate clutch in oil.

Cycle parts: Lugged and brazed tubular open diamond frame, telescopic front forks and swinging-arm rear suspension. Six-inch drum brakes front and rear.

Dimensions: Wheelbase – 54 in. Dry weight – 350 lbs. Ground clearance – 6 1/4 in. Fuel tank capacity – 3 1/2 gallons. Saddle height – 29 1/2 in.

Owners' Club: Active. Membership secretary – John Cherry, Meadow Lodge Farm, Henfield, Coalpit Heath, Avon.

Sources of help: Spares – Keith Benton, Via Gellia, Grange-over-Sands, Cumbria; Burton Bike Bits, 152A Princess Street, Burton-on-Trent, Staffs DE14 2NY; L & D Motors, 367-369 Bath Road, Brislington, Bristol; Hitchcock's Motorcycles, Long Close, Glasshouse Lane, Hockley Heath, West Midlands B94 6PZ. Advice – Owners' Club has appointed specialists to advise on all Bullet models.

Johnny Brittain and Royal Enfield

Royal Enfield's trials team for 1952 included a fresh-faced 20-year-old with a lot of promise. By the end of the year, Johnny Brittain, son of a famous trials-riding father, was one of the sport's top stars. When he lined up for the start of the Scottish Six Days, few thought the new-

20-year-old Johnny Brittain made history in 1952 as the youngest winner of both the Scottish Six Days Trial and later the British Experts title. The growing success of the sprung-flame Royal Enfield finally convinced other makers to change from rigid rear ends.

comer who had never won a National trial would threaten the top men.

Johnny Draper (Norton) led at the end of Monday, the first day, but after Tuesday's Highlands tour, J. V. Brittain (Royal Enfield) and the promising Brian Martin (250 BSA) were tying. 'Everyone was saying I'd crack up,' Johnny says of that memorable ride. 'But I'd got nothing to lose. I'd never won a National trial, so I just got on with it. It just seemed that I couldn't do anything wrong from then on.'

John was four marks ahead of David Tye (BSA) on Wednesday evening, and made it a six-point margin on Thursday after footing at the Ravine on the Lochailort to Kinlochmoidart road, where David Tye stopped. Tye closed the gap to three on Friday, but the final day included no observed sections apart from a simple stop-and-restart on the ride back from Fort William to Edinburgh. 'Unknown to me, Jack Booker and Jack Stocker from the factory had brought my dad up,' recalls John. 'Someone said to me "Your father's at the top" when I got to the test, but I didn't believe it. It was a good job I didn't know he was watching, or I'd have gone to pieces. As it was, I got to the top all right, which meant I'd won the trial, and there was my dad! It was a marvellous surprise.'

Johnny remembers his Royal Enfield days with affection: 'I rode in 15 International Six Days trials for them and won 13 Gold Medals, which wasn't bad. The twin broke its crankshaft on the final day in 1952, but that was the only bad spot of that year.

'I thought the 350 was a good bike, not the fastest but very reliable. It was a challenge, being the underdog and riding the bike people thought was the underdog, too. But Enfield were quite forward looking with the spring frame; I don't I could have wished for better.'

After wins in the Shropshire Cups and Greensmith trials, Johnny faced the toughest opposition in the British Experts trial. Two 30-mile laps around a blizzard-swept Stroud in Gloucestershire made it hard for the most experienced, but when the marks were counted the same 20-year-old was two marks ahead of Hugh Viney's AJS. Johnny was the youngest winner of the trial at that time and confirmed a family habit – father Vic won in 1936 and jointly in 1939. 'Confounding the theorists, Brittain's 350cc Royal Enfield used a normal spring frame,' said *Motor Cycling*; the underdog had done it again!

ROYAL ENFIELD TWINS

Fast and furious

500 Twin was the title Royal Enfield gave to their first parallel twin, announced at the end of 1948. A typical practical Redditch product of that unglamorous era, it came with deeply valanced mudguards to keep road dirt off the rider, while two-way damped telescopic forks and a swinging-arm rear end looked after his comfort. With a compression ratio of 6.5 to 1, the 64mm bore × 77mm stroke engine produced a claimed 25 bhp at 5,750 rpm, enough to take it to a top speed of 86 mph in a *Motor Cycling* road test.

For the 1953 season came the 'Meteor 700', the biggest vertical twin on the market and an apparent doubling-up of the popular 346cc 'Bullet' with its 70mm × 90mm dimensions, giving 692cc of flexible muscle.

Motor Cycling gave it a top speed of 94 mph, enough to compete but not a sports model; the standard photographs of the 700 issued by the factory showed it complete with panniers. As well as its appeal to the long-distance man who wanted effortless cruising, there was a demand for flexible power to pull the family along in a sidecar, and when *The Motor Cycle* tested a Meteor in 1954 they had it to sidecar specification with a Canterbury Victor child-adult model attached. The 69 mph in both third and top suggests slight overgearing, but with the ignition retarded and a careful throttle hand, the engine would pull as low as 12 mph in top gear – flexibility of a high order!

Changes came in 1958 with the legendary

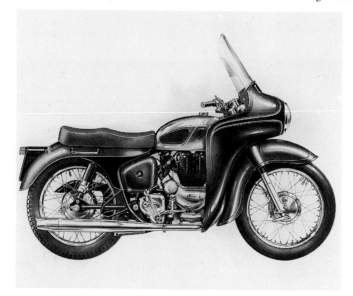

Left *Interceptor Mk IIs outside the entrance to the underground Bradford-on-Avon factory of Enfield Precision Engineers. On the left is hill climb champion Chris Ludgate, with plant manager Roger Shuttleworth standing.*

Below far left *The 1962 700cc Constellation in Airflow touring trim shows how comprehensive the fibreglass was.*

Below left *The final form for the Interceptor power unit was in a Metisse rolling chassis, with an early use of a disc front brake making it even more unusual. Derek Rickman tries a 1970 example around the Hampshire heathlands.*

'Constellation', a development of the 700cc theme and offering a claimed 51 bhp at 6,250 rpm with 8.5 to 1 compression ratio and its tuned engine breathing through either an Amal Monobloc or 30mm TT9 racing carburettor. The 500 Twin was replaced by the short-stroke Meteor Minor, with 70mm bore and a short stroke of 64.5mm, giving 496cc and an output of 30 bhp at 6,250 rpm. The Meteor Minor came with 17-inch wheels.

1958 also saw the introduction of the Airflow fairing, a substantial dolphin-style enclosure developed in co-operation with Bristol Aircraft and their wind tunnel. It was part of Royal Enfield's forward-looking way of catering for riders from sporting to committed tourers, and was available in due course on models from 125 to 700cc. Around this time, the factory also loaned a Super Meteor to the Road Research Laboratory for development work on anti-lock brakes based on the Maxaret system that had been proved on the Ferguson racing car. But Tony Wilson-Jones, technical director, saw little future in the idea and it was quietly dropped.

In 1963 came the final capacity increase, with the introduction of the 750 Interceptor that claimed an output of 52.5 bhp at 6,000

Below *Steve Lightfoot's 1959 Meteor Minor is far from standard, but the chunky power unit still looks ready for action, whether at a gentle potter or cruising around the legal speed limit.*

Mike Griffiths' Interceptor

The 1963 Mark One Interceptor that Bristolian Mike Griffiths still rides in hill climbs has a history of success that started with the 1969 National Hill Climb Championship. Built from scrap parts by factory tester Chris Ludgate, it was ridden by him to the National title again in 1970, beating the experienced Chris Williams on the very special Triumph-powered Hill Waye. Soon after, it was sold to its present owner.

'I bought it for £85, after Chris refused an offer of 75,' Mike recalls. 'I have to pay nearly that much for a set of oversize pistons today! I was second to the great Paul Spargo in the 1974 championship and managed to beat him once.

'It's been a really good bike, reliable apart from breaking one cam follower. That came out through the crankcase and I had the hole welded up with a piece from a Triumph case, so it's not a completely genuine Royal Enfield. And it bent a valve ten years later on that same side.'

The Interceptor is an amalgam of standard parts, the stock chassis fitted with the 3-inches-longer US specification swinging-arm and the front forks shortened to reduce the bike's height. The result has impressed Mike: 'I used to have a Norton Commando and I'd say the

Enfield handles better,' he says. 'On fast sweeping bends it's particularly good.

'The engine isn't really highly tuned. The crank was lightened and the cylinder heads were gas-flowed. It uses standard pistons and a standard exhaust camshaft for both inlet and exhaust to boost the valve lift a little. It uses Amal 930 Concentric carburettors and fuel is normal pump petrol. It's such a tractible engine that I never change the gearing, wherever I'm riding it. The engine has been in there more than 20 years and the bottom end has never been touched. I don't use a rev-counter, but I'd guess it revs to about 7,000.

'The gearbox is the standard Albion with close ratios. I've never had to touch that or the clutch, never even changed a clutch plate, just strip and clean it occasionally. Mind you, I believe Chris Ludgate split a box on take-off once – I suppose I don't ride as hard as he did.'

The Interceptor and other big 1960s' British twins found themselves outpaced when modern moto-cross bikes brought a combination of wide power bands and very light weight to the hills. Mike retired from regular competition on the twin until the National Hill Climb Association introduced its Classic class for the 1988 season, when he came back to take third in the title chase, and runner-up in 1989. 'It's ideal for the Enfield, which is the best £85 I've ever invested,' he grins.

The 750cc Interceptor's flexible power makes it ideal for hill climbs and twisty sprint events. Mike Griffiths blasts off to another fast time at Curborough sprint course, using the same gearing for this level track as he uses on steep hill climbs.

rpm. The 750 survived when the 500 was discontinued in 1965, the time when the Redditch factory was closed and production moved literally underground at the old secret munition works at Bradford-on-Avon in Wiltshire. From there it was exported mainly to America, where a batch of Police-specification versions was sent in 1965. Royal Enfield were good at the export business, including supplying a Constellation to the butler of Her Majesty's Ambassador in Rumania with no frame or engine numbers. When the new owner made contact with the Owners' Club, that gave them a pretty problem to solve, not to mention the small matter of getting spares in Eastern Europe before the Curtain was lifted a little; tractor valves can be adapted to fit Royal Enfields, it seems!

The twin came to the end of the line in 1970, when production ceased. A final batch of engine and gearbox assemblies was built up and fitted into a special Rickman Brothers' Metisse chassis and these sold until 1972, when another noble line petered out. At the end, the engines had dynamically balanced crankshafts, and improved machining had largely cured oil leaks, but more glamorous names survived and it was left to a coming generation to realize how good a Royal Enfield twin can be.

Steve Lightfoot discovered the twins' smooth-running appeal and adaptability after a car driver's insurance company paid for their client's mistake in knocking Steve off his BMW. He spent part of the proceeds on a 1959 Meteor Minor which had been mildly customized by its second owner, and has no plans to bring the 500cc twin back to original specification. 'I chose it because it was different and I don't plan to change it,' he insists. 'I thought the standard bike was ugly and I like this the way it is.'

Steve's bike has had the cast alloy instrument nacelle replaced by a 250 model's instrument cluster, and the export model fuel tank was repainted by the previous owner without the standard knee pads. A battery box from a 750 Interceptor confirms how twin parts can be interchanged, and removing the side panels is something that spirited

riding might have done automatically! This is Steve's first Enfield and he finds it smoother to ride than the Triumphs he had before. Performance naturally falls short of the modern machines he has owned: 'It cruises easily at about 65 mph, but it's a bit underpowered two-up,' he reports. 'I get about 60 to 70 miles to the gallon, but that's because I don't use hard acceleration. And the single-leading-shoe front brake limits what you do – it doesn't do a lot to stop you.'

American-style swept-back handlebars suit Steve's relaxed riding style: 'It doesn't have a stunning performance and with these bars you're not tempted to play at cafe racers anyway, so the layout suits the bike,' he says. 'The worst part is the gearbox, with lots of neutrals when you change down. It's got a neutral selector, but I never need to use it!'

Steve Lightfoot's individual approach to Royal Enfielding and recognition of a 1950's machine's limitations in modern traffic leaves him free to enjoy the Meteor Minor on his own in the way he chooses, away from the crowd. Quite typical of the company's image when it was alive – a little bit different.

ROYAL ENFIELD TWINS

Engine: 1948 500 twin – air-cooled four-stroke vertical twin cylinder, with two pushrod-operated valves per cylinder. 64mm bore × 77mm stroke, 6.5 to 1 compression ratio, claimed power 25 bhp at 5,750 rpm. 1970 Series II Interceptor – 71mm × 93mm, 8.5 to 1 compression ratio, claimed power output 52 bhp at 6,000 rpm.
Transmission: Four-speed gearbox with integral footchange. Primary and secondary transmission by chain. Multiplate clutch in oil.
Cycle parts: 1948 500 twin – lugged and brazed tubular frame, 6-inch drum brakes front and rear. 1970 Series II Interceptor – welded tubular frame, with 8-inch drum front brake, 7-inch rear. Both with telescopic front forks and swinging-arm rear suspension.
Dimensions: 1948 500 twin – Wheelbase – 54 in. Saddle height – 29^1/$_2$ in. Dry weight – 400 lbs. 1970 Series II Interceptor – Wheelbase – 57 in. Saddle height – 30 in. Dry weight – 426 lbs.
Owners' Club: Active. Membership Secretary – John Cherry, Meadow Lodge Farm, Henfield, Coalpit Heath, Avon.
Sources of help: Spares – Keith Benton, Via Gellia, Kirk Head Road, Grange-over-Sands, Cumbria; Burton Bike Bits, 152A Princess Street, Burton-on-Trent, Staffs DE14 2NT; L & D Motors, 367-369 Bath Road, Brislington, Bristol; Hitchcock's Motorcycles, Long Close, Glasshouse Lane, Hockley Heath, West Midlands B94 6PZ. Advice – The Owners' Club have appointed specialists to advise on most models.

SUNBEAM

Much quality, little speed

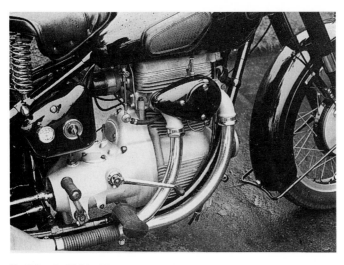

In March 1946, *The Motor Cycle* whetted its readers' appetites with the description of a brand new design. 'Instead of a collection of components, motorcycles conceived as a whole – how often has this been urged over the last decade?' the magazine asked, conveniently overlooking the country's preoccupation with other, more urgent, matters during the Second World War. 'The Sunbeam . . . has been designed from the front mudguard right to the ingenious rear lamp as a complete entity.'

It was all part of a long-term promotion of the new twin that was to be sold under the Sunbeam name as a flagship for the parent BSA Group, a model that Managing Director James Leek said was '. . . as modern as tomorrow, but built in the familiar tradition'. Designed by Erling Poppe, it drew heavily on BMW R75 detail and was powered by an overhead camshaft vertical twin with the crank running fore to aft. The 4.75 × 16-inch balloon tyres, handlebar control cables hidden from view, wide cantilever saddle, Poppe's unique style of telescopic forks, sprung rear frame and shaft drive

added up to a luxury mount. The engine was rubber-mounted to insulate the rider from vibration, smoothly contoured mudguards had a section deep enough to keep road dirt off both bike and rider, and every part looked like it was designed to be just where it was.

Compared to the basic transport most makers were offering in the austere 1940s, the Sunbeam looked something special. But for anyone looking for performance, it was a disappointment: 'I rode one at Alec Bennett's showroom in Southampton and I was disappointed,' said one industry notable. 'It had no power, no guts. Alec didn't like it, either.' As a professional racer in the past, who won the 1924 Senior TT on a Sunbeam, Bennett knew his bikes. And as a dealer, he like others found the handsome heavyweight a slow seller.

In 1949 a brother was born, the S8. It was £32 cheaper and used BSA's forks and front brake, normal size tyres and conventional handlebar controls with exposed cables. The compression ratio was up from 6.8 to 7.2 to 1, to give one extra claimed bhp. It sold better than its bulky forebear, but between

Far left *The S7 and 8 shared the same motive unit, a handsome piece of engineering, with cylinder barrels and crankcase in one casting. The use of an air-cleaner was unusual in the '40s and '50s, and may account in part for the long mileages some owners report between overhauls.*

Left *The S7 used basically BSA forks by 1951, but retained its balloon tyres, sensible mudguarding and a host of quality detail fittings. The shield by the cylinder head protected the spark plugs from rain and kept a flapping Belstaff coat out as well.*

Below *Rescued from terminal neglect as a field bike, Peter Ashen's S8 is a used example of the breed with individual touches to the owner's liking. The carefully built engine shows no sign of oil leaks, thanks to a rocker box gasket to Peter's own design.*

the two versions, BSA only sold some 8,000 Sunbeam twins from the S7's 1947 arrival in the showroom to the final clearing of stock in 1958. The official end of production was in 1956, but they were still listed two years later, which hints at how fast they were selling. The S7 was priced at £222 in 1947, putting it in the top three most costly road bikes; for 1958 it was priced at £301.28, beaten only by Ariel's mighty Square Four for the 'Most Expensive British Bike' title.

Modest performance may have limited the Sunbeam's appeal (and the worm gear in the rear wheel limited any aspirations to tuning), but it set a high standard for quality that the discerning still recognize, and it would run for many miles when treated properly. Sunbeam twin specialist Bob Stewart has seen the proof: 'We had one customer who did 300,000 miles, with an engine rebuild every 100,000 miles,' he says. 'We had it in for the third rebuild and after another 100,000 miles there was half a thou wear on the crank.

'He was very particular about oil changes, drained it off every 2,000 miles, and then put

in 20SAE and went for a quiet ride around the block. Then he drained the light oil off and filled up with the right grade.'

Bob Stewart has found that the single-plate clutches last well if treated properly, and a life of 100,000 miles is not unknown. And Sunbeam Fellowship member Chris Armour has used an S8 for ride-to-work duties and reports a fuel consumption varying between 55 and 65 mpg. Regular use in modern traffic conditions has persuaded Chris to convert the front brake to a disc, but he can swap back to Sunbeam standard quickly without spoiling the originality of the bike.

The author was once a Sunbeam owner, using an S8 with sidecar chassis as regular transport to work and to carry an ancient OK Supreme sprinter to events all over the South and the Midlands. Despite a regular diet of neglect, it gave no memorable problems apart from occasionally spitting back when starting and setting the carburettor alight. It was even ridden in the sidecar class of a sprint at Ramsgate's Western Undercliff, finishing an inglorious last but providing a light-hearted change from the more serious competition. Its ultimate fate is unknown after it was sold on for a nominal sum; perhaps it suffered ignominy as a children's plaything in the fields, as so many unwanted British machinery has.

SUNBEAM TWINS

Engine: Air-cooled vertical in-line twin, with two valves per cylinder operated by single overhead camshaft and rockers. 70mm bore x 63.5mm stroke, claimed output 24 bhp at 5,800 rpm (S8 – 26 bhp at 6,000 rpm). Alloy cylinder barrel and crankcase in one casting; alloy cylinder head.
Transmission: Four-speed gearbox in unit with engine, driven through single-plate clutch. Integral footchange. Final drive by shaft to worm gear.
Cycle parts: Telescopic front forks (single central damper on early S7) and plunger rear suspension (undamped). Twin cradle frame. Eight-inch drum brakes front and rear (7-inch front).
Dimensions: Wheelbase – 57 in; Saddle height – 30½ in (S8, 30). Ground clearance – 4½ in (S8, 5½). Tank capacity – 3½ gallons. Weight 430 lbs (S8 405).
Owners' Club: Sunbeam Owners' Fellowship. Secretary – 'Rotor', c/o Stewart Engineering, PO Box 7, Market Harborough, Leics LE16 8XL.
Sources of help: Advice – Owners' Fellowship and Stewart Engineering. Spares – Stewart Engineering, Church Terrace, Harbury, Leamington Spa, Warks CV33 9HL.

Some badly neglected bikes are brought back to life by a caring owner with a sense of history. Few can have given the restorer's kiss of life to a Sunbeam twin more effectively than Peter Ashen, a customer furniture maker based in Birmingham with a collection of Sunbeams ranging from a V-twin made for the Russian Army in the 1914-18 War to an S8 twin. His S8 was rescued in 1975 when it was being used as a 'field bike', and took four years to bring to full glowing health.

Peter's older 'beams are noted for their authentic period details, but his S8 is modified for practical riding and his own aesthetic pleasure. Alloy rims complement the similar material of the dominant engine and gearbox unit, while black-painted centres of the rims set off the lustrous paintwork. The sump is a special large-capacity version made by specialists Stewart Engineering, increasing the reservoir by 1½ pints and a wise addition if the model is to be ridden any distance. 'You have to keep an eye on the oil level, as they tend to burn it a little,' explains Peter.

The rear mudguard is a carefully repaired original, but the front is a glass-fibre copy; both were hand-painted with a good quality coach enamel, while other cycle parts that did not need repairs were stove enamelled. The original front brake has been replaced by a BSA Gold Star unit: 'A very good brake,' says the owner. 'But the original was pathetic.'

The engine has the optional 7.2 to 1 pistons and gives an easy cruising speed of 50 to 55 mph for touring in comfort. And comfort for the rider and passenger comes from the correct saddle and a pillion seat that looks just right with the bike. Few people realize that it actually is a Lambretta scooter unit, and Peter enjoys the bike too much to worry about purists' attitudes to such inter-marriage of parts. 'It's the most comfortable bike I've ever ridden,' he says. 'But it's not fast and you have to ride it sensibly. If I want to go fast I use my 1932 Model 90.'

Leading Sunbeam authority Bob Cordon-Champ knows and respects the Ashen S8: 'That's what a good one should be like,' he says with admiration.

Harold Taylor and the S7

Harold Taylor is part of British motorcycling folklore. His role as manager of the British team in the Moto Cross des Nations in the 1950s was the one best known to the public, most of whom recognized the one-legged gent waving his wooden crutch in the air and urging his men on in a crisp military tone. Arthur Lampkin remembers Harold getting excited as he looked for a chance to pass a Swedish rival, finally managing to elbow past right in front of the gaffer. Next time around, Harold threw his crutch at Lampkin with the admonition: 'Don't cheat. Get past fairly!'

Riders respected Harold Taylor's demands and advice as a man who knew a lot more than filling in forms and getting his team to the start of international matches in time to parade with the Union Jack. Despite the loss of his left leg, Harold Taylor could drive a sidecar outfit better than most, including the 1948 International Six Days Trial on a 1000cc Vincent outfit. The next year, with the ISDT held in Wales, he took an even more eccentric step and entered a Sunbeam S7 and BSA sidecar for the hectic dash around the hills.

The S7 was built with the standard 6.8 to 1 compression ratio, but expert opinion suggests slightly bigger valves gave a power boost. 18-inch wheels were used, fitted with Dunlop Universal tyres and the gearing was the standard sidecar overall ratios of 16.6 to 1 first, 10.3, 7.4 and 6.13 top gear. In the conventional ISDT manner, control cables were duplicated, and the BSA sidecar was slimmer than the standard version, mounted on a special chassis with a narrower track. On the side of the body were clips to hold Harold's crutch.

The Welsh hills were tough terrain for the mild-mannered S7, and Harold was reported as screaming along at 20 mph in first gear for many miles. But while the motor stood up to the thrashing, the worm gear in the final drive unit proved to be the Achilles' heel of the design and gave up the struggle. Unofficial reports leaked in later years said that the rear drive worm was changed three times! 'That's not an official statistic, but the worm wheel runs at a million degrees if you do anything like hard work with it,' says Sunbeam historian Bob Cordon-Champ. 'You can bet there were quick rear drive changes behind a shed when they were needed.'

Whatever the final drive problems, Harold Taylor came through those six hard days without loss of marks to claim a Gold Medal. When *Motor Cycling* tried the outfit later that year they mentioned Harold's 'apparently effortless Six Days'. It did less than justice to the S7's finest hour and a great drive.

When Harold Taylor won his Gold Medal in the 1949 ISDT, crash helmets were worn by very few competitors, despite those menacing Welsh rocks. Even if tales of replacement rear drive units are true, getting the S7 through such a demanding event was a great achievement.

TRIUMPH SINGLES

The little Cub could roar

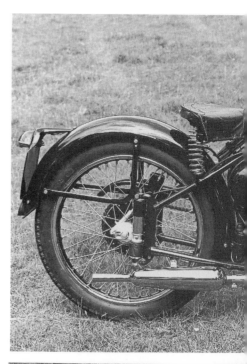

Triumph caused a sensation when it unveiled the stylish little 150cc Terrier at the 1952 Motorcycle Show. Finished in the Amaranth Red shade long associated with its 500cc Speed Twin model, it reflected its bigger brother's styling with a smaller version of the headlamp nacelle, the same tank-badge styling and the smooth lines expected of an Edward Turner design. Plunger rear suspension was different from the unique Sprung Hub of the larger models, but the family characteristics were there in every other respect. No power output was quoted for the four-speed single, the first Triumph with less than two cylinders to be made since the old '30s-style 350s built for dispatch riders in the 1939-45 war.

The idea caught the public imagination, enough for the factory to show the 200cc Tiger Cub the following year, to sell at £127.20p in 1954. The Cub came in the same dashing silver shade as the sporting Tiger 100 twin, and by 1956 the little Terrier was dropped and the Tiger Cub carried on, to become an essential part of British two-wheeled history.

The Turner styling made it attractive to look at, but a four-speed gearbox in unit with the engine was better than the three speeds of most of the opposition, and 10 bhp from the 63mm x 64mm pushrod power unit gave better performance than most. Driven carefully, it would return around 100 miles for every gallon of fuel, an important consideration to the teenagers who flocked to buy it. If they neglected to change the engine oil the plain bush big-end bearing could clank its

Above *This Terrier was restored by owner Mike Estall, who also sleeved the motor down to give his daughter a British 125cc model on which to take her test.*

Left *Stephen Hill's 1961 Tiger Cub is one of an all-British collection in the family garage. The silencer was made in his own business workshop and gives an interesting and non-standard bark.*

Right *Johnny Giles tests the waterproofing of the competition department's preparation as he fords a stream on his factory-entered Cub.*

expensive protest, but the sweet-handling little Cub made a lot of friends.

One 1955 model proved its worth twice over for author and broadcaster Anthony Smith. He bought it in Cape Town, South Africa, for £155 when it was less than a year old, quickly passed his driving test, then loaded the Cub and set out for London! Few African roads had tarmac in the mid-'50s, and amongst Anthony's memories of the 7,000-mile trip is a photograph of a signpost at Kapiri M'poshi; one direction is for Algiers and the other for Egypt. With a tank capacity of only 2½ gallons and up to 300 miles between fuel pumps, careful use of the throttle was needed while picking a path

through hub-deep sand or around potholes deep enough to damage a lorry, but the little Cub made the journey as far as Switzerland with no major problems. Then deep snow on the Brenner Pass proved too much and the rest of the journey was completed by train.

Twenty-seven years later, Smith Senior and Junior made the return trip, Anthony planning to show his son Adam how Africa looks from the saddle. Father was on the very same 1955 Tiger Cub and Son was on a 1964 version. With a blend of traveller's guile, good luck and Triumph dependability, they made it to Cape Town. Problems along the way were few, including a split fuel tank on the older model, welded by an Egyptian

1959 Scottish Six Days Trial

The simple little Tiger Cub engine was used in every sphere of motorcycle sport, but one particular record that it set in 1959 still stands 30 years later.

The Scottish Six Days Trial, regarded all over the world as one of the most arduous tests of man and machine, was the province of traditional 'big bangers' until the Tiger Cub changed the course of history. The man in the saddle was Roy Peplow, who had joined the works team two years before upon completing his National Service. In his second National trial he finished third in the Wye Valley event, proving his rapid adaptation to the Cub, and by 1959 he was well established as a Triumph star.

Peplow's Cub victory came on a machine he says was 'not very special at all, just a good little bike and like all the other works riders had.' But with a combination of his determined and skilled riding and the small Cub's good traction and manoeuvrability, he rode the rocky hazards and long hills to beat AJS star Gordon Jackson, with 18 marks lost to Jackson's 20; Sammy Miller on his legendary Ariel was in third place.

It was naturally not an easy ride, but Peplow did not realize until years later what a handicap a small machine could be with the traditional Scottish starting order. It was long established that small-capacity models would have the early starting numbers, to give them time to cover the long road sections before darkness caught them out. But what seemed fair in early days when lightweight machines could not approach the larger models for sheer cross-country speed proved to be a handicap when lightweight machines came into the serious competition sphere.

'I never realized it until I rode a 500 years later.' Roy explains. 'But the small bikes used to arrive at the sections when they'd just put all the rocks in and they hadn't been disturbed. On a big bike, there was a path pushed through by the time you arrived on the scene and it was much easier to get through.'

In an illustrious career with the Triumph factory, Roy won seven gold medals in the International Six Days Trial and was a natural choice for the prestigious Trophy Team for Britain, but that landmark victory in the Scottish Highlands he rates as his greatest achievement. Not that he had much time to celebrate the victory clinched on Saturday, 7 May 1959; on the morning of Monday, 9 May he opened Roy Peplow Motorcycles in his native West Midlands. Nobody could have planned the timing better, as the man who had made history two days before opened the business where he still trades to this day!

Roy Peplow, the most successful of Triumph's Cub-mounted trials team, picks a careful path over Scottish rockery in the 1960 Six Days Trial. The year before he set a record for the smallest capacity machine to win the event, unequalled to this day.

blacksmith who simply drained the fuel off and then lit his torch and did the repair, never thinking of such basic fire precautions as filling the tank with water.

The Tiger Cub evolved during its life, with a swinging-arm frame for 1957 and a Zenith carburettor fitted for the following year. Poor starting and tickover came with the Zenith, but the factory persisted for three years, taking the precaution of stating in the instruction manual that all guarantee claims about the carbs should be referred direct to the makers of the unloved instrument. In 1959 came the T20S Sports Cub, with welcome Amal carburettor, a more sporting camshaft, compression up to 9 to 1 and a power output of 14.5 bhp at 6,500 rpm.

In 1962 came major changes to the range. The service department at Meriden was pleased to see Amal carburettors fitted to all models, and a roller big-end bearing (from engine number 84270 onwards) and an uprated oil pump meant greater strength and potentially longer life. With the introduction of the TR20 Trials and TS20 Scrambles versions, there were a lot of Tiger Cubs due to work hard, and uprating the heart of the engine was no more than common sense. Even road racers were looking at the Cub, fitting 220cc USA-made cylinder barrels and competing in the 250cc class, without spending a difficult-to-find fortune on a foreign two-stroke.

The Tiger Cub is a good choice for today's British enthusiast, either as a starting point for an amateur restorer or as an economical supplement to a patriot's collection. 28-year-old Stephen Hill is typical of the younger riders who do not remember the Cub as a contemporary model, but can still appreciate its blend of economy and classic Triumph styling. His 1961 example had been standing for 12 years when he bought it and set about bringing it back to full health. £400 later he has the ideal supplement to his immaculate 1970s 750cc Bonneville.

A director of the family engineering business that specializes in tube work, Stephen had no problem replacing the badly rusted silencer – he made his own, which keeps the snappy exhaust note of the Cub legal, but

deeper than that of the original Triumph unit. Paintwork is Stephen's own work, using Jaguar silver metallic paint that is very near to the original Silver Sheen that the factory used. Wherever possible, the Cub now has stainless steel or chromed nuts and bolts, adding to appearance and resistance to corrosion.

'It's a lovely little bike,' reports Stephen. 'Easy to ride and a nice handler. That 6-inch front brake may not look very impressive, but in fact it's very good. And if I cruise at around 50 mph, the engine's happy and I get about 85 miles to the gallon.' Rebuilding a bike that had stood for 12 years was a good test of spares availability, and Stephen had few problems. 'I could get everything I needed apart from the tank badges.'

Curious onlookers often ask Stephen why his share of the family garage contains only British bikes, with the Tiger Cub next to the Bonneville and a 250 BSA C15. 'I suppose it started when I used to work on my brother's A65 BSA,' he tells them. 'That's a typical British bike – so simple and easy to work on.'

TRIUMPH SINGLES

Engine: Air-cooled, four-stroke single, with two pushrod-operated valves. Alloy cylinder head, cast iron barrel. 63mm x 64mm stroke, with output varying from 10bhp at 6,000 rpm (standard engine) to 14.5 bhp at 6,500 rpm (T20S/H Sports). Unit construction of engine and gearbox throughout the model life from 1954 to 1968.

Transmission: Four-speed gearbox with integral footchange. Primary drive by duplex chain, secondary by single-row chain. Multi-plate clutch in oil.

Cycle parts: 1954-57 – plunger rear suspension. After 1957 – swinging arm type. Telescopic forks, 5¹/2-inch single-leading-shoe drum brakes front and rear.

Dimensions: Wheelbase – plunger frame, 49 in; swinging-arm standard frame, 51 in; Sports and Trials frame, 50 in. Dry weight – plunger frame model, 182 lbs; swinging-arm road model, 220 lbs (variations according to model specification).

Owners' Club: Very active; 35 UK branches. UK Secretary – Edna Page, 101 Great Knightleys, Basildon, Essex SS15 5AN.

Sources of help: Spares – Charlie's Motorcycles, 169-171 Fishponds Road, Bristol; TMS, 92 Carlton Road, Nottingham NG3 2AS; Barry Cooper, 3 Orchard Avenue, Berkhamsted, Herts (Cub specialist); L. Vale-Onslow, 104-116 Stratford Road, Sparkbrook, Birmingham. Restoration – Hughie Hancox, r/o 21 Bayton Road, Exhall, Coventry CV12 6HD. Paint to original factory colours – MS Motorcycles, same address as Hancox.

Edward Turner's design for a 500cc parallel twin was first shown at the 1937 Show, priced at £75. And a 500 twin stayed in Triumph's range until 1973, outlasting many other designs that followed the astute Turner's trend.

From its debut with rigid rear frame and girder forks, the twin progressed to telescopic forks in the 1940s, with the famous Sprung Hub next, followed by the smoothly-styled nacelle that tidied up the headlamp mounting and handlebar area. What if the handlebars were just a little too far swept back for real comfort, the bike looked terrific!

In the 1950s, the Triumph was the most popular 500, with a name for quality and performance, even if the handling was not of the very best. It came from a factory where a happy workforce liked the bikes and liked their work, as restorer Hughie Hancox remembers. 'You couldn't wait to go to work there. You'd ride into the yard and smell the new paint, the new tyres and the new metal, and it all hit you.' Hughie started his Triumph days in the Service Department, where a team of skilled fitters sorted out production line snags and helped customers with service work or just friendly advice. And if an owner was really hard up, there was a selection of refurbished parts that came at bargain prices.

The Triumph's reputation for reliability

TRIUMPH 500 TWINS

The best-looking twin

Left *A 1952 Tiger 100 restored to original condition by expert Hughie Hancox, who worked at the old Meriden factory for 20 years. This immaculate reminder of his own reliable transport in the 1950s was rebuilt from a rusted heap that had stood under a sheet of corrugated iron in a back garden for 20 years.*

Below *Reliable transport today for Mark and Sue Hand are his 1966 ex-Ministry 5T Speed Twin and her 1967 Tiger 100SS. The bikes are kept in the front entrance of their house and used regularly, giving 85 miles to the gallon.*

makes it practical transport today, as Mark and Sue Hand of the Triumph's Owners' Club know. Bike mechanic Mark rides a 1966 5TA Speed Twin and Sue – who also holds a City and Guilds certificate in bike mechanics – has the more sporting Tiger 100SS of 1967. Both bikes are kept in the front hall of the house, and they give a regular 85 miles to the gallon with a top speed of 100 mph available if the coast is clear.

Mark and Sue restore bikes as a team, and when Mark's black-painted Speed Twin was rebuilt it was Sue who sprayed the paint, baking the smaller parts in her kitchen stove! 'People say Speed Twins were only ever painted in Amaranth Red, but these Ministry

bikes were supplied in black,' says Mark. 'When we were stripping the paint off, it was black down to the factory undercoat.' With only a regrind of the crank and new main and big-end bearings, the trusty twin has recorded over 70,000 miles on its chronometric Ministry issue speedometer; pistons are still standard and the same set of piston rings that Mark fitted 45,000 miles ago are working well. Both the Hands' bikes are run on SAE 40 oil except when the weather gets really cold, when they are swapped to Castrol's GTX multigrade.

Well-used Triumphs are known to leak oil around the base of the pushrod tubes and from the front fork oil seal holders. Mark uses a smear of plastic rubber compound at these vulnerable points, to ensure oiltight bikes that have covered mileages as high as 780 in one 30-hour stint on the 1986 BMF National Rally. Not aiming for concours-winning originality with the family's only transport, he uses stainless steel nuts and bolts where possible. 'You'll find some domed nuts on the bike, which aren't correct as original fittings,' he admits. 'But I just like them like that.' With 45,000 miles of one Triumph to call on, he has one criticism of a basically very sound design: 'I wish Triumph had sorted out access to the sludge trap in the crank, so it could be cleaned easily without stripping the motor.'

Such a tough engine proved its versatility in many areas of the sport. Works rider Jimmy Alves won the very first ACU Trials Drivers Star in 1950 and Triumph was the standard engine for Britain's Trophy Team in the 1970 ISDT. It would go fast, too – fast enough for sprinter John Hobbs to take world speed records from racing giants like the Italian Gilera team, while Percy Tait rode a works development racer to second place in the 1967 Belgian Grand Prix, averaging 116 mph to be beaten only by the legendary combination of Giacomo Agostini and his MV-Agusta. Drag racer Tony Weeden screamed his engine to 10,000 rpm to beat machines many times bigger, and when an impressed American racer asked 'How many runs do you do on a motor?', Tony laughed and told him that he had replaced one piston in two years, putting in a second-hand one that a friend had given him! For a bike that once reached a speed of 155 mph at the end of a standing start quarter mile, it was quite a remarkable collection of used parts.

The Triumph 500 grew to be the world leader in its class because the factory kept standards high. No wonder, with Edward Turner himself inclined to take a bike at random from the dispatch bay and go for a spin to see that the Meriden factory was making them as he intended. 'He was quite a little bloke, but always immaculate in his Savile Row suit,' one old factory man recalls. 'The word would go round that Turner was coming and the place would be tingling in anticipation.' That tingle inspired quality, with every bike off the assembly line given an eight-mile road test until changing management philosophy installed a rolling-road testbed to save the time and cost of a year-round team of testers. That did little to improve quality control, however, and the Service Department had one bike sent back that had been despatched minus its oil pump, a sad reflection on declining relations and standards at a time when opposition from Japan was beginning to grow. That wasn't what Turner wanted his factory to produce, but he retired in 1964, shortly before the tried and trusted production testers were replaced.

Edward Turner died of a coronary thrombosis in 1973, but the 500 Triumph, which had set a trend to last for a third of a century until four-cylinder units took over, lives on in many enthusiasts' hands as a tribute to the little man with a cigar and an eye for style.

TRIUMPH 500 TWINS

Engine: Air-cooled, four-stroke parallel twin, with two pushrod-operated valves per cylinder. Early versions had iron barrel and head, 63mm bore × 81mm stroke (1937 Speed Twin developed 26 bhp at 6,200 rpm); alloy head introduced on Tiger 100 in 1949, with alloy barrels available only to 1959. Unit construction introduced in 1959, with engine changed to 65.5mm bore × 69mm stroke. Final production year 1974, when Tiger 100 Daytona produced 39 bhp at 7,400 rpm.

Transmission (all models): Four-speed gearbox with integral footchange. Primary and secondary transmission by chain. Multi-plate clutch in oil.

Cycle parts: 1937 – rigid frame and girder forks, 7-inch drum brakes front and rear. 1946 – Telescopic forks introduced. 1948-54 – Sprung Hub optional. From 1954 – swinging-arm frame and 8-inch single-leading-shoe drum front brake. From 1964 – twin-leading-shoe brake on Tiger 100.

Dimensions: Wheelbase – 1938 Speed Twin, 54 in; T100, 55 in; 1974 T100R Daytona, 53.6 in. Dry weight – 1939 Tiger 100, 361 lbs; 1974 T100R, 337 lbs.

Owners' Club: Very active; 35 UK branches. Secretary – Edna Page, 101 Great Knightleys, Basildon, Essex SS15 5AN.

Sources of help: Spares – Charlie's Motorcycles, 169-171 Fishponds Road, Bristol; Carl Rosner, Station Approach, Sanderstead, South Croydon, Surrey; Roebuck Motorcycles, 354 Rayners Lane, Pinner, Middlesex; TMS, 176 Belvedere Road, Nottingham. Restoration (and paint matched to factory colours) – Hughie Hancox Restorations, r/o 23 Bayton Road, Exhall, Coventry CV12 6HD.

1952 500cc Clubman's TT

The big win for a 500 Triumph with the Sprung Hub rear came in the 1952 Clubman's TT. A long series of Norton wins was ended by Lancashire lad Bernard Hargreaves, a 22-year-old engineer entered by dealer and ex-works rider Alan Jeffries, who supplied the Tiger 100. 'Absolutely standard,' Bernard describes it. 'Father and I sorted it out, just cleaned up the ports and lowered the front mudguard close to the tyre – it was a bit light at the front end and I didn't want the wind lifting it. That Sprung Hub was a bit better than a rigid back end, but only just.'

Practice for the TT showed that 9½-stone Hargreaves could gear up for a better fuel consumption, to cover the four-lap race on one tankful. But trouble with handling started early in the race. 'The back end was lively, and I put it down to a broken chainstay,' Bernard recalls. What he couldn't see was a rear wheel spindle nut missing!

In the pits, Bernard's dad was having his own problem, with Edward Turner himself coming down from the grandstand to tell him the non-stop run couldn't work. 'If you can stop him, we'll fill him up,' replied Hargreaves Senior, and Turner went back to his seat. Bernard carried on, fighting the bike for 151 miles to the finish, where he took the flag with just half a pint of fuel in the tank. His average of 82.45 mph gave Triumph's sporting image a boost, with three rival Nortons behind him. It was an heroic ride against the odds, but Bernard suffered physically: 'I finished with a water blister from the tip of my index finger to the end of my thumb and my knees were bleeding where I'd been gripping the tank. I was so exhausted they had to lift me off the bike.'

Delighted Edward Turner congratulated the weary winner, and when Bernard's father suggested it was time Triumph offered a swinging-arm frame, he confided 'We've already got that in hand'. At the end of 1954 the new frame was announced, and the Sprung Hub's days were numbered.

Bernard Hargreaves was never certain why the spindle nut went walkabout. He normally tightened it with a huge ring spanner, but that detail may have slipped through the final pre-race fettling. To commemorate what Bernard still regards as the best ride of his life, the factory presented him with a chrome-plated spindle nut, mounted on a plinth and engraved with the simple legend, 'Lest we forget'. Certainly the Norton factory did not forget, for the next year it announced that its 500 International roadster would be fitted with the Featherbed frame similar to its Manx racer, and Triumph couldn't catch them in the 1953 Clubman's TT.

Bernard Hargreaves on the standard Tiger 100 he prepared with his dad for his winning ride in the 1952 500cc Clubman's TT. The rev-counter was hanging loose after vibrating off, and the rear wheel spindle nut on the right-hand side of the bike went missing on the first lap.

TRIUMPH 650/750 TWINS

The Bonneville Legend

Right *Triumph was represented by star names in its 1950s' trials heyday. Their team in the 1958 International Six Days was (left to right) Ken Heanes, Johnny Giles and Roy Peplow.*

Far right *Roy Shilling's T120C Bonneville was originally built for the American market, boasting straight-through exhaust pipes and no lights. Today, the sharp edge of the Triumph's bark is subdued by flutes in the pipes.*

Triumph's parallel twin was a clear leader of the field as the bike industry struggled back to prosperity after the 1939-45 war. But as other factories followed its design trend, Edward Turner realized that Meriden needed something more to keep the place busy, and his visits to America convinced him that a bigger engine was the answer. The 500 design was sound, and easily stood an increase in bore and stroke to 71mm × 82mm to give a capacity of 650cc, and in 1949 the 6T Thunderbird was launched.

As usual, Turner did it in style. Three of the new models were ridden to Montlhéry in France, and a team of riders thrashed them for 500 miles at an average of more than 90 mph. This was the stuff of dreams, but the dreams were already in dealers' showrooms – Turner had made sure that 2,500 of them were delivered before the model was officially announced. A whole new era of Triumph twin success had begun.

The bike was priced at £153 in 1950, with Purchase Tax adding another £41.86. If the Sprung Hub was wanted that would cost extra, but at least one dealer with a competition background advised his customers to

opt for the rigid rear end and better handling! In 1955 Thunderbirds could be ordered with a swinging-arm rear end, or conservative sidecar men could have the Sprung Hub.

The first 650 to use Triumph's swinging-arm frame was the Tiger 110, announced in 1953 with 42 bhp on tap at 6,300 rpm. When Bernal Osborne, *Motor Cycling*'s Midlands editor, came to Meriden to report on the new model, he was given a standard model for the morning's country lanes and urban roads riding. Then, as Edward Turner took him for a lavish lunch, the Service Department stripped the engine, fitted the sporting E3134 camshafts and had the bike back in place waiting for the afternoon speed tests at the nearby Motor Industry Research Association testing ground. The Tiger that had purred along in the morning roared through the speed trap at some 116 mph!

America demanded variations on the 650cc theme, and a favourite for off-road use was the 650 Trophy. The USA team in the 1965 was Trophy-mounted and included film star Steve McQueen, a very capable rider who only gave way to stunt riders on location when the film director and insurance company insisted! Steve proved his mettle in the Six Days in East Germany that year, including flattening the exhaust pipe in a fall and relieving the engine's resultant asthma by chopping slots in the pipe with a borrowed woodman's axe!

The versatility of Triumph's 650 can be measured by its range of use, from breaking the world speed record to patrolling the

The Tiger 110 was certainly a handsome bike, in its livery of silver and black, and sleek lines from its 8-inch front brake and stylish nacelle to hold the headlamp and speedo neatly, back to the Twinseat (£12.10p extra if you wanted one on your Thunderbird). It was naturally a strong seller in America, and was a popular choice for tuners to persuade more power from, something that was to spawn a legend later in Triumph's life when the name Bonneville honoured the 214.47 mph world record set by Johnny Allan at Bonneville Salt Flats, Utah, in 1956.

The Bonneville was announced in October 1958 for the 1959 season, and those early versions were built with the traditional Triumph nacelle. But that changed for 1960, when the more sporting separate headlamp was fitted in the style that remained throughout the model's life.

1969 Isle of Man TT

The Bonneville was named to commemorate the breaking of the world solo speed record by 650 Triumph power in 1956, when Texan Johnny Allan averaged 214.47 mph over the measured mile on Bonneville Salt Flats in America. But Triumph built bikes for normal roads, and the final proving of the model came with the first 100 mph lap of the Isle of Man TT course.

Malcolm Uphill, a quiet young man from the Welsh valleys, was a natural choice for the 1969 team and before the race was quietly confident, despite troubles with the ignition cut-out button vibrating loose and causing a practice session misfire. But a polite request to mechanic Jack Shemans to 'check everything from front to back, just in case some silly little thing gives us trouble' saw the Bonneville in prime race condition on the day.

Malcolm's pre-race nerves weren't helped when a commentator looking for a newsworthy quote pushed a microphone in front of him and asked if he would be lapping at 100 mph. 'It doesn't matter if I only average 50, what I want to do is win the race,' was the dismissive reply.

Malcolm's quiet determination struck the right chord with Jack Shemans, who remembers him with respect: 'Easy on the bike and such a nice, polite chap. Easy to get along with.' Jack's magic fingers had produced a strong engine, and Malcolm was told, 'Go to 8,000 rpm if you're pushed.'

It wasn't necessary. Using no more than 7,500 revs on his first lap, the Welsh Wizard lapped at 100.09 from a standing start, which put him 18 seconds ahead of Rod Gould on another factory Bonnie. Uphill's mastery of the Mountain course was confirmed with a second lap speed of 100.39 mph, even though he was easing off and only revving to 7,200. Gould's engine clonked to an expensive stop, its crankshaft broken through enthusiastic revving, and Uphill sped to the flag with half a minute in hand over Paul Smart's Norton Commando. Confirmation of Uphill's ability to lap fast without thrashing the engine came with the publication of the speed trap figures taken at 'The Highlander', one of the fastest stretches on the 37$\frac{3}{4}$-mile course: Uphill was timed at 134.6 mph, while Gould broke the light beam at 140.1!

Malcolm Uphill says of the Bonneville's handling: 'I was racing a Manx Norton, so really had nothing to compare it with. But it was a bit of handful at the speeds I was riding at.' He was simply riding the Bonneville faster than it has been ridden before, but he must have found the bike attractive, because he still owns it!

Elbows tucked well in, Malcolm Uphill sets a new standard for production bikes with his stunning 1969 TT win at over 100 mph.

roads as a police mount, and from winning production machine races for aces such as Hailwood and Uphill to serving many International teams in the annual Six Days Trial. And between all that, serving owners as faithful transport – Brian Brook of Birmingham has a 1959 Thunderbird that he thought deserved a thorough overhaul after 209,000 miles!

Triumphs attract great loyalty, from the people who built them to those who collect and ride them today. Chairman of the thriving Triumph Owners' Club, mining engineer Roy Shilling, has no fewer than seven twins in his stable of 11 Trumpets! Amongst the Shilling rarities are an ex-Yorkshire Police experimental 750, with electric start and anti-vibration rubber mounting of the engine; it was one of numerous experiments to refine the twin as the Meriden entered its final years before the factory closed.

But Roy's favourite is an American market special, never listed for the British market. It's one of the very last T120C 'TT' models, made for the USA from 1965 until 1968, with the East Coast version fitted with lights while the West Coast variant had none. Intended for competition use, the TT was supplied with straight-through pipes, but Roy makes a concession to the local constabulary by fitting flutes in the tail of the pipes and muting the powerful bark while cruising around town.

The well-worn engine blew up in dramatic style soon after Roy bought the bike, coming apart so completely that a piece of camshaft hit him on the leg. But Triumph engines are easily swapped between models, and into the frame went a 750cc engine with a 20-tooth engine sprocket that gives leisurely high-speed cruising. Boyer Bransden electronic ignition gives accurate spark timing, with full advance not locking in until the crankshaft is turning at 5,000 rpm. 'It is a great system,' vows the owner. 'Power comes in below 2,000 rpm and it pulls a treat. I suppose you could say it's a bit of an evil tool, this one.' Finished in stark Alaskan White with not a single piece of unnecessary equipment, the T120C TT may look spartan compared with Roy's luxurious faired T140

Bonneville with matching sidecar, but as it growls its way out into the country its appeal as a one-man machine is obvious to anyone.

The bigger Triumph twins have a pedigree going back to the announcement of the original 5T Speed Twin in 1937; the type stayed in production until 1938 with L. F. Harris making 750cc Bonnevilles and Trophies in Newton Abbot, Devon. The 650 is a good choice for a first move into British biking, with spares still readily available. And if today's owner wants to know original factory details about his bike, the red leatherbound dispatch records that were kept in a strongroom near Edward Turner's office are now in London's Science Museum.

TRIUMPH 650/750 TWINS

Engine: Air-cooled, four-stroke parallel twin, with two pushrod-operated valves per cylinder. Early 650cc model had iron cylinder barrel and head. Single Amal carburettor gave 34 bhp at 6,300 rpm (6T), and 42 bhp at 6,500 rpm (T110). Alloy cylinder head on 6T from 1960, and on T110 from 1956. 1959 – 650cc T120 introduced, with twin carburettors and claimed output of 46 bhp at 6,800 rpm. 1973 – 750cc Bonneville and Trophy introduced, with 75mm (later 76mm) x 82mm engine. 1982 – four valves per cylinder introduced, for TSS and TSX 8 models only, with limited deliveries until closure of Meriden factory in 1983.

Transmission (all models): Four-speed gearbox with integral footchange, until five-speed on T120RV Bonneville in 1972; fitted to other twins for 1973. Primary and secondary transmission by chain. Multi-plate clutch in oil.

Cycle parts: 1949 – Sprung Hub rear with telescopic forks, rigid frame option. 1954 – swinging-arm frame on T110 in 1954; on Thunderbird from 1955. Seven-inch drum brakes front and rear on rigid Thunderbird, 8-inch rear drum with Sprung Hub; 8-inch front and 7-inch rear standard from 1966. Disc front brake introduced in 1973.

Dimensions: Wheelbase – 1950 Thunderbird, 55 in; 1955 Tiger 110, 55¾ in; 1960 Bonneville, 56½ in; 1967 Bonneville, 56 in. Dry weight – 1950 6T, 370 lbs; 1966 6T, 369 lbs; 1960 T120, 393 lbs; 1967 T120, about 363 lbs; 1975 T140, 395 lbs.

Owners' Club: Very active; 35 UK branches. Secretary – Edna Page, 101 Great Knightleys, Basildon, Essex SS15 5AN.

Sources of help: Spares – Charlie's, 161-71 Fishponds Road, Eastville, Bristol BS5 2PR; Hamrax Motors Ltd, 328 Ladbroke Grove, North Kensington, London W10; Roebuck Motorcycles, 354 Rayners Lane, Pinner, Middlesex; Carl Rosner, Station Approach, Sanderstead, Surrey; TMS, 92/4 Carlton Road, Nottingham NG2 2AS; Wileman's Motors, Siddals Road, Derby DE1 2P2. Restoration (and factory matched paints) – Hughie Hancox Restorations, r/o 21 Bayton Road, Exhall, Coventry CV12 6HD. Information – Owners' Club specialists.

TRIUMPH TRIDENT

Everything but high sales

Below *Martin Jones has covered over 145,000 miles on the T160 Trident he bought new in 1975. The earlier-pattern silencers give a better spread of power and the mudguards are the second set – the originals rusted from the inside while the chrome still looked good.*

Triumph's three-cylinder Trident, a bike destined to become a legend in its brief production life of only seven years, was announced officially in 1968. Rumours about the new development from the famous Meriden factory had been circulating, and lorryloads of engine units seen in Birmingham confirmed that the unusual models that showed a fast-disappearing trade plate to curious drivers were going to be on the production line. When it arrived, the reception from the press was euphoric, *Motor Cycle News* saying it was 'the most explosive motorcycle to sear up the highway in two-wheel history'. With a top speed near 130 mph, it was as fast as a 500cc Manx Norton, and the unique fishtail-styled silencers gave out a satisfying muted roar as 58 bhp moved 482 lbs of machinery.

The engine was a rational adaptation of the established Tiger 100 twin, with revised measurements of 64mm bore and 70mm stroke being the significant change internally; the tried and trusted Triumph layout of camshafts fore and aft and pushrods in external tubes were all pure tradition. Braking by an 8-inch twin-leading-shoe drum brake at the front may have seemed enough on the road, but as soon as the model began to get into production racing the lack of braking power began to show. The Trident was about 100 lbs heavier than the 650cc Bonneville and relied on the same brakes, which proved inadequate when a fast man worked them hard. Malcolm Uphill took one to victory in the 1970 750cc Production TT after a titanic last-lap scrap with Peter Williams on the works Norton Commando, but it was no easy ride. 'The engine just lost its edge after the first lap and it was like a

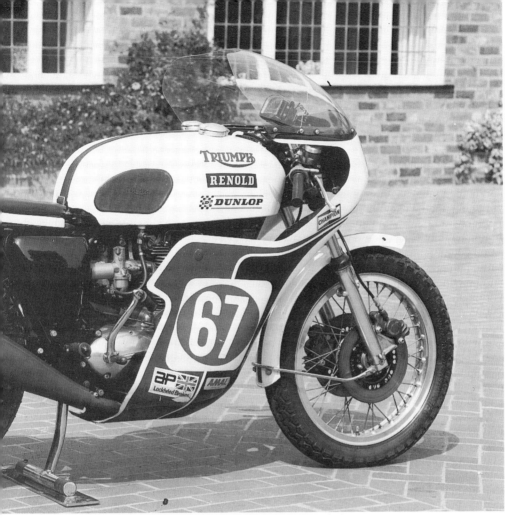

side-valve; I couldn't use top gear apart from the downhill stretches,' he recalls. The problem was the timing losing its setting and retarding as the race progressed; when the bike was put on the development shop dyno back at Meriden it gave only 47 bhp, but with ignition reset it was back up to 70! The factory's racing machines were fitted with an extra bearing on an outrigger plate and timing proved spot-on at 7,500 rpm when checked, whereas the old system could vary by 12 degrees from one cylinder to another!

The development of the Trident into a dominant force in racing was in the hands of Doug Hele, with a crew of devoted specialists in support and a team of the Best of British to ride the bikes. The aim of the team was to win, and Doug Hele would accept nothing less than perfection from his men; cylinder heads took a skilled fitter 16 hours

Les Williams built 'Slippery Sam', the most famous Trident of all, and later bought it from the factory. Sam has the unique record of winning the 750cc Production TT five years in a row.

to fettle, and the rockers were machined from a solid billet. There was an experiment with rockers forged in titanium, and after a lengthy wait for space in the supplier's production schedule, a set was presented to Hele for tests. Norman Hyde, who has stayed faithful to the Trident from those days at Meriden to his present specialist business catering for the model, remembers the brief experiment Hele made to establish if they would work: 'Doug clamped one up in a vice, got hold of a hammer and looked at the rocker to measure the sort of torque it would be subject to when the motor was peaking, then swung the hammer at the rocker. It broke.

'Doug just said "Well, that won't work" and walked away. So far as he was concerned he'd tried the idea and there was no benefit. The poor guy who sweated to get these super expensive rockers made after interrupting the normal production schedule just stood there and looked as if he could cry.' Doug Hele was never one to waste words without benefit, preferring to concentrate on the development of the Trident, which was also raced under the BSA name, though built in the Meriden Race Shop. The pure Formula 750 racers used a frame designed and made by Rob North in a small workshop in nearby Bedworth, and amongst the developments was the first bike to race with disc brakes front and rear. Detail like metal-sprayed alloy discs for short races and longer-lasting cast iron discs for long races were typical of the Hele-inspired attention to detail that made the Trident the dominant 750 on the race tracks of the early '70s.

On the road models, a five-speed gearbox replaced the original four-speeder in 1972 and the custom-styled X75 Hurricane was introduced the same year for the American market; about 1,000 of this early attempt to catch the laid-back were sold, which makes them quite a collector's item today. A 10-inch single disc front brake was the big change for 1973 and in 1975 the T160 with electric start and left-foot gearchange to comply with the American market's demands was the Trident in its final form. The unhappy time of Triumph production being moved to the BSA factory in Small Heath and the subsequent collapse of the BSA-Triumph group is too recent history to be detailed here; they stopped making the Trident when it had reached maturity and acceptance by a discerning market which did not always want the fickle fashion and constant changes of Japanese ranges.

The Trident is still a practical everyday rider's motorcycle, as the prosperity of specialists like Norman Hyde and Les Williams and their world-wide market confirms. A bike that cost just under £1,000 in 1975 can fetch more than that today if it is in good running order! One owner who knows that is Martin Jones, a Midlands-based express train driver whose 1975 Trident is his sole powered transport.

Martin must like the Trident's way of travelling, because he wasn't put off when his first one was delivered with no oil in the gearbox! He had only covered short local journeys before checking it over prior to a touring holiday in Europe only to find the box dry; he has learned to service his bikes himself after that experience and along the way has come to know the Trident's good and bad points. His present T160 has covered 145,000 miles from new, the only major engine work in that time being a rebore at 60,000 and a second rebore and the crankshaft reground at 130,000 miles. Early in his time with the bike he fitted Rita ignition and finds that 70 mph cruising gives him 45 to 50 miles per gallon.

Oil changes at 2,000-mile intervals and proper servicing are Martin's secrets of long life. 'And don't thrash it,' he adds. 'I cruise at about 4,000 and it will accelerate really well from that if I need it.' And would he sell it? 'I can't see that happening. It's like an old friend,' he smiles.

TRIUMPH TRIDENT

Engine: Air-cooled, four-stroke parallel three, with two pushrod-operated valves per cylinder. Alloy cylinder head and barrel, each cast in one piece. 67mm bore × 70 mm stroke, claimed output 58 bhp at 7,250 rpm.
Transmission: Four-speed with integral footchange from 1968 to '72, then five-speed. Primary and secondary transmission by chain. Single-plate clutch in oil, with diaphragm spring.
Cycle parts: Welded full cradle frame, swinging-arm rear suspension and telescopic front forks with two-way damping. Eight-inch twin-leading-shoe front brake and 7-inch single-leading-shoe from 1968; 10-inch disc brakes front and rear for 1975.
Dimensions: Wheelbase – 1968-71, 56¼ in; 1971-5 58 in; X75 Hurricane, 60 in. Dry weight – 1968, 482 lbs; 1975, 493 lbs.
Owners' Club: Very active; 35 UK branches. Secretary – Edna Page, 101 Great Knightleys, Basildon, Essex SS15 5AN.
Sources of help: Spares – Les Williams, Common Lane Industrial Estate, Kenilworth, Warwickshire CV8 8EF; Norman Hyde, Rigby Close, Heathcote, Warwick CV23 8UY; Triple Cycles, 228 Henley Road, Ilford, Essex IG1 2TW; Carl Rosner, Station Approach, Sanderstead, Surrey. Rob North frames – Miles Engineering, Unit 4, Princes Road, Teddington, Middlesex. Advice – Owners' Club specialists.

1972 World Sidecar Speed Record

The Trident holds one version of the World Sidecar Speed Record for ever, thanks to one brave Triumph development engineer and the FIM – the sport's governing body – changing the qualifying rules. Norman Hyde was one of Doug Hele's assistants who was a keen sprinter, and when the rules for sidecar records changed by demanding passenger-weight ballast and a sidecar able to carry a passenger, Norman got the factory's agreement to go for the newly vacant speed title.

His supercharged Trident was already proven and with a little financial help he had a streamlining designed and made by Grand Prix car body builder Don Woodward, while a friend built a sidecar for a total cost of £1.50! The engine capacity was boosted to 831 cc with a set of barrels Norman had designed and in the autumn of 1972 the record quest was under way.

'Things got done at the last minute, as they always were,' Norman remembers. 'The 830 engine first ran three days before the record meeting, and I managed to get a run at the Motor Industry Research Association, where the rear tyre left a black mark from the start as far as you could see.' Before he even had a chance to ride the outfit with the full fairing on, Norman had packed it in the van and headed for RAF Fairford, the Gloucestershire base of Concorde's early flight tests. He set records for the standing start events, then on the second day came the big one, the World Sidecar Speed Record.

'It was revving near to 10,000 rpm in the gears and it was hot inside the shell,' Norman recalls with a grin. 'Somewhere around 150 mph the front wheel was coming off the ground and moving across to the right. I was trying to keep right down in the fairing, listening to the engine, watching the rev counter, all stuck in there wrestling with the front wheel.'

In a search for lightness, the bike was fitted with Tiger Cub front forks and brake and stopping before the end of the 2^1/2-mile runway was a close thing. Then the plugs were taken out and the bike pushed around in gear as the team attempted to cool the engine before the return run, only stopping to mend a broken fairing bracket by Jubilee-clipping a spanner on as a temporary splint.

The return run was made, to get the necessary two-way average, and as Norman lay on the grass – 'I had to lie down for five minutes after each run, after the physical effort and the adrenalin pumping – the timekeeper's news came through. Norman had averaged 161.8 mph to set a record that no one beat until the FIM changed the rules yet again in 1985, leaving the 1972 Hyde Trident figure to stand for all time.

Crouched behind the fairing to keep wind resistance at a minimum, Norman Hyde braces his arms to keep the Trident and sidecar pointing in the right direction as he arrows towards a World Sidecar Speed Record that a change of regulations has left untouchable.

VELOCETTE VENOM AND VIPER

Hard stuff from Hall Green

Below *Dave Houghton bought his Thruxton Venom in 1967 and has a host of sprint wins and three championships to his credit on the bike, raced while it was also his ride-to-work transport.*

The 500cc Venom and its little 350cc brother the Viper were logical developments of Velocette's touring singles. The Viper always lived in the shadow of the Venom, which grew to become a true legend in its own life, as the definitive British sporting single after BSA and the great Gold Star had given up the fight for superiority.

The new models were first shown in November 1955 and, after a test ride on one, racing journalist Vic Willoughby teamed up with Velocette director Bertie Goodman to ride one in the 1956 Thruxton Nine Hours race for production bikes. They didn't come home with a fairy-tale win, but Bertie's old racing instincts were aroused by the bike leading its class before a broken primary chain put it out, and soon the list of optional extras included all a private owner needed to go production racing. By 1961 Velocette's racing habits had developed the Venom far enough for an attempt to be made on the World 24-hour Speed Record at Montlhéry, near Paris. Six French riders were recruited, with Bertie Goodman inviting journalist Bruce Main-Smith to join the team.

Bruce doesn't remember the organization as the best possible. 'There was supposed to be a quick filler laid on for the fuel stops and it turned out to be a big bucket and funnel. And the oil supply was Esso 10/30 – for an engine with a roller big-end! It must have been a good motor to last.'

Riding through the night with only track-side lights for illumination brought out the true abilities of the riders, with Main-Smith putting in best lap at 107 mph and one of the French losing time before stopping and

handing over to the next rider. 'Came in and complained about the fog – and it was a clear night,' remembers Main-Smith. But after 24 hours of flat-out top gear work with only breaks for fuel and rider changes, the Venom took the record with an average of 100.05 mph. The record breaker was naturally shown off at every opportunity and passed on to journalist John Griffith when the Velo factory closed; it is now owned by Ivan Rhodes, President of the Owners' Club.

The Venom revived Velocette's sales, proving to be the best seller in its range of sports and touring singles. But the Viper, head and shoulders above the other sports 350s after the demise of BSA's Gold Star, never sold anything like the numbers of MAC 350 tourers. As the fashion for sporting bikes with aggressive racer appearance

Above *At the 1958 Earls Court Show, Velocette showed the Venom and Viper with the optional fibreglass enclosure of the bottom of the central working parts. Here Bertie Goodman explains the advantages of the clean look to Lord Montagu of Beaulieu.*

developed, so the Venom became one of the accepted examples of the type. *Motor Cycling* showed one burdened with sidecar and caravan in 1961, but what attracted attention was the Venom's ability to go fast, on road or track. Dealers Reg Orpin from Stevens of Shepherd's Bush and Geoff Dodkin of Putney developed the model, Dodkin's entry winning the 500cc class of the 1966 500-mile Grand Prix d'Endurance at Brands Hatch by no less than ten laps, with Dave Croxford and Tom Phillips aboard.

Simon Goodman, son of director Bertie

1967 500cc Production TT

Velocettes started winning TT races in 1926, when Alec Bennett topped the field in the 350cc Junior race. Forty-one years later, the Venom gave the factory its final victory in the 1967 500cc Production race, with Manxman Neil Kelly having his first race on a Velo.

Prepared and entered by Londoner Reg Orpin, the Venom was in Thruxton trim, with a rather special engine built to Bertie Goodman's orders in the Hall Green works. Nimonic 80 valves set in a squish band cylinder head, actuated by valve gear that included titanium tips to the pushrods; titanium was also used for the valve caps. A Manx Norton piston forging was machined at Velocette and cam followers on needle rollers shared timing cover space with alloy timing wheels.

With a race for production bikes back in the TT programme from 1967, Reg Orpin wanted the very best performance possible in the 500cc class for the Velocette name, and if his man could get amongst the 750cc class who were due to start one minute before the 500s, so much the better. But whatever dreams Orpin had were looking a bit shaky when Neil Kelly had trouble starting the Venom during practice – and the race featured a Le Mans-style start, with riders running across the road and kicking the bikes into life. Practice problems meant Neil didn't complete his quota of laps and only a special dispensation agreed two hours before the start got him to the line.

When the flag fell for the 500 class riders to sprint across Glencrutchery Road and kick their bikes into life, most of the field tore away, leaving Neil frantically kicking at the Venom. A quick squirt from an aerosol carried by Orpin for such emergencies got a secret mixture up the inlet tract and the big Velo finally fired – last away.

Neil Kelly rode in what he later admitted was a red mist of fury on that first lap, catching others within three miles of the start. The sight of Percy Tait stopped at the roadside with his works Triumph meant the accepted favourite for the 500cc class was out, and with an even greater effort he got past Keith Heckles on Geoff Dodkin's Venom, the Orpin machine's arch rival. He couldn't believe a simple '1' signal from his pit at the end of the frustrating first lap, but confirmation came with another

signal at Ballacraine. With a second lap at 91.01 mph, during which he was clocked at 121 mph past the Highlander speed trap, Neil kept his head and his lead. The revived Production TT saw the Velocette name back at the top in a TT race – and only John Hartle (factory 650 Triumph) and Paul Smart (Dunstall 750 Norton) were ahead when the flag fell.

The Venom in flight. Neil Kelly in a hurry at Ballaugh Bridge as he makes an historic dash through the field after a slow start to give Velocette its last TT victory.

Goodman, remembers how fast one of the special Venoms could be. 'I borrowed one of the bikes that had been prepared for the Production TT just to nip over to Worcester from home. It was so fast. I was doing up to 90, but I never got into top gear. People didn't realize how fast they were going, because the engine didn't sound in a hurry; in fact, we used to paint over the speed-ometers on the production racers because riders who weren't used to the bikes didn't realize how fast they could go. If they'd known, they might have slowed down.'

The ultimate road-going Venom made by the factory was the Thruxton, introduced in 1964 and named after the Hampshire circuit that had seen so many successes for the model. Breathing deeply though a 1³/₈-inch Amal GP and a 2-inch inlet valve, the Thruxton claimed an output of 41 bhp in road trim. One man who knows the model well is glass-worker Dave Houghton, who bought his from Horsman's of Liverpool in 1967. 'It was the most expensive British bike at the time,' he says. '£400 1s 1d, and the BSA 650 Spitfire was £395. I actually went to buy a second hand BMW, but I ordered the Thruxton instead!

'It's registered NKB 27F, and Neil Kelly's Production TT winner was NKB 31F. Mine was used for everyday transport as well as sprinting, because it was the only bike I had. We used to go to dances on it, and I'd use it to go to work every day. It only let me down once on the road, when I was coming back from Darley Moor races: it pushed the end of the main bearing out through the crankcases and it had to come home in the back of a van.'

Dave's Venom has led a hard life, being regularly used for sprinting. 'It was ridden to meetings in the early days. We'd leave home at Haydock and ride down to Duxford in Cambridgeshire with the tent on the back and my wife Lynn with a bag of tools on her back. After we'd finished at Duxford, we'd ride up into Yorkshire to Topcliffe, camp out overnight to sprint on Sunday, then ride back home Sunday night.

'The only real tuning work was having the inlet gas-flowed by Harold Hall, the rest was

standard. It did 125 mph on a flying start quarter mile at Elvington airfield and its best time for the standing start was 13.7 seconds with a finishing speed of 99 mph. I won the National Sprint Association production championship in 1970, '71, and '77, which was an unlimited capacity class, against big stuff like Norton Commandos and these Kawasakis.'

The bike was supplied in the traditional Velocette finish of black with gold lining, but Dave resprayed it British Racing Green him-self early in its life. 'I don't use it in the wet now, if I can avoid it,' he admits. 'The paint is prone to cracking around bolt heads and the rain and rust soon gets in. Keeping it as clean as this is not an easy job.

'Sprinting is hard on an engine – when I started I just revved it 'til the valves bounced, then changed up. I've been through about six big-ends and the barrel is on maximum oversize, so it rattles a bit with piston slap. I know there are some parts on it that aren't standard, so it won't ever win a concours – but it's what I want, and to me that's more important.'

VELOCETTE VENOM AND VIPER

Engine: Air-cooled four-stroke single cylinder, with two valves per cylinder operated by pushrods. Alloy cylinder head and barrel. Claimed output – 1956 Venom, 34 bhp at 6,200 rpm; Viper 26 bhp at 7,000 rpm; Venom Thruxton 41 bhp at 6,200 rpm; Viper, 28 bhp at 7,000 rpm.
Transmission (all models): Four-speed gearbox with inte-gral footchange. Primary and secondary transmission by chain. Multi-grade clutch in oil.
Cycle parts: Swinging-arm rear suspension with adjustable dampers, telescopic front forks. Single-leading-shoe drum brakes, 7-inch diameter front and rear (7.5-inch diameter front brake on later Venom model).
Dimensions: Wheelbase (all Models) – 53.75 in. Dry weight – Viper 399, 404 lbs; Venom Thruxton, 375 lbs.
Owners' Club: Very active; 23 UK sections. Secretary – Vic Blackman, 1 Mayfair, Tilehurst, Reading, Berkshire RG3 4RA.
Sources of help: Spares – R. F. Seymour Ltd, Hawthorne Works, Park Street, Thame, Oxfordshire OX9 3HT; Geoff Dodkin, 346 Upper Richmond Road West, East Sheen, London SW14 7JS; Fred Cheshire (Motorcycles) Ltd, 19-23 Prestbury Road, Cheltenham, Gloucestershire GL52 2PN; Veloce Spares Ltd, The Old Chapel, Cheney End, Huncote, Leicestershire LE9 6AD; Lynn Drury Spares, Unit 1b, Beechings Way, Alford, Lincolnshire LN13 9JA. Restoration – R. F. Seymour and Geoff Dodkin (addresses above). Advice – Owners' Club specialists.

Velocette's reputation for building high-quality single-cylinder tourers with smooth engines was established long before it announced its revolutionary LE twin. The 250cc MOV pushrod single announced for the 1933 season was developed over the succeeding years into the 350cc MAC and the 500cc MSS, both of them long-lasting models that typified the British flair for simple design at its best.

The MAC and MSS sold so well when they were put back on the market after the 1939-45 war that the bigger model was withdrawn in 1948 so that the full order book could be dealt with and production concentrated on the sweet little MAC with its Dowty oleo-pneumatic tele forks and rigid rear frame. A cylinder head and barrel in cast

iron was not at all sporting, but the ride-to-work motorcyclist appreciated the slim build, a low weight of 320 lbs and an engine that would tolerate the low-grade petrol of the day with a compression ratio of only 6 to 1. Not until 1953 did the factory offer rear suspension on its roadsters, even though its KTT racer had featured a swinging-arm rear end as long ago as 1938. But for the '53 season a new frame went one better than most rival factories, with the Woodhead Monroe dampers mounted in slots at their top, allowing movement to vary the damping effect. Velocette's own telescopic forks replaced the Dowty type at the front end (as Dowty concentrated its expertise on developments for the aircraft and mining industries) and a dual seat with two distinct levels for

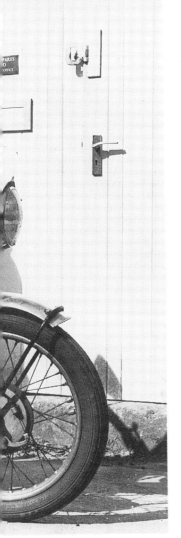

VELOCETTE MAC AND MSS

Singles built to last

Left *Brian Hoy's 1955 MSS has had an eventful life over 150,000 miles, fitting foreign touring and racing into a schedule that includes regular ride-to-work duties.*
Below *Trevor Davies' 1955 MSS was bought from its original owner with only 15,400 miles on the clock in 1989.*

rider and passenger was a gift for sharp cartoonists who could picture a large lady towering over a small chauffeur in those pre-equality days! The cylinder head and barrel were now in alloy, but the bore and stroke stayed at the old long-stroke 68mm × 96mm in an engine that gave a shade over 14 bhp to power the MAC to its 75 mph top speed. It may not sound exciting, but for the connoisseur who appreciated quality of engineering and finish, the simple MAC was in the top bracket.

The MSS came back into the range for 1954, using the same swinging-arm frame, but with the engine changed from the old 81mm x 96mm formula of the 1930s to an all-alloy unit with a 'square' 86mm × 86mm measurement. Charles Udall, Velocette's

chief designer, had to come up with a revised form for the tall old engine when it wouldn't fit in the new frame, but he could not have foreseen what a legend the engine would father. Look at an MSS of the mid-'50s and you can see the lines of the Venom that was to come!

The Velocette single in its milder form has no lack of supporters. Geoff Steele, Technical Secretary of the Velocette Owners' Club, uses his 1960 example for two-up touring at home and abroad, but finds the big gap between top and third gear impedes rapid overtaking and prefers the closer gears of his Seymour Metisse, with a Venom power unit in the famous Rickman-built frame that dealer Ralph Seymour offered as high-speed roadster or out-and-out racer.

Geoff has put 50,000 miles on the MSS since he bought it in 1972 with 42,000 already on the clock, and the engine has been treated to one big-end bearing in that time. Cruising two-up at 60 mph, he found the fuel consumption on the original small Amal carburettor could be as good as 90 miles to the gallon, but long trips on motorways showed evidence of the engine running a little hot. As a precaution, he has rejetted the carburettor for a slightly richer mixture and accepts the heavier 70 mpg consumption with greater security for the engine. When the MSS was pulling a sidecar in its spell as the only family transport, Geoff saw 90 mph on the speedo as he chased a foreign four-cylinder model around the Isle of Man TT course!

The factory used the MSS as the basis for off-road models like the Scrambler listed in the 1950s, but never had success in competition with the bigger factories, even with European Moto-Cross champion-to-be Johnny Draper in the saddle for a brief period in 1953. An Endurance model was produced for the American market, but it proved too heavy at 375 lbs complete with full lighting set and proper mudguards. In the perverse way history has of turning the unloved into the cherished, a Scrambler in original trim is now something to make a Velo enthusiast drool.

The ease with which the touring MAC or MSS can be uprated to sporting Viper or Venom specification can catch the casual onlooker out. Brian Hoy is a committee member of the Owners' Club and uses his 1955 MSS to commute, for foreign touring and for regular trips to meetings at the Club's headquarters in Leicestershire. What began life as an 80 mph touring bike has been altered as it has covered over 150,000 miles, and it now has late Venom power hidden beneath the well-worn fairing and panniers essential for long-distance touring in comfort. 'It does go quite well, and it gets up to a genuine 100 mph quite quickly if you want it to,' says the owner, with a quiet grin. 'It's funny to see people's faces if I get it wound up on the motorway and this funny old motorbike comes past something new and shiny!'

Brian reports a regular 65 miles to the gallon when he cruises at 70 mph, even with the engine breathing through a big Amal GP carburettor, but in original form he could rely on a steady 90 mpg. Other alterations are made by owners to keep regularly ridden bikes on the road, and Brian relies on a Citroen car alternator to power the 12-volt lighting and coil ignition system. With long journeys abroad to meet other Velocette owners, he wants to know he is not dependent on finding some rare part if he hits a problem: 'When you're abroad, what you need are the simplest and easy-to-find bits,' he reasons. 'If I have a problem in the middle of France or Germany, I can get bits for this system quickly. If I was really pushed I could probably find some breaker's yard and buy a complete alternator for a fiver or thereabouts.'

Since buying the MSS in 1960, Brian has raced it, ridden it through 24-hour National Rallies and used it just to ride to work. A collection of trophies remind him that the good times far outweigh the cost of only two big-ends in all those miles!

VELOCETTE MAC AND MSS

Engine: Air-cooled four-stroke single cylinder, with two pushrod-operated valves per cylinder. MSS – 81mm x 96mm to 1948, then 86mm x 86mm from 1954 (MAC 68mm x 96mm). Cast iron cylinder head and barrel to 1948; alloy from 1954 (MAC alloy from 1953). Claimed output 25 bhp at 5,800 rpm (MAC, 14.3 bhp at 6,000)

Transmission (all models): Four-speed gearbox with integral footchange. Primary and secondary transmission by chain. Multi-plate clutch in oil.

Cycle parts: Brazed, lugged frame, rigid rear end and girder front forks from 1945 to 1948. Dowty telescopic forks to 1953, then Velocette teles. Swinging-arm frame introduced 1953, with adjustable rear damper mounting. Seven-inch single-leading-shoe drum brakes front and rear.

Dimensions: Wheelbase – rigid frame, 52.3 in; swinging-arm frame, 53.6 in; Weight – swinging-arm MSS, 385 lbs; rigid MAC, 320 lbs; swinging-arm MAC, 355 lbs.

Owners' Club: Very active, 24 UK centres. Secretary – Vic Blackman, 1 Mayfair, Tilehurst, Reading, Berks RG3 4RA.

Sources of help: Spares – R. F. Seymour, Hawthorne Works, Park Street, Thame, Oxon OX9 3HT; Geoff Dodkin, 346 Upper Richmond Road, East Sheen, London SW14 7JS; Fred Cheshire (Motorcycles) Ltd, 19-23 Prestbury Road, Cheltenham, Glos GL52 2PB; Veloce Spares Ltd, The Old Chapel, Cheney End, Huncote, Leics LE9 6AD; Lynn Drury Spares, Unit 1b, Beechings Way, Alford, Lincs LN13 9JA (Cycle parts). Restoration – R. F. Seymour, Geoff Dodkin; also Brian Thompson, Elton Vale Works, Elton Vale Road, Bury, Lancs. Advice – Owners Club specialists.

The Holmes Velocettes

An MAC Velocette and its MOV smaller brother set a new standard in vintage racing in the late 1980s. Developed by Nottingham ordnance engineer David Holmes, the 250 and 350 Velos embarrassed riders of bigger bikes by beating opposition up to 650cc in size!

David's 250 first made its mark in the experienced hands of Scott specialist Ian Pearce, and when David suggested that a matching 350 could be built his rider was naturally very keen. From a collection of assorted bits including a mid-1930s frame and a 1950 MAC motor, David produced the race-ready bike in ten months of devoted part-time labour. It was no mere careful assembly of standard parts, as David made his own flywheels, connecting rod and 13.5 to 1 compression piston in his home workshop. The 230 lbs MAC finished third in its first race in 1985 and ended the season winning the Vintage Unlimited cc final at Cadwell Park.

In 1986 Derbyshire rider Stephen Tomes took over the riding and ended the year as Unlimited Class champion on the little 250. In 1987 Stephen won the 250 and Unlimited titles on the smaller MOV and added the 350 title on the MAC. At the traditional end-of-season meeting at Cadwell Park in Lincolnshire he was uncatchable, winning six races from six starts and putting in a lap on the 350 MAC that was beaten only by a 750 Norton and a 1065 Vincent!

1987 was the last year the Holmes Velocettes were seen in action, as David devoted his time to restoring a 1934 Singer Le Mans car and his 600cc Norton 'Big Four' road bike. The 350 MAC had been remarkably reliable, never stopping for mechanical reasons, although a crash at Donington Park did arrest its meteoric progress. The very special engine, running on methanol alcohol fuel, gave some 35 bhp when checked on a dynamometer, $2^1/2$ times the factory's claimed power for the 1950 version and a tribute to the effectiveness of Holmes' engineering skill.

Under strict rules that govern the building of machines for vintage events, the Holmes Velocettes were not able to use all the tricks in the tuning trade. The 350 MAC confirmed its humble origins with a four-speed gearbox with a sandcast shell dating from the 1930s, and standard MAC hubs and brake drums; only the use of a Mark 8 KTT backplate in the front helped the braking. The impact of the two little black-and-gold racers was such that even after his withdrawal from racing, David is still in demand to prepare engines for both cars and bikes, leaving little time to complete his Singer car. But the Velocettes are still in his workshop and one day may be back to shame bigger and younger machines.

A talented rider who has moved on to modern machines, Stephen Tomes first made his mark with winning ways on David Holmes' Velocettes. Determination in every limb as he heads for another win on the MAC confirms his dedication to the art of riding fast.

Philip Vincent had a single aim for his motorcycle factory on the A1 Great North Road in Stevenage, Hertfordshire. He wanted to produce quality machines with a level of performance other makers could only dream of – and for years he could honestly claim to offer 'the fastest standard machine in the world'.

Vincent refused to compromise on quality, nor would he follow conventional design trends. So when he announced his 998cc Rapide V-twin in 1946, its unit construction of engine and gearbox, its use of a steel-box-section back-bone to hold oil as well as sling the engine underneath, and the idea of a triangulated cantilever rear suspension were the stuff of dreams. Many riders had finished their military service on side-valve plodders capable of some 65 mph with a tail-wind, but here was a bike with a top speed in excess of 110! And better was to come, with the announcement of the higher performance Black Shadow, fitted with a huge

Above left *The factory used the title Vincent-HRD from Philip Vincent's takeover of the HRD (Howard R. Davies) factory until American dealers advised him that the old logo was easily confused with Harley Davidson. From 1950, the tank transfer was changed and the HRD cast into the engine timing cover was ground off and polished over!*

Above *The Rapide could be ordered in this optional Touring form, with upright bars and deeply valanced mudguards in black enamel.*

5-inch diameter speedo that read to 150 mph – when all the opposition dared offer was a 120 mph instrument. Tested by Charles Markham of *Motor Cycling*, the prototype Black Shadow hit a top speed of 122 mph and established a legend that lives on today.

But it was not just a top speed 20 mph ahead its few rivals that made Vincent's flagship such an outstanding machine. Twin 7-inch drum brakes at the front helped to stop the 450-lb twin in only 22ft 6in (6.9m) from 30 mph, when others tried to complete that task in less than 30 feet (9.1m)! The Feridax

VINCENT TWINS

Built to last and built to blast

Above *John Richardson's 1952 Black Shadow has been modified in the light of over 150,000 miles experience of the long-legged Stevenage twin. His future plans for refinement include replacing the alloy cylinder barrels and their cast iron liners by his own cast iron barrels. This example runs on 19-inch wheel rims instead of the original 20-inchers, to make tyre replacement simple.*

dualseat was a Vincent design, with two distinct areas for rider and passenger, and chain adjustment didn't even mean touching the tool-kit mounted in a stainless steel tray under the seat – slacken the wheel spindle off by the stout tommy-bar on its end, then turn the large knurled knobs on the adjusters to get the chain tension correct. At the front of the crankcase, a prop-stand on either side offered parking whatever the road camber, and if you used both the propstands together the front wheel was off the ground and easy to remove in the event of a puncture.

By 1950, the updated Series 'C' used the same power unit, transmission and chassis, but Vincent's own 'Girdraulic' forks were used, with the facility to alter fork trail from solo to sidecar options in a matter of minutes. Also with the 'C' models came hydraulic damping at the rear, as assistance to the friction damping. It was around this time that Phil Vincent returned from a trip to his American agents, who told him that

the Vincent-HRD title was too easily confused with their native Harley-Davidson make; he ordered the HRD logo to be machined off all castings and then polished, but some 1950 models still show the HRD below the surface in the right light!

The Rapide touring model was offered with optional raised handlebars and deeply valanced mudguards enamelled in the best Pinchin Johnson paint that gave the standard black finish a deep lustre, but most riders preferred the gleam of stainless steel guards, as fitted to the Black Shadow.

The mighty Vincents saw their final form in the Series 'D' introduced for 1955, with

1954 Solo and Sidecar World Speed Records

The Vincent twin was a natural choice for riders who wanted to break records; with its immense power in road trim, it offered even more with only a little tuning. Two New Zealand enthusiasts thought so in 1955, when they combined their talents to break the world speed records for both solos and sidecars.

Bob Burns was a Scot who emigrated with his family in 1947, while Russell Wright was born down under of British parents. Burns developed a streamlined home-tuned Rapide roadster to reach a speed of 157 mph in 1954, and Wright was quick to suggest that his own Black Lightning racer fitted with Burns' home-made streamlining could be a winner. On 2 July, on the 22-feet wide Tram Road at Swannanoa, near Christchurch, they proved the point.

The narrow road was wet from overnight rain, but Wright would let nothing put him off. His first run was against a headwind, with the rear wheel spinning and throwing up spray as the revs reached 6,000 rpm and the projectile averaged 182.94 for the kilometre distance. The return run, with the limited room in the streamlined shell making gear-changing by knee necessary, saw the revs as high as 6,400 and a frightening wobble when Russell shut off at the end of the measured distance, then opened the throttle again to steady the weaving

bike. But that second run – one in each direction to negate any benefit from a tail wind – was at over 187 mph and the world speed record was set at a new high of 185.15, taking the honour from the German NSU factory.

Then came 43-year-old Bob Burns' turn, with a third wheel bolted to the bike by aero-foil-section struts to make it legally a sidecar outfit. Bob rode with the rear suspension bolted up solid, but kept the same 2.5 to 1 overall top gear.

The bumpy Tram Road surface threw the minimally sprung outfit around as the speed rose, and Burns had to stand on the footrests and brace his arms to keep the handlebars in the dead-ahead position. A first run at 160.4 mph was well above the old record speed of 156, and when the return was made at almost 166 mph, Burns smashed the record with an average of 163.06 mph.

It was an outstanding success, with no help from the British factory apart from a pair of big-port cylinder heads, using a streamlined shell made in Bob Burns' home workshop, and riding on a closed public road far removed from the Bonneville Salt Flats where most world speed record figures were set.

A Vincent factory spokesman summed it up: 'The record attempts came as a complete surprise to us at the factory. I was happy to transmit our profound admiration and joy at the achievement of these magnificent milestones in motorcycling history.'

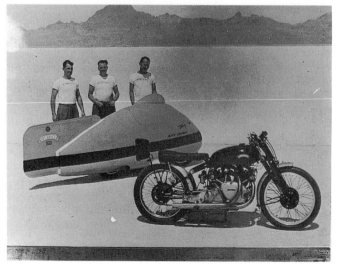

Following the Solo and Sidecar World Record speeds set on the narrow Tram Road in Swannanoa in New Zealand, Russel Wright tried to reach 200 mph on the vast space of the Utah salt flats in America. Despite a revised streamlining that completely enclosed him, Russell (left) was unsuccessful. But he and Bob Burns (centre) and a helper did seem to enjoy the sunshine.

l enclosure of mildly altered Rapide and ack Shadow models giving the Black night and Black Prince variants. The glass- re bodywork offered good weather protec- n, but the models did not sell well and it as not long before the Vincent-HRD name ssed into legend with the end of bike pro- ction as 1955 neared its close.

The big twins remain the definitive ritish long-distance machine, with mem- rs of the world-wide Owners' Club cover- g mileages that would shame bikes 30 years unger. Like Stuart Jenkinson, whose 1955 lack Shadow has covered something over 0,000 miles from new, and can occasion- ly be seen cruising down a British highway he sets off to meet another party of urists that he will lead across Europe.

John Richardson has been riding bikes nce 1947, and this laboratory technician in e Mechanical Engineering Department of runel University has covered over 150,000 iles on Vincent twins. But he does not gard bikes in a sentimental way. 'I don't ok upon motorcycles as a thing of pleasure, really use them as transport,' he explains. he 1952 Black Shadow that carried him for ost of those 150,000 Vincent miles pleased ith its ability to cruise at 75 to 80 mph and ill return over 50 miles to the gallon, but ear in the two carburettors limited per- rmance above 85 mph and gave a weak ixture, with the risk of a holed piston. So hn changed to Amal Concentric MkII rbs, and revelled in a higher cruising speed n continental trips with little difference in nsumption.

Only once was a long trip across Europe terrupted by mechanical problems, when e was returning from an FIM Rally in udapest. A gear selector pinion worked ose and fell through the whirling cogs, aving John with only second gear and the urney from the Swiss border to England head of him. Cruising at a lowly 50 mph, he ade it home with no further problems, to build the box and carry on riding. 'The box enormous inside,' he says. 'Big enough for lorry. You can't wear them out.' That bike as sold on to a Swiss enthusiast after a build with 230,000 miles covered, and

John rebuilt his present 1952 Black Shadow with modifications in the light of many miles' experience.

Bought for only £70, John's present mount has a steel idler timing gear with a life expectancy double the 40,000 miles of the factory's alloy one. Ignition is a personal mixture of Lucas Rita with a Dolphin Engineering twin contact breaker points set, the latter developed by ex-Vincent sidecar racer Peter Russell. The carburation is by Amal Concentrics, with a Mark II Vincent cam helping the mixture into the cylinders. 'It's a different animal with that cam. It goes up the road like a scalded cat!' enthuses the proud owner.

The Vincent seat has been changed for a BMW unit that allows John more room to shift about on long trips and leaves room for a stainless steel pannier rack. Mudguards are painted black with durable yachting paint and the final touch is the simple legend on the speedo face: 'Do not exceed 104 mph in third'. In the world of six-speed superbikes, that makes younger riders look twice at a living example of yesteryear's finest!

VINCENT TWINS

Engine: Air-cooled, 50° V-twin, with two pushrod-operated valves per cylinder; alloy head and barrel, with stepped iron cylinder liner. Claimed 55 bhp at 5,700 rpm (Rapide, 45 bhp at 5,300 rpm). Lucas magneto ignition until Series 'D' intro- duced in 1954, when changed to coil. Black Lightning racing version gave a claimed 68 bhp in 1951.

Transmission: In unit with engine, four-speed gearbox with integral footchange. Primary transmission by triplex chain, secondary by single row chain. Single-plate first stage clutch, with drum second stage.

Cycle parts: Series 'B' used Brampton girder forks; Series 'C' (from 1950) 'Girdraulic' forks. Rear suspension by cantilever with friction damping (Series 'B') and additional hydraulic damping (Series 'C'). Double 7-inch single- leading-shoe brakes front and rear on Series 'C'.

Dimensions: Wheelbase – 56 in. Dry weight – 458 lbs (455 lbs or 470 lbs for Rapide in Touring trim).

Owners' Club: Very active; 30 UK branches. Secretary – Adrian Cattell, 15 Grenfell Ave, Sunnyhill, Derby DE3 7LA.

Sources of help: Spares – The Vincent Owners' Club Spares Co Ltd, The Wharf, Burford Lane, Lymm, Cheshire (available to members only); Conway Motors, 224 Tankerton Road, Whitstable, Kent CT5 2AY; Maughan & Sons, 42 Townend, Wilsford, Nr Grantham, Lincs NG32 3NY; Ron Kemp, 'Ty Vin', Llanddewi, Llandrindod Wells, Powys LD1 6SE. Restoration – Bob Dunn, Elton Vale Works, Elton Vale Road, Bury, Lancs; also Ron Kemp (address above).

VINCENT 500 SINGLE

Half a Shadow

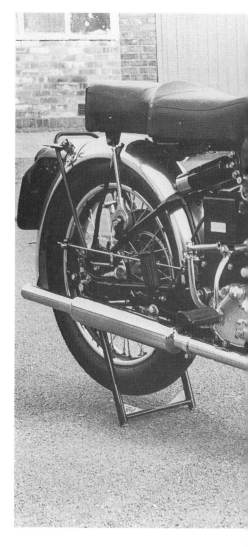

Dave Clarke's 1951 Comet took 18 months to rebuild from a mouldering heap to this concours-winning beauty, but some of the detailed assembly jobs proved to be time-consuming. The paintwork is Dave's own, including his first attempt at lining a tank.

Vincent's single-cylinder Comet was destined always to live in the shadow of its V-twin bigger brothers. It shared cycle parts with the rest of the Vincent family, which made its 390 lbs (154 kg) weight a little on the heavy side. The factory's claim for 28 bhp may have been more than other single cylinder road models aspired to, but a 1950 price tag over £241 added to the burden – no other factory asked over £200 for a pushrod road single in that year's listings. So the Comet, available with slim stainless steel or deeply valanced black mudguards, was a model for the man who wanted Vincent's uncompromising quality without the performance of the mighty twins.

A Comet rider was rewarded with a bike that would cruise easily at 70 to 80 mph, and if he was in no great hurry it also rewarded him with a modest thirst. Up to 100 miles to the gallon was not unknown when an experienced rider ran a new motor in with a gentle touch, and 70 mpg at more normal cruising was easy to get. And brakes designed to stop 458 lbs of V-twin from over 100 mph made the Comet stop on the proverbial sixpence, even if the single only had a single rear drum brake and not the twins' double drum arrangement. When *Motor Cycling* magazine tested a Comet in 1950, its man stopped

from 30 mph in only 21 feet (6.4m) to record the best braking figures in the journal's history. At a steady 30 mph, suggested the same test, the fuel consumption would be 118 mpg, but few riders would expect to waste the Comet's near-90 mph ability crawling along like that.

The Comet engine was very strong and would stand a lot of tuning, as was proved by successes from John Surtees and Leicester schoolteacher Johnnie Hodgkin in road racing to amazing drag-strip performances by Essex carpenter Brian Chapman on his knee-high 'Mighty Mouse'. And George Brown, factory tester and habitual

VINCENT 500 SINGLE

Engine: Air-cooled, four-stroke single, with two pushrod-operated valves per cylinder, opened by highmounted camshafts. Alloy cylinder head and barrel, with cast-in iron liner. 84mm bore × 90mm stroke, claimed output 28 bhp at 5,800 rpm (Meteor touring version, 24 bhp).

Transmission: Four-speed Burman gearbox with integral footchange. Primary and secondary transmission by chain. Multi-plate clutch.

Cycle parts: Series 'B' – Brampton girder front fork. Series 'C' – Vincent 'Girdraulic' front forks. Both Series built with cantilever sprung rear frame, with twin friction dampers below seat. Twin 7-inch drum brakes at front, single 7-inch drum at rear. Both wheels quickly detachable via tommy bars built into wheel spindles.

Dimensions: Wheelbase – 56 in. Dry weight – 380 lbs.

Owners' Club: Very active; 38 UK sections, 62 overall worldwide. Secretary – Adrian Cattell, 15 Grenfall Ave, Sunnyhill, Derby DE3 7LA.

Sources of help: Spares – The Vincent Owners' Club Spares Co Ltd, The Wharf, Burford Lane, Lymm, Cheshire (members only). Maughan and Sons, 42 Townend, Wilsford, nr Grantham, Lincs NG32 3NY. Ron Kemp, 'Ty-Vin', Llanddewi, Llandrindod Wells, Powys LD1 6SE. Conway Motors, 224 Tankerton Road, Whitstable, Kent CT5 2AY, Restoration – Maughan and Son and Ron Kemp (addresses above); Bob Dunn, Elton Vale Works, Elton Vale Road, Bury, Lancs.

world record breaker, used one in local trials! But the bike never appealed to the great buying public, requiring careful maintenance to keep in top form.

Nottingham's Dave Clarke, an engineering fitter who needs a bigger sideboard to hold all the concours trophies his rebuilds have won, takes a view of the Comet through glasses definitely not rose-tinted by memory. His award-winning 1951 Series 'C' Comet was bought as a mouldering heap and took 18 months of hard work to bring back to immaculate order, using parts from Tony Maughan's specialist service in nearby Grantham.

'It's so complicated and over-engineered,' says Dave. 'Some of the castings are very poor quality, but other parts like the spindles and bearings are much better.'

As a newcomer to Vincents, Dave also found the 'Girdraulic' front forks a time-consuming rebuild task. 'It took me three days to assemble the front end, shimming up the taper roller bearings and shimming the brake plates to get the right clearance.' Dave recognizes that an experienced pair of Vincent hands would do it much quicker, but when asked about fuel consumption a grin begins to break through: 'It's giving me about 90 mpg running it in!'

1951 season – Surtees' Grey Flash

John Surtees, the only man to win world championships on both two wheels and four, first rode to stardom on a Vincent Grey Flash, the racing version of the Comet roadster. The racing single was priced at £330.20 for the 1951 season when the teenage son of a London Vincent agent showed just how fast it could go with a future world champion in the saddle.

Johnnie Hodgkin had shown what an effective racing tool the 'Flash' could be on a tight circuit, setting a new Cadwell Park lap record and winning the 500cc Invitation Race at a soaking wet Hutchinson 100 meeting at Silverstone during 1950 season. For 1951, the youthful Surtees switched from keeping the sidecar wheel of his father's Vincent twin outfit near the ground to start his solo racing career; not on an established racing model like a Manx Norton, but on a Grey Flash he prepared himself after normal hours at the Stevenage factory.

At the first Thruxton meeting of the year, pouring rain made conditions difficult, but Geoff Duke was expected to dominate the results on factory-entered Nortons. In fact, the cheeky 17-year-old Surtees on his pushrod-engined production racer pushed Geoff so hard that the Vincent actually took the lead at one stage! Duke's experience showed in the end,

but young Surtees was a strong second, and then repeated the performance in the Invitation Race. John Surtees and the Grey Flash had definitely arrived!

At the Festival of Britain meeting at Boreham Airfield in Essex, the cream of non-works riders gathered to contest the first meeting on what is now the Ford Motor Company's high performance development unit. The big race of the day was the Chelmsford 100 Senior Championship, with a full grid of determined men after the title, but after three laps there was no doubt who was going to take it. 'J. Surtees Jnr (499 Vincent)' was the programme's official description, but his rivals must have thought the young Londoner simply uncatchable. Ironically, the next man to finish after John was Vincent's chief tester, George Brown, riding a Manx Norton!

Later in the season, John was a strong third at a dry Thruxton meeting, beaten only by Les Graham on the MV-Agusta 500-4 and Norton's new works rider Dave Bennett. And in 1952 he mixed the Vincent with a Manx Norton according to the suitability of each machine for the circuit; at Brands Hatch he was the dominant 500cc rider of the year, including one win in a 25-lap race when he lapped the great Ray Amm, the Vincent thrashing the Norton. Nobody was surprised when the Norton team signed up John for the 1953 season, but that simple pushrod Vincent had served to show his great talent.

17-year-old John Surtees on his Grey Flash worried established stars on works machinery in the 1951 season. Here he heads for third place at the end-of-season Thruxton International meeting, in a race won by ex-World Champion Les Graham on his four-cylinder MV-Agusta.

INDEX